HAUGHEY'S FORTY YEARS OF CONTROVERSY

D0473239

T. RYLE DWYER

MERCIER PRESS

MERCIER PRESS
Douglas Village
Cork
books@mercierpress.ie
www.mercierpress.ie

Trade enquiries to CMD DISTRIBUTION,
55a Spruce Avenue, Stillorgan Industrial Estate, Blackrock, Dublin

© T. Ryle Dwyer 1992, 2005

ISBN 1 85635 426 1

10 9 8 7 6 5 4 3 2 1

DEDICATED TO
FIONA, DAVE, AND NORA DEENEY

Mercier Press receives financial assistance from the Arts
Council/An Chomhairle Ealaíon

Printed by J. H. Haynes & Co. Ltd., Sparkford

CONTENTS

CJH Diary

16 September 1925: CJH born in Castlebar, Co. Mayo.

1928: Seán Haughey's retired from army and the family settled in Dunshaughlin, Co. Meath.

1933: family moved to Donnycarney, Dublin.

7 May 1945: sparks riot in Dublin after burning Union Jack.

1946: earned Bachelor of Commerce degree from UCD.

1948: joined Fianna Fáil.

1949: called to the bar.

1951: joined with Harry Boland in establishing Haughey Boland accountancy firm.

30 May 1951: defeated as Fianna Fáil candidate in general election (lost deposit).

18 Sept 1951: married Maureen Lemass.

1953: co-opted to Dublin Corporation.

18 Jun 1954: CJH defeated as Fianna Fáil candidate in general election (lost deposit).

23 Jun 1955: fails to hold seat on Dublin Corporation to which he was co-opted.

30 Apr 1956: defeated in Dáil by-election in Dublin North East.

5 Mar 1957: elected to Dáil Éireann.

9 May 1960: appointed parliamentary secretary to Minister for Justice.

4 Oct 1961: re-elected to second Dáil term at head of poll in general election.

11 Oct 1961: appointed Minister for Justice.

22 Nov 1961: announces re-activation of Special Criminal Court.

17 Jun 1964: introduces Succession Bill.

8 Oct 1964: appointed Minister for Agriculture.

7 Apr 1965: re-elected to third Dáil term at head of the poll.

28 Apr 1966: ICMSA farmers jailed for picketing Leinster House.
   Over 500 arrested and jailed in the ensuing dispute.

26 May 1966: concedes most of ICMSA demands.

June 1966: National director of elections for President de Valera's re-election campaign.

28 Sept 1966: protests to RTÉ over contradiction of his statement.

7 Oct 1966: National Farmers' Association set out on protest march to Dublin.

19 Oct 1966: refuses to meet NFA, who begin a sleep-in outside his office.

31 Oct 1966 story of impending retirement of Seán Lemass breaks.

8 Nov 1966: Lemass and Haughey patch up deal with NFA.

9 Nov 1966: Jack Lynch elected leader of Fianna Fáil.

11 Nov 1966: appointed Minister for Finance.

11 Apr 1967: announces free travel for elderly.

May 1967: George Colley, in Galway, refers to low standards in high places.

20 Sept 1968: badly injured when he crashed his state car at Cooadnagan Bridge.

7 May 1969: announces income tax concessions for writers and artists.

29 May 1969: reports that Haughey sold Grangemore for £204,500.

18 Jun 1969: re-elected to fourth Dáil term at head of the poll.

2 Jul 1969: re-appointed Minister for Finance.

16 Aug1969: authorised by government to provide money for victims of unrest in Northern Ireland.

20 Aug 1969: tells cabinet of secret meeting with IRA chief of staff, Cathal Goulding.

19 Mar 1970: CJH instructs customs to admit arms consignment without inspection.

17 Apr 1970: Garda commissioner informed of plot to import guns.

18 Apr 1970: asks Berry if guns will be admitted if they go straight to Northern Ireland.

21 Apr 1970: hospitalised after fall from horse; Lynch delivered his budget address.

29 Apr 1970: visited in hospital by Lynch.

1 May 1970: Lynch informs cabinet that there will be no action over arms affair.

5 May 1970: CJH sacked as Minister for Finance.

6 May 1970: Arms crisis erupts.

28 May 1970: arrested and charged with conspiracy to import arms illegally.

9 Sept: 1970: secret meeting with Minister for Justice Des O'Malley.

22 Sept 1970: Arms trial begins.

29 Sept 1970: mistrial declared by judge.

6 Oct 1970: new Arms Trial begins.

19 Oct 1970: Haughey testifies at arms trial.

23 Oct 1970: CJH and others acquitted.

2 Mar 1971: begins testimony before Dáil Committee of Public Accounts.

17 Jan 1972: begins affair with Terry Keane.

19 Feb 1972: elected vice-president of Fianna Fáil.

10 Feb 1973: Frank Aiken retires from politics in protest at CJH's ratification as Fianna Fáil candidate.

28 Feb 1973: re-elected to Dáil at head of poll.

16 Feb 1974: elected joint national secretary of Fianna Fáil.

30 Jan 1975: appointed Fianna Fáil front bench as spokesman for Health and Social Welfare.

16 June 1977: re-elected to Dáil at head of the poll.

5 July 1977: appointed Minister for Health and Social Welfare.

2 June 1978: CJH meets bishops to discuss Family Planning legislation.

2 Aug 1978: introduces bill to curb tobacco advertising.

28 Feb 1979: declares Family Planning Bill 'an Irish solution to an Irish problem'.
7 Dec 1979: elected Fianna Fáil leader.
11 Dec 1979: elected Taoiseach.
10 Jan 1980: warns that the country is living beyond its means.
21 May 1980: meet Prime Minister Margaret Thatcher in London.
8 Dec 1980: Anglo-Irish summit at Dublin Castle.
14 Feb 1981: Fianna Fáil Ard Fheis called off after Stardust disaster.
11 June 1981: re-elected to Dáil at head of the poll.
30 June 1981: replaced by Garret FitzGerald as Taoiseach.
27 Jan 1982: unable to contact President Hillery by telephone.
18 Feb 1982: re-elected to Dáil at head of the poll.
25 Feb 1982: re-elected leader of FF after O'Malley withdraws challenge.
8 Mar 1982: signs deal for support of Tony Gregory.
9 Mar 1982: elected Taoiseach for second time.
30 Mar 1982: Haughey appoints Dick Burke to European commission.
6 May 1982: announces that Ireland will be asking EEC to end sanctions against Argentina.
22 June 1982: disclosure of override facility to intercept all Leinster House calls.
17 Aug 1982: accepted Patrick Connolly resignation as AG and gives rise to GUBU.
6 Oct 1982: staved off heave led by Charlie McCreevy.
4 Nov 1982: government lost confidence motion.
25 Nov 1982: re-elected to ninth Dáil term at head of poll.
14 Dec 1982: replaced by Garret FitzGerald as Taoiseach.
19 Dec 1982: Haughey says he would not countenance tapping journalists' phones.
7 Feb 1983: Haughey won re-election as Fianna Fáil leader.
16 Dec 1983: broke down weeping at New Ireland Forum meeting.
26 Feb 1985: Des O'Malley expelled from Fianna Fáil.
29 Sept 1985: rescued after boat sank off Mizen Head.
25 Oct 1985: said he considers Col Gaddafi a friends and supports him.
17 Feb 1987: re-elected to tenth Dáil term at head of the poll.
10 Mar 1987: elected to third term as Taoiseach.
27 Mar 1987 cabinet approved draft bill to regularise withholding part of pensions of patients in nurshing homes
7 July 1988: report that Haughey retained gifts from Saudi royal family.
15 June 1989: re-elected to eleventh Dáil term.
28 June 1989: failed to win re-election as Taoiseach.
11 July 1989: concluded coalition agreement with PDs.
12 July 1989: elected Taoiseach for fourth time.
30 Oct 1990: dismissed Brian Lenihan as Tánaiste.
6 Nov 1991: motion challenging leadership tabled for Fianna Fáil meeting.
7 Nov 1991: sacks Albert Reynolds for backing motion and refusing to resign.
9 Nov 1991: Haughey survives leadership challenge.

13 Nov 1991: *withdraws nomination of James McDaid as Minister for Defence.*

15 Jan 1992: *Seán Doherty says that Haughey was aware of taps on journalists in 1982.*

30 Jan 1992: *announces that he will resign as Taoiseach the following week.*

7 Feb 1992: *formally announces his resignation as Taoiseach.*

11 Feb 1992: *replaced as Taoiseach by Albert Reynolds.*

20 Feb 1992: *Ben Dunne has panic attack in Miami.*

1 Oct 1992: *honoured by Fianna Fáil national executive.*

13 Oct 1992: *began four days of testimony at Beef tribunal.*

5 Nov 1992: *retires from Dáil Éireann after more than 35 years.*

11 May 1994: *Des Traynor died.*

3 Dec 1996: *report that senior figure in Fianna Fáil received over £1 million from Ben Dunne.*

6 Dec 1996: Phoenix *magazine identifies Haughey as unidentified individual.*

7 Feb 1997: *McCracken tribunal set up.*

15 July 1997: *Haughey testified before the McCracken tribunal.*

25 Aug 1997: *McCracken report published criticising Haughey's sworn testimony.*

27 Aug 1997: *mistaken report that CJH was rescued by helicopter having fallen off his yacht in Dingle Harbour.*

21 Jul 1998: *summoned to appear in court on charges of obstructing McCracken tribunal.*

15 Dec 1998: *Appeals commissioner rules CJH had no tax liability for Dunne money.*

14 May 1999: *Terry Keane speaks of affair on* Late Late Show.

17 Sep 1999: *reports that Keane is auctioning Haughey memorabilia.*

3 Apr 2000: *paid £1,009,435 in tax and interest on Dunne money.*

26 Jun 2000: *Judge Kevin Haugh postponed obstruction trial indefinitely.*

3 Jul 2000: *High court upholds Judge Haugh's ruling.*

21 Jul 2000: *begins testimony at Moriarty tribunal for two hours a day over five days.*

21 Sep 2000: *begins 12 further days testimony at Moriarty tribunal.*

18 Jan 2001: *begins 20 days of testimony – one hour a day in camera.*

15 Mar 2001: *concludes testimony at Moriarty tribunal.*

18 Mar 2003: *announcement that revenue have agreed €5 in gift tax and penalties for money received (bringing total in back taxes and penalties to €6.28m).*

Sept 2003: *agrees to sell Abbeville and Kinsealy for €45 million.*

PREFACE

Charlie Haughey and controversy seem almost synonymous. He has been involved in major political scandals of Watergate proportions in five different decades.

The major scandals could be compared not only with the Watergate scandal in the United States but with the major scandals involving all the twentieth century American presidents – from the perjury and philandering accusations that led to the impeachment of Bill Clinton, to the arms controversy surrounding Ronald Reagan, to the telephone-tapping of Watergate and Richard Nixon, to the tax evasion that led to the resignation of his vice president Spiro Agnew, and even back to the business affairs of the Tea Pot Dome Scandal, which rocked American politics in the 1920s. Haughey was involved in different major scandals that could be compared with each of those. In the midst of his dispute with the National Farmers' Association in 1966, his father-in-law, Seán Lemass, resigned as Taoiseach. Four years later in 1970 came the arms crisis, which was undoubtedly the most serious political crisis in the state since the civil war. In 1983 he found himself implicated in Liffeygate – a controversy surrounding taps on the telephones of two journalists. It was a hang-over of this controversy that eventually brought him down in 1992. Then while he was in retirement Charlie's past came back to haunt him with the exposure of a whole series of scandals surrounding his financial affairs, getting the banks to write off a significant portion of his loans, borrowing, bumming and misappropriating money.

In his final address to the Dáil as Taoiseach on 11 February 1992, Charlie quoted from *Othello*: 'I have done the state some service, and they know't,' he said. 'No more of that.'

This is not the story of his service much less his achievements, though the ways in which – in the face of considerable adversity – he bounced back from a whole series of political controversies were in themselves tremendous achievements. The four major controversies already mentioned were just the more notorious.

There were also many others, beginning with the Macushla Affair, which involved the virtual mutiny of extensive elements of the garda síochána shortly after Charlie took over as Minister for Justice in 1961. In this and other controversies Charlie was really blameless. He inherited the mess.

This book seeks to examine dispassionately the various political controversies extending from 1961 through the 'secret courts', his role in the presidential election of 1966, and his disputes with the farmers and RTÉ the same year, his role in *Taca*, his long-standing feuds with George Colley and Dessie O'Malley, the arms crisis, arms trial, the Gibbons confidence vote, the public accounts inquiry, his election as leader of Fianna Fáil, the 'flawed pedigree' controversy, the leadership heaves, the GUBUs, the deals and strokes, problems with telephones, political u-turns, leading Fianna Fáil into coalition, sacking his own Tánaiste, his resignation as Taoiseach and his retirement from politics.

Part of this book initially appeared under the title *Haughey's Thirty Years of Controversy* in 1992 and *Fallen Idol* in 1997. In the decade since then the opening of the State Papers up to 1972 has thrown new light on a number of the earlier incidents, especially events surrounding the arms crisis.

Even in retirement Haughey has been at the centre of controversy over the handling of his financial affairs going back over a quarter of a century – the writing off of part of his AIB loans, the Ben Dunne money, the misappropriation of money donated either to Fianna Fáil, or for his Tánaiste's liver transplant operation. His prevarications were to lead to him being charged with obstructing the McCracken tribunal, and his affairs are still the focus of the Moriarty tribunal.

TRD
Tralee

As Taoiseach Charles J. Haughey was described as the acceptable face of fantasy – the poor boy who grew up to become a powerful and fabulously wealthy man.

Unlike his great political rival, Garret FitzGerald, who was born into comfortable surroundings as the son of a cabinet minister, Charlie was the son of an army officer who retired early and then developed multiple sclerosis when Charlie was only a boy. Times were hard for the family of nine dependent on the sick father's small pension during the depression of the 1930s and the early 1940s. But young Charlie was a brilliant student and got through secondary school and university on academic scholarships.

In 1951 he married Maureen Lemass, the daughter of Tánaiste Seán Lemass. Six years later at the age of thirty-one he was elected to the Dáil, at his fourth attempt. After more than four years on the backbenches he was selected as parliamentary secretary to the Minister for Justice in the government of his father-in-law Seán Lemass, who had taken over from Eamon de Valera as Taoiseach in 1959.

Charlie quickly established a reputation for himself as a legislator by successfully piloting a whole series of bills through the Oireachtas. These included bills on defamation, civil liability and rent restrictions.

As the legislative decks were being cleared to make way for a general election in 1961, James Dillon, the leader of Fine Gael, complimented Charlie in the Dáil not only 'on the skill with which he has had recourse to his brief', but also on 'his extraordinary erudition', together with 'his exceptional and outstanding ability'. It was a tremendous tribute for the leader of the opposition to pay to a young opponent, especially right before a general election.

At the start of his second term in the Dáil Charlie was appointed to the cabinet as Minister for Justice by Lemass, but there was no question of nepotism. He deserved the post and this was recognised even by the opposition which welcomed his appointment.

He got on well with his staff at justice. Peter Berry, the secretary of the department, had a good though sometimes stormy working relationship with him. 'Haughey was a dynamic minister,' Berry recalled years later. 'He was a joy to work with and the longer he stayed the better he got'. He was quick to master bureaucratic ways of formulating and implementing policy. Having served in the department under

14 different ministers beginning with Kevin O'Higgins back in the 1920s, Berry noted that 'Haughey learned fast and was in complete control of his department from the outset'. In fact, he rated him 'the ablest' of all those ministers.

'He did not interfere in minor details,' Berry explained, 'but where political kudos or political disadvantage might arise he was sharp as a razor'.

The department had often been frustrated by a lack of money until Charlie's appointment. 'Successive Ministers for Justice had failed to get the necessary monies from the Department of Finance but Mr Haughey proved very adroit at extracting the necessary financial support,' Berry noted. He was a good man to cut through red tape.

Working long hours – on average a ten-hour day – Charlie prided himself on efficiency and getting things done. He could be a good listener, but he became irritable when people became long-winded. He sought to emulate the capacity of his father-in-law to make decisions quickly without agonising interminably over them as had been the practice in the de Valera governments.

As Minister for Justice, he was responsible for a phenomenal volume of legislation dealing with adoption, extradition, the abolition of capital punishment, the introduction of free legal aid and a number of bills to update the antiquated legal system. In 1964 he introduced the succession bill, a novel piece of legislation designed to ensure that dependents were provided for in any will. This was to prevent a repetition of cases in which the bulk of estates were bequeathed to a church for something like masses while dependents were left virtually destitute.

As the succession bill was being considered in the Dáil, Charlie was made Minister of Agriculture in place of Paddy Smith, who had resigned in protest over government policy. The move was widely considered a promotion.

Charlie remained in the new post for two-and-a-half years. Towards the end of his stay things became somewhat stormy, but, following the resignation of Seán Lemass in November 1966, he secured what was seen as the second most important post in the government. He was appointed Minister for Finance by the new Taoiseach, Jack Lynch.

Although critics often depicted him as an uncaring capitalist, Charlie demonstrated a distinct social concern. He admitted to being fascinated by politics and being lured into political life by his wish to get things done. 'What politics should be about,' he once said, 'is making the world a better place for those you serve.'

It was he who introduced the farmers' dole to help the agricultural sector during the winter months, but it was his assistance to pensioners which attracted most attention. His budgets were remarkable for a whole series of novel and comparatively cheap give-aways. Ever mindful of his late father's plight, he introduced imaginative schemes to help people on the old-age pension, such as free rail and bus travel during off-peak hours, free electricity and free telephone rental, as well duty-free petrol for disabled drivers of all ages. He also won a reputation for himself as a champion of the arts by introducing legislation to exempt the earnings of artists and writers from income tax. Another novel proposal was an exchequer grant of £100 for the birth of triplets, and £150 for quads. The whole thing would not even cost £1,000 in a year, because there were so few triplets born, and he admitted that there was no known case of quads being born in Ireland.

Some critics dismissed these as gimmicks to win votes. 'No one will dispute,' the playwright Hugh Leonard once wrote, 'that to catch a vote Mr Haughey would unhesitatingly roller-skate backwards into a nunnery, naked from the waist down and singing *Kevin Barry* in Swahili.' Yet pleasing people is the very essence of representative democracy, as far as Charlie was concerned.

He was prepared to help people and be generous even when there was no political advantage to be gained. This side of him has not been generally recognised, except by those who know him. It helps to explain his enormous popularity, especially in his own constituency.

As a minister he adopted the same facilitory attitude towards deputies looking for his assistance. He was always available to backbenchers and he made a particular point of making them feel welcome. This applied not only to those members of Fianna Fáil who might one day help him to realise his ambition for power, but also to those on opposition benches.

During his early years in politics Charlie somehow assembled a personal fortune. He has persistently refused to explain how, or to talk about his private business affairs, but he has flaunted his wealth. He moved into a palatial mansion on a 240 acre estate in the outskirts of Dublin. It had served as a summer residence for the British viceroy in the late eighteenth century. Charlie also bought an island on which he built an expensive holiday home off the south-west coast. He has owned yachts, and has gone in for breeding and racing horses – the so-called sport of kings. He also set up one of his sons in a helicopter business.

'Coming to terms with Charlie Haughey is like making your confirmation or losing your virginity,' according to Anne Harris of the *Sunday Independent*. 'He has a way with women. Young women and matrons alike ache for him.'

He exuded a mesmerising charm with his uncanny ability to make even a woman he just met in a crowded room feel that he thought that she was the most interesting person in the place. He flattered many women by flirting with them.

Conor Cruise O'Brien, one of his most trenchant critics, wrote that people have liked Charlie 'for lending some colour to life in a particularly drab period'. He had become an inspiration for Irish people wishing to fantasise about money, power and the good life.

Those that Charlie liked got sworn at ribaldly with no expletives deleted. He demanded an unwavering personal loyalty from his friends and tended to regard any questioning of his motives or actions as a betrayal. Although he got on great with photographers, his relations with reporters were frequently strained.

'I could instance a load of fuckers whose throats I'd cut and push over the nearest cliff,' he told one interviewer. In particular he singled out the pontificating breed of knowall political commentators. 'They'll say something today and they're totally wrong about it – completely wrong – and they're shown to be wrong about it. Then the next day they're back pontificating the same as ever,' he said. 'I suppose if anything annoys me, that annoys me.'

He was often the victim of unfair media criticism, with the result that his relations with reporters were difficult. When an *Irish Times* reporter approached him in the street one day, Charlie took the offensive. 'Who writes the *Irish Times*' editorials, anyway?' he asked. 'They read like they have been done by an old woman sitting in a bath with the water getting cold around her fanny!' With that he walked off.

Charlie was a man with real *charisma*, which should not be confused with charm or popularity. The charismatic leader, in the true sense, is one whose followers believe him to have superhuman powers. In his case, these have been demonstrated in his extraordinary ability to survive politically.

For over forty years he was involved in a whole series of controversies. Some of the scandals have been of Watergate proportions. Although written off many times, both by his political opponents and the media, he has managed to extricate himself each time. After one escape in which the media was virtually unanimous in writing him off, one writer noted that the chastened press would wait for three days after Charlie's death before reporting the event – just in case!

In October 1988 *The Cork Examiner* had a sensational report that Charlie's heart had stopped in the midst of a severe bout of coughing. His doctors were able to confirm his denial of that story, because he had not suffered a cardiac arrest, but a respiratory arrest. He had stopped breathing for a short time before being revived. That was but another of his many escapes against seemingly impossible odds.

In June 2003 there were further rumours of his imminent demise from prostate cancer. All of the newspapers prepared pages covering his career and RTÉ made arrangements for programmes covering his anticipated death, but he rallied to confound those who were again writing him off prematurely. It all added to the aura of Charlie – the Great Survivor.

Shortly after talking over as Minister for Justice on 11 October 1961, Charlie found himself in at the deep end. He was faced with a virtual mutiny within the garda síochána.

Over the years the force had become demoralised as a result of low pay, poor promotional prospects, and a feeling that its leadership was out of touch with the problems of the rank and file. The garda commissioner was invariably drawn from the civil service, rather than from the force, with the result that the men on the beat felt that he had little appreciation or understanding of their problems.

When a request from the garda representative body for a pay increase was turned down, some discontented elements began holding meetings in Dublin stations. These were banned by the commissioner, Daniel Costigan, under the force's disciplinary code, so a meeting was arranged for the Macushla Ballroom, Amiens Street, Dublin on 5 November 1961.

Charlie directed Costigan to issue a circular to members of the force warning that attendance at unauthorised meetings was a serious breach of discipline warranting dismissal. A total of 815 gardaí ignored the warning, but the inspectors outside only recognised 167 of the men, and they only got the name of one of 30 leaders on the stage.

The *Irish Times* depicted the dispute as 'undeniably the most serious of its kind to have faced any government since 1922'. Haughey insisted that disciplinary proceedings be taken against the 167 gardaí who were identified. They were to be fined and transferred from Dublin within four weeks. Some disgruntled gardaí decided on a 'go slow' campaign.

Dublin traffic was thrown into near chaos as gardaí stopped directing traffic and refused to give out parking tickets. Costigan responded on 8 November by asking Charlie to dismiss eleven of the ring leaders. He duly complied, but was smart enough to open the door for possible negotiations by issuing a statement emphasising his willingness to enquire into garda grievances 'on receiving an assurance from the commissioner that discipline had been fully restored throughout the force'.

With a crisis looming, Charlie turned to the Catholic archbishop of Dublin, John Charles McQuaid, for help. As parliamentary secretary to the Minister for Justice, Haughey had been in charge of the department's legislative programme and he visited McQuaid frequently, possibly to clear the legislation with the archbishop who had been exerting a virtual veto on legislation ever since the Mother and Child controversy of 1951. McQuaid liked Charlie and recognised him as a young man who would go far. Now when Haughey came for help, the archbishop gladly intervened. He announced publicly that discipline would be restored, if garda grievances were investigated by the Justice Department.

'The fact that the guarantee has been given by the archbishop is good enough for me,' Charlie announced on 13 November. 'I am satisfied that full discipline has now been restored to the force and the commissioner agrees with me.'

The eleven dismissed men were reinstated and disciplinary proceedings against others were dropped. Charlie assured the Dáil that there would be no victimisation of those taking part in the affair. 'The dismissed men express their gratitude and appreciation to the archbishop and complimented Mr Haughey on his readiness to accept their guarantees to his grace.'

'May I thank you for the bigness with which you handled the garda settlement,' McQuaid wrote to the Taoiseach on 15 November 1961. 'The minister has achieved something that could not otherwise have been obtained – a genuine loyalty. And it will help him at the beginning of what, please God, will be a most successful term of office.'

In the end, the Macushla Affair, despite its threatened gravity, turned out to be little more than a storm in a teacup.

Prior to Charlie's appointment as Minister for Justice, charges against prominent politicians or their friends for things like drunken driving would never get to court, but he adopted a different approach. Those who approached him were told they would have to go into court and face the music, but he was ready to help them by ensuring the case would not be reported in the press.

As all district justices were political appointments, a friendly one could be found to rise at five o'clock in the evening and go to his rooms. Journalists would naturally leave for the evening, thinking that their work was done for the day, and the judge would then return and hear the case. The politician would plead guilty, accept his punishment, and that would be the end of the matter. In this way the needs of justice were served without subjecting the accused to damaging publicity. Charlie was satisfied, and in fairness to him, he had some justification. At least it was better than fixing the case so that the accused got off scot free.

'He didn't see his secret courts as a piece of smart-assery in which he exploited the known habits of the court reporters and that he ran his secret courts at the professional expense of the reporters', one Dublin editor later wrote. In any public challenge in the Dáil the reply would make the media look, at worst, as accomplices who might have taken a backhander to kill the case or, at best, people who were slovenly and lacked basic contacts in the building in which they worked for half a lifetime. As far as Charlie was concerned, it was a just a case of helping someone in trouble.

'As editor of a Sunday paper,' the late John Healy recalled, 'I had heard three of four instances where Fianna Fáil bigwigs dodged the press punishment by way of extra early or extra later sittings by obliging district justices.' These went unreported until one of the accused got a bit too greedy and tried to fight a case. As a result it was postponed and the press were ready when it reconvened.

That should have been the end of the so-called 'secret courts', but of course it wasn't. 'When the next one was held,' Healy noted, 'I was editing the *Evening Mail*. I got a tip from the courts. Charlie had pulled the wool over our eyes again.'

Donagh O'Malley, parliamentary secretary to the Minister for Finance, had been quietly prosecuted for drunken driving the previous evening. He had pleaded guilty and was fined and put off the road for six months.

He had been stopped while driving the wrong way on O'Connell Street.

'Did you see the arrows?' Garda James Travers is reported to have asked him.

'Arrows!' O'Malley exclaimed. 'I'm so drunk I couldn't see the fucken Indians.'

It was characteristic of his cavalier attitude towards the law. There was another celebrated story of a night that a garda raided a bar in which O'Malley was drinking after hours, and he reportedly asked the garda if he would 'have a pint or a transfer'.

'I remember the sense of frustration of the morning,' Healy wrote more than thirty years later. The board of the *Irish Times* had just informed him that it was closing the *Evening Mail*. He assigned a reporter to investigate the O'Malley case, and the reporter came back with the story, which Healy passed to a sub-editor with instructions to put it 'on page one where people will see it ... I was still in the boardroom working out details of the funeral of the paper when the first edition was brought down to me,' he continued. 'We spread the drunken drive charge, which was not even the day's news, across the front page as a lead story. In the shoulder, under the banner head was a single column saying the *Mail* was going to die.'

'It was so wrong,' he went on. 'You rarely lead an evening paper with a drunken driving court case. A strong single column would have done it. To make it worse it looked as if we were, in our death throes, trying to bring down a politician with us.'

'Are you the fucker that crucified me in the *Mail*?' Donagh O'Malley asked Healy when they next met.

The editor said he was unapologetic. 'We weren't crucifying O'Malley,' he later told Charlie to his face. 'We were crucifying you and your secret courts.' According to Healy that 'was the end of the *Mail*, and the end of Charlie's secret courts.'

It made a fascinating story, but unfortunately Healy embellished it out of all recognition. He was friendly with both Charlie and O'Malley and he possibly liked to think that he had broken the story, but the banner headline on the front page that evening actually read: '"Mail" Publication will be Suspended'. The story about O'Malley's arrest and the secret court was true all right, but the *Evening Mail* did not report it in that edition or any other before finally folding.

John Healy may have been confusing it with the 'Backbencher' column, which he started along with Ted Nealon in a sister paper, *The Sunday Review*. The following Sunday, Backbencher reported that the Fine Gael knives were out for Charlie. 'I cannot see the minister with all his resourcefulness come out unscathed,' he continued.

The case took a particularly unseemly turn shortly afterwards when James Travers, the garda who had arrested O'Malley, was transferred to new duties. Contending that his transfer amounted to victimisation, the garda – a six year veteran – refused to move. He was then given the option of resigning voluntarily or being dismissed from the force. In the circumstances he resigned.

The issue was raised in the Dáil when Richie Ryan of Fine Gael accused the government of conducting 'a reign of terror' within the garda síochána and the Department of Justice. Charlie replied accusing the opposition of political scavenging, much to the irritation of Gerard Sweetman, the deputy leader of Fine Gael. He threatened to ask embarrassing question about 'an amazing coincidence' concerning another garda who had also been asked to resign recently.

'There are some "quare" files in my office too,' Charlie warned. It seemed like a threat to reveal information that would be embarrassing to Fine Gael.

'Let us not be pushed too far,' James Dillon, the Fine Gael leader, cautioned, but he and his colleagues did not dare pursue the garda's case any further. 'This ended the discussion', the *Irish Times* noted with a certain finality.

An Image Problem

While Minister for Justice, Charlie introduced voluminous legislation covering a wide area, extending from family law to international law. Some of the more minor bills were to cause as much trouble as complicated ones, especially in the prevailing political climate in which the minority government was unable to depend on majority support in the Dáil.

A bill to increase the salaries of judges, for instance, was particularly controversial, because of the attitude of some members of the opposition. Charlie realised the bill would be unpopular with many people, but he contended that substantial salary increases were necessary to ensure the best and most capable people were on the bench.

'It is a natural tendency of people to be envious of highly-paid people and I accuse the opposition of playing on that simple human emotion and trying to make political capital out of it,' he told the Dáil. 'A man who is only earning £9 or £10 per week is going to resent an already highly paid member of the judiciary getting an increase. It is difficult to explain to such a man why this is necessary and the opposition are doing their best to make sure that the people will be as envious as possible.'

'Do we not all know that a man's work or value is judged by what he earns?' he asked on introducing that bill. 'It is a human and natural thing and it is something which is very common here – to look down on a man who does not earn as much as you do. I think it applies to all levels of our society.'

While that kind of thinking may have been fundamental to Charlie's philosophy, it had no appeal whatever to a Socialist like Noel Browne. 'I do not agree with that at all,' Browne said. 'I think the complete contrary is true.'

People like the Little Sisters of the Poor or the Carmelite fathers earned very little, but this did not mean that society placed more value on the services of brothel keepers just because they were paid more money.

'I do not know anything about them. I leave them to the deputy,' Charlie replied sarcastically.

There was little empathy between Browne and Charlie. As Minister for Justice, the latter was involved largely with legislation which had little to do with the needs of the poor or underprivileged. He contended, however, that he cared about the poor as much as any politician. In fact, he introduced the first bill to provide free legal aid, though the circumstances were very restrictive because of financial constraints.

In supporting the introduction of a controversial sales tax in the budget of 1963, Charlie argued that the new tax would give the government the financial resources necessary to increase children's allowances and social welfare benefits.

Noel Browne objected that this form of tax would hurt the poor more than the rich because both would have to pay it equally. His criticism led to some rather unseemly exchanges in which Charlie charged that Browne had 'difficulty proving he is not a Communist'.

'Oh, shut up,' Charlie exclaimed when Browne sought to question him in the Dáil on 11 July 1963.

'The minister will not make me shut up by his puppyish tactics,' Browne replied. Later the same day he had his chance to tell Charlie to be quiet. He was complaining that there would be an exemption from the turnover tax for medicines for animals but not for humans. Charlie tried to explain, but Browne cut him off.

'I am not finished,' he said. 'Do not interrupt me.'

'Do not be so dictatorial,' replied Charlie.

'Do not be so damned imperious,' Browne snapped.

'This is arrogance indeed. I was only trying to be helpful.'

'Do not be so supercilious. Sit down and behave yourself.'

'This is the Communist mentality,' said Charlie.

Browne appealed to the chair to order that the remark be withdrawn as it was an indication that he was a Communist.

'It is not,' Charlie insisted. 'It is an indication of the Communist mentality.

'I do not see any implication that the deputy is a Communist,' the acting speaker ruled.

'I say the minister's behaviour is the behaviour of a Fascist,' Browne retorted.

'That rubs off me much more lightly,' Charlie replied.

By squabbling with Browne, a recognised champion of the poor and underprivileged, Charlie was inevitably seen as a friend of the rich, and his ostentatious lifestyle exacerbated the impression. Fianna Fáil had for long been proud that it consisted of the men with the cloth caps, but Charlie was one of those in the mohair suits who were representative of a new breed. A wealthy businessman who owned racehorses and rode with the hunt, he enjoyed his prosperity and flaunted it, with the result that he became the object of gossip and colourful rumours, both ribald and vicious.

There were all kinds of unfounded rumours about his love-life and how he supposedly got involved in scrapes with husbands and the boyfriends of women all over the country. Some seemed to take on a life of their own, no matter how often denied. The late Eamonn Andrews was supposed to have hammered Charlie at a function one night. It would, of course, have been a total mismatch physically, and the incident never took place. Yet the rumours haunted Andrews for the rest of his life. In later years it would even be published, but most of the rumours were never printed because of the country's libel laws, which were, incidentally, updated by Charlie himself in 1963.

The *Sunday Independent* provoked his wrath by publishing a cartoon depicting him in the midst of a group of drunken people in evening dress being off-loaded from a paddy wagon outside a garda station, as a garda was saying: 'Come on out, you tally-hoing, hunt-balling pack ... Oh sorry Mr Minister, I didn't see you in there.' Although this was mild in comparison to some later cartoons, Charlie threatened legal action and the *Sunday Independent* settled by making a contribution to a charity of his choice.

In the eyes of reporters Charlie 'was too clever by half', according to John Healy, who noted that 'it was probably at this stage in his career and the affair of the secret courts which started the love-hate relationship between Haughey and the media'.

'Nineteen sixty-four was one of the best years ever for Irish agriculture,' Charlie told the Dáil in his first annual review as Minister for Agriculture on 29 April 1965. On average farm income had risen by an phenomenal 20%. The increase had been largely due to a dramatic rise in cattle exports. There had been an 11% increase in store cattle exports and a 66.6% increase in fat cattle. Beef shipments to the continent almost quadrupled in value from £3.3 millions to £12.7 millions.

The following year he was still talking in extremely optimistic terms in his next report. 'The prospects for the agricultural industry was never better,' he said. The whole country had been attested for bovine tuberculosis, and he rather rashly proclaimed that the disease was almost eradicated. 'From now on,' he said, 'there is very little excuse for an outbreak of bovine tuberculosis in a herd.'

The marked increase in agricultural production did not, however, guarantee an increased income for farmers. In 1965 the average rise was about 5%, which was slightly higher than the average rise in industrial wages, but Charlie warned of ominous indications as 'food surpluses were appearing everywhere'. The highly protective nature of the Common Agricultural Policy of the European Economic Community (EEC) was particularly worrying, because it was rapidly curtailing the opportunities for Irish expansion.

'We were planning for major increases in our agricultural production and exports, while the markets in which we could dispose of them were becoming more and more restricted,' Charlie later admitted. Hence he enthusiastically welcomed the Anglo-Irish Free Trade Agreement, due to come into operation in June 1966. The country's quotas for butter exports to Britain would be doubled, and store cattle were being given free access to the British market.

'It is impossible to exaggerate the importance of the breakthrough represented by the fact that the agreement provides for the extension of the British agricultural support price system to our finished products,' he said. 'If we work together, this agreement will surely mark the beginning of a period of development and progress in Irish agriculture unparalleled in our history.'

His optimistic projections would begin to haunt him even before the end of the month when he ran into difficulties with the Irish

Creamery Milk Suppliers Association (ICMSA), which was demanding higher milk prices.

The ICMSA advocated the introduction of a new two-tier price system in accordance with which all farmers would receive an extra 4 pence per gallon for the first 7,000 gallons of milk they produced annually and 2 pence per gallon for any milk above that quota. Since the average milk delivery was only around 3,600 gallons per year, it meant that almost all dairy farmers would enjoy the full benefits of such an increase. Only the very largest farmers, who were more likely to be members of the rival National Farmers' Association, were likely to exceed the quota.

Under the leadership of its president, John Feely, the ICMSA placed a picket outside Leinster House on 27 April 1966. The government responded rather high-handedly by having the 28 picketers arrested under the Offences Against the State Act, but Feely defiantly announced the picket would remain until his organisation's demands were met. Seventy-eight farmers were arrested while picketing next day and a further 80 the following day as the dispute escalated.

As with the Macushla Revolt, Charlie refused to talk while the protesters were acting illegally. He said that he would discuss 'other ways in which the income of the dairy farmer can be increased', he made it clear that he would not concede the price increase demanded.

The ICMSA responded by removing its picket so that discussions could be held with Charlie on 4 May, but there was no progress. 'They gave me to understand clearly that they were only interested and would accept nothing less than their original two-tier price system,' Charlie told the Dáil.

He had strong objections to this two-tier system, both from the philosophical and administrative standpoints. For one thing, he argued the government simply could not afford the extra £6 million a year that the ICMSA scheme would cost, as this amounted to more than 15% of the annual agricultural budget at the time. Moreover he contended that reducing the price for milk above the quota would be an administrative nightmare and act as a disincentive.

'It would be bad economics to discourage more efficient and more largescale production,' Charlie argued. Prompted by his own capitalist instincts, he also had reservations about granting any price increase under the circumstances for fear it would lead to socialised agriculture. 'There is a danger that agitation directed only to getting higher prices may develop a kind of dole mentality which would eventually make agriculture subservient to the state,' he contended. 'What I want to achieve is a self-reliant, independent and progressive agriculture, fully backed by, but not utterly dependent on, the state.'

Before the end of the month, however, he was sounding a more sombre note from the exuberant optimism of April. 'The task which confronts me, indeed any Minister for Agriculture,' he told the Dáil on 26 May 1966, 'is of such vast proportions and the problems are so intractable that I do not think it is possible ever to be enthusiastic about the progress which is being achieved at any given moment compared with what still remains to be done.'

Charlie proceeded to back down on the milk price issue that day. He announced an immediate increase of two pence per gallon with a further penny per gallon for quality milk after 1 April 1967. Counting the one penny per gallon extra previously given for quality milk, this meant that those farmers who had not been producing milk with a high enough cream content previously would actually get the requested four pence per gallon extra within twelve months, if they got their milk up to the desired quality.

In view of the strong, reasoned stand taken by Charlie against any increase only weeks earlier, questions must be asked about his eventual surrender. Why did he virtually capitulate on the issue?

There was no doubt in the minds of the opposition that the concessions were related to the presidential election campaign being conducted at the time. Fine Gael's candidate, T. F. O'Higgins, was running very well in Dublin and other urban areas, with the result that the incumbent president, Eamon de Valera, needed Fianna Fáil's traditional rural support to win a second term. This support would obviously be endangered if the government was still at odds with farmers over the price of milk.

As de Valera's national director of elections, Charlie pulled a political stroke and shored up the president's rural support by conceding on the milk price issue. In view of the narrowness of de Valera's subsequent victory, the concession quite conceivably made the difference between victory and defeat. It appeared that Charlie had backed down under ICMSA pressure, and he would pay for this dearly before the year was out.

Figuratively speaking Charlie was flying high at this time and it was the start of a particularly crucial period because his father-in-law, Seán Lemass, had indicated his intention to retire as Taoiseach within the next twelve months. Charlie, who had never made any secret of his aspirations for the office, was clearly in an advantageous position. As Minister for Agriculture, he was in one of the most influential posts in the government and his comparative youth was a decided advantage because, on his next birthday, he would be the same age as John F. Kennedy was when he became the youngest president ever to be elected in the United States. Kennedy had made a profound impression on the Irish people, and Charlie never seemed averse to being compared with the late president. And those comparisons extended beyond the political arena.

Much of Charlie's success as a politician was due to his ability to sell himself. Having talked so favourably about the prospects for Irish agriculture in early 1966, he came in for strong criticism when things began to go wrong, especially when the bottom virtually fell out of the cattle market that summer.

Eighty per cent of Irish cattle and beef were exported, with the result there was little that he, or the Department of Agriculture, could do about controlling those markets. When the EEC virtually closed its doors to beef imports from outside the community in April 1966, Irish farmers had to turn to the British market to sell their surplus cattle, but they ran into serious difficulties here, too. A seaman's strike in Britain initially blocked imports and, after it was settled, a glut developed as the backlog was dumped on the market. This was further complicated by a credit squeeze which impaired the ability of British importers to keep Irish cattle for the two months necessary to claim a British government subsidy. Hence the demand for Irish cattle dropped.

As prices tumbled Charlie was criticised. It was not his fault, but he had left himself wide open to censure by his failure to prepare farmers for the slump, which became virtually inevitable following the closing of EEC markets in April. Apprising farmers at that stage would, of course, have meant giving them bad news before the presidential election and that was not Charlie's way of doing things.

At the annual general meeting of the National Farmers' Association (NFA) in August, Rickard Deasy, the organisation's president, criticised the minister's handling of events. Always highly sensitive to criticism at the best of times, Charlie was particularly sensitive now that his father-in-law was due to step down within the next six months. He over-reacted to the criticism by cancelling a planned meeting with NFA leaders. And his problems were compounded by his own arrogance as he got into a controversy with Radio Telefís Éireann (RTÉ) over the whole affair.

On 29 September he told the Dáil that farmers should hold on to their cattle to await better prices. The NFA, on the other hand, advised them to sell as soon as possible because prices would continue to drop. That night RTÉ reported Charlie's statement followed by the NFA's contradictory advice on its nightly television news. Charlie immediately telephoned the news department to protest.

'I felt compelled in the public interest to protest that the NFA statement should be carried immediately after mine,' he explained. 'I gave specific advice to farmers in reply to questions from deputies in the Dáil as the responsible minister, and I felt that to have my advice followed by a contradiction from an organisation could only lead to confusion and damage the industry.' As a result of his protest, the item was dropped from further bulletins that evening. Consequently questions were asked in the Dáil, where Charlie came across rather arrogantly.

'I think it was a very unwise thing to say the least of it, for Radio Telefís Éireann to follow that solemn advice of mine given as Minister for Agriculture with a contradiction by one organisation,' he said. 'I pointed this out to the news room of Telefís Éireann and I think I was absolutely right in doing so.'

The RTÉ affair was not only as an attempt 'to hinder the democratic right of freedom of speech', an NFA spokesman argued, but also 'one further example of the arrogance of Mr Haughey'. The latter suddenly found himself embroiled in a controversy over the freedom of broadcasting.

RTÉ journalists had been uneasy for some months over the station's role in the recent presidential election campaign. As de Valera was in his mid-eighties and almost totally blind, he had been unable to match his younger opponent on the campaign trail. It was therefore decided that he would not campaign at all. As his director of elections, Charlie sought to minimise the Fine Gael candidate's physical advantages by persuading RTÉ not to cover the campaign in the supposed interests of fairness.

RTÉ was asked to ignore the Fine Gael campaign, because the president would not be campaigning himself as he was supposed to be above politics. RTÉ's news department accepted the argument, which was unfair to Fine Gael's T. F. O'Higgins. Unlike the president, he campaigned actively but got practically no news coverage, whereas Charlie dispatched ministers around the country, where they highlighted de Valera's bid for re-election by making newsworthy announcements. Charlie was credited with pulling a political master stroke, but the pent up frustrations of RTÉ journalists exploded during the controversy with the NFA.

Matters were compounded when Charlie withdrew from a scheduled television appearance on a current affairs programme. He was supposed to debate the cattle situation with Deasy. Despite strong objections from Charlie, RTÉ went ahead with the programme, using one of its own reporters, Ted Nealon, to put forward the minister's case.

With Charlie refusing to talk, NFA leaders decided to exert public pressure with marches and a massive protest rally. On 7 October 1966 Deasy and other members of the NFA set out from Bantry to walk the 210 miles to Dublin, where it was planned to hold a protest rally outside Leinster House. In the following days other marchers set out from different centres and gathered support on the way. By the time the various marchers reached Merrion Square on 19 October, there were several thousand protesters. After a rally Deasy and eight other leaders went over to Department of Agriculture to talk to Charlie, but he refused to meet them.

The refusal seemed churlish after they had walked such a long way. Charlie had blundered tactically, because the NFA leaders set about dramatising his refusal in a novel way. Deasy announced that they would wait outside the Department of Agriculture for 'a bloody month' if necessary until Charlie met them. The nine of them literally camped outside the front door of the Department for the next three weeks.

Charlie was becoming desperate. He travelled to the continent and tried frantically to find a market for Irish cattle. He was actually depicted on the cover of *Dublin Opinion* magazine as a cowboy driving cattle to the ends of the earth. But the only concession he came back with was a German promise to purchase 2,000 cattle. He promptly announced this to the Dáil, much to the embarrassment of the Germans, who had not had time to clear the matter with their European partners.

In the midst of the controversy with the farmers, Lemass formally announced his decision to retire and the quest for a successor began in earnest. Charlie and George Colley were initially seen as the main contenders.

'There is great appreciation of the sheer ability of Mr Haughey in the Dáil, in the party, and in the government,' according to the political correspondent of the *Irish Times*. 'The only snag, it is generally agreed, is that his public image is not favourable.'

And that image was not being enhanced by either the RTÉ controversy or his problems with the farmers camped on the steps of his office. When he went to Athlone for a Fianna Fáil meeting on 21 October, his car was attacked by a mob of protesting farmers. Four days later the same thing happened outside a hotel in Dublin.

'Rat, rat, come out of your sewer, sewer rat', many of the 200 farmers chanted as they tried to prevent his car entering the hotel grounds. Later they attempted to block the road as he was leaving. Some stood in front of the car and pounded on it.

'Go on, go on,' an elegantly dressed woman shouted from the sidelines. 'I hate him.'

Such scenes really put paid to Charlie's chances for the leadership. Lemass, who initially stayed in the background, led some correspondents to believe he was supporting Colley, but this may have been just a ploy to help Charlie by discouraging others from entering the fray.

With backing from senior party figures like Frank Aiken and Seán MacEntee, Colley was seen as the candidate of party traditionalists, who were more concerned with the revival of the Gaelic language than with economic matters. On the other hand, Charlie's support came largely from those interested in a more pragmatic, business-minded approach.

Charlie was the epitome of the men in the mohair suits who were changing the face of Fianna Fáil. He and fellow ministers, like Donagh O'Malley and Brian Lenihan, were urban realists with little time for the pastoral idealism inspiring de Valera's dream of comely maidens dancing at the cross roads. Instead, Charlie and friends were to be found in the company of self-made men, speculators, builders and architects, the very people it seemed to some who were destroying the pastoral dream with their concrete jungles.

By working hard and also playing hard, Charlie had already become the subject of an elaborate mythology of rumours. His *bon-vivant* lifestyle with its aristocratic trappings commanded attention, but not always the approval of those he seemed to be imitating. Many of them despised him as *nouveau riche*. Others, possibly jealous at his successful rise, questioned how in a relatively short time he made money to live in such opulence, especially when most of his career was in public life at a time when politicians were not particularly well paid. He was secretive about his business dealings, and the unanswered questions led to speculation, which was easily exploited by enemies spreading defamatory rumours.

Although the *Irish Times* described Charlie as 'far and away the strongest candidate,' the political correspondent of *The Cork Examiner* believed that Colley was virtually certain to win a contest, because Haughey was so unpopular at the time.

Some rural deputies like Tom McEllistrim of Kerry and Eugene Gilbride of Sligo called on Jack Lynch, Minister of Finance, to run, but he expressed no interest.

Haughey was rebutted when he approached Neil Blaney for support. 'No, Charlie,' Blaney told him, 'you haven't got the background.' Blaney decided to run himself, and Kevin Boland announced on 3 November 1966 that he would be nominating him. This changed everything. Donagh O'Malley, Haughey's campaign manager, promptly threw his support to Blaney. At that point, the Taoiseach decided to put pressure on Lynch to stand.

Lemass told Lynch 'that several backbenchers wanted me to run and that the party generally favoured me as his successor,' Lynch recalled. 'He pointed out that I owed the party a duty to serve, even as leader. He gave me to understand that the other contenders, to whom he had already spoken, were prepared to withdraw in my favour. I told him I would consider my position and would discuss it with my wife.'

When Lynch agreed to stand, Lemass called in the other candidates and informed them that he would be backing Lynch. He basically wished them to withdraw. Colley told him that he would first have to consult his wife, Mary.

'What kind of people have I got when one man has to get his wife's permission to run and the other has to get his wife's permission to withdraw?' Lemass asked in exasperation.

Haughey's chances had already been undermined by the defection of Donagh O'Malley, so when the Taoiseach talked to him, he immediately agreed to withdraw and even offered to nominate Lynch.

'I'm glad someone can give me a straight answer around here,' Lemass remarked.

The Taoiseach then called in Blaney and asked about his plans.

'What are George and Charlie doing?' Blaney asked.

'Charlie is no problem,' Lemass replied.

'What about George?'

'George is going out to Mary to allow him to withdraw.' With that Blaney agreed to stand down.

'We were foolishly blinded by the necessity for unity in the party,' Blaney said afterwards. 'Lynch literally didn't have a Fianna Fáil background at all.' Both Blaney and Boland were the sons of founder members of Fianna Fáil and both of their fathers had served in the Dáil. In their sneering arrogance, they essentially questioned Lynch's party pedigree from the outset. 'Look,' Boland said to Blaney, 'let him on so long

34

as he does what we tell him.'

Haughey and Blaney publicly announced that they would be supporting Lynch. But George Colley – who was one of those with an impeccable party pedigree as the son of a former Fianna Fáil deputy – announced that he would not be withdrawing. There would be a contest, but the outcome was a foregone conclusion. Lynch won easily and was promptly elected Taoiseach.

His selection was widely welcomed, even in opposition circles, where there was obvious relief that Charlie had not succeeded. James Dillon, the Fine Gael leader, rejoiced openly. Now Charlie would never become Taoiseach, he gloated.

'Remember,' Dillon told the Dáil, 'when he failed to land his fish last Wednesday night, he will never land it. He is finished. He stinks, politically, of course.'

Having backed Lynch in the end, Charlie was rewarded with a prestigious promotion to what was generally seen as the second most powerful post in the government. He was appointed Minister for Finance.

Charlie was an innovative Minister for Finance. Each of his budget addresses incorporated popular giveaways, which reduced the opposition to impotent frustration. Richie Ryan of Fine Gael described the various concessions as a 'payment of conscience money'.

'You are a reflection on the dignity of this house,' Charlie snapped. 'You are only a gutty.'

'Our people will get the government they voted for,' James Dillon declared. 'If it is *Animal Farm* they want, they should vote for Fianna Fáil, but if it is democracy and decency they want, I suggest they will have to look elsewhere. I think the acceptance of corruption as the norm in public life is shocking.'

'Is it not another form of corruption to take people's character away, to spread false rumours about them?' Charlie asked. Fine Gael was vilifying and slandering him with malicious rumours, he said. 'That is all you are good for, the lot of you.'

On the night of 20 September 1968 he was seriously injured in a car accident in Co. Wicklow while driving home following an election rally. The circumstances of the crash were never explained publicly, but it was widely believed in political, garda and media circles that Haughey was driving at his own insistence. As Charlie was seriously injured, the opposition did not press the matter on this occasion. Thereafter, however, ministerial drivers were ordered not to allow anyone to drive their cars, even their respective ministers.

Haughey recovered in time to be appointed national director of elections for the general election of June 1969. This time he was the subject of some particularly strong opposition criticism in relation both to his own finances and his fundraising tactics for the party.

Fianna Fáil had been adopting American methods. Charlie had helped to draw up the blueprint for *Taca*, a support group made up mostly of businessmen who were invited to join at £100 a year. The money was deposited in a bank until election time, and the interest was used to fund lavish dinners at which members of *Taca* could mix with cabinet ministers.

Taca was 'a fairly innocent concept,' according to Charlie. 'In so far as it had any particular motivation it was to make the party independent of big business and try to spread the level of financial support right across a much wider spectrum of the community.' Some members had previously been subscribing 'substantially more' to the party at election times than the £500 that would accumulate in *Taca* subscriptions, if the Dáil ran its full five-year term, he contended.

Although Charlie was the politician most associated with *Taca* in the public mind, the idea had come from somebody else and he had no control over the funds, but he embraced the scheme with enthusiasm and organised the first dinner – a particularly lavish affair attended by the whole cabinet. 'We were all organised by Haughey and sent to different tables around the room,' Kevin Boland recalled. 'The extraordinary thing about my table was that everybody at it was in somehow or other connected with the construction industry.'

Opposition deputies promptly questioned the propriety of such fraternisation between the property developers and members of the government. In particular, there were questions about the selection of property being rented by government departments and agencies as they mushroomed in the midst of the unprecedented economic growth.

Boland insisted that he 'never did a thing' within his department for any member of *Taca*, but he admitted that other ministers might have been 'susceptible'. A cloud of suspicion was cast over the operations of *Taca* and it 'unfortunately provided a basis for political attack which,' Charlie said, 'did us a lot of damage at the time'.

Insinuations of corruption were widespread and these had been fuelled in May 1967 when George Colley urged those attending a Fianna Fáil youth conference in Galway not to be 'dispirited if some people in high places appear to have low standards'. It was widely assumed that Colley was alluding to Charlie in particular, in view of the intensity of their rivalry over the party leadership some months earlier, but Colley rather disingenuously denied this intent.

Haughey was involved with Donagh O'Malley in Reema (Ireland) Ltd., a property company of which O'Malley was the chief executive and Charlie was secretary. Reema bought property around Limerick on the road to Shannon airport. At the time, there were suggestions that he and O'Malley used inside knowledge.

When it came to money matters Charlie was very much a mystery man. Following their marriage the Haugheys initially lived in a semi-detached house in a Raheny housing estate, but in 1957, they moved to Grangemore, a large Victorian mansion on a 45 acre site in Raheny. The builder Matt Gallagher advised Haughey to splash out £13,000 to buy the house and lands in Raheny, with the promise that when the time was right and planning permission had been secured to build houses on the property, he would buy it from him.

In his early years in the Dáil, Charlie projected a high public profile and enjoyed a good press, but he was quiet about his own private life and especially his business dealings. He appeared to amass a considerable fortune at a time when politicians were not a particularly well paid. 'Now to be a wealthy politician was the sin of the day – and Charlie Haughey was indecently wealthy,' according to columnist John Healy. 'If a pub changed hands, Haughey was the secret buyer.' At one point, he supposedly owned about five on the north and south sides of Dublin.

In 1968, Haughey bought a 127-acre stud farm in Rathoath, Co. Meath for £30,000 without taking out a mortgage. He was a full-time politician, and was no longer earning from the accountancy firm that he had established with Harry Boland. His only visible income was his ministerial salary of £3,500, but the subsequent profit that he made from the sale of his Raheny property some months later would have more than accounted for the purchase price of the farm. Of course, he protested that his business dealings were all legitimate, but his subsequent behaviour cast serious doubts on both his veracity and his financial probity.

In the midst of the general election campaign of 1969 Charlie found himself implicated in further controversy, following a sensational report in the *Evening Herald* about the sale of his Raheny home, which the newspaper stated was sold to his developer friend, Matt Gallagher, for over £204,000. Charlie used this money to purchase Abbeville and the surrounding 240 acres for £144,997, so even with the purchase of the farm in Co. Meath, he would still have had about £25,000 left over.

'I object to my private affairs being used in this way,' Charlie declared. None of the figures could be given with certainty, because he did not give details to any reporter. 'It is a private matter between myself and the purchaser.'

Planning permission would inevitably be granted for the land, regardless of who owned it, once Dublin began to spread out. Gallagher's advice was not particularly inspired, but Haughey had the advantage of knowing that he had an eventual buyer when he purchased the land. By hanging on to the property for a decade its value appreciated greatly. Some opponents tried to suggest that there was something immoral about the profit he made on the whole venture. Maybe what they should really have been questioning was the cost of new land at Kinsealy, because that would seemed to have been an equally propitious purchase, seeing that he sold just 17.5 acres of that land to Cement Roadstone for a quarry in December 1973 for £140,000, which was under £5,000 less than he had paid for the house and the 240 acres four years earlier.

Matt Gallagher, who had made a small fortune in wartime Britain, returned to Ireland and began building houses in the public and private sector in the 1950s. There was a great deal of housing deprivation in urban Ireland, especially in Dublin, where several families often lived in the one tenement. Gallagher was one of the builders most involved in *Taca*, and some of those people were prepared to help Haughey in their own interest.

'Haughey was financed in order to create the environment which the Anglo-Irish had enjoyed and that we as a people could never aspire to,' according to Patrick Gallagher, who believed that his father saw the construction of a modern Ireland as a great patriotic enterprise.

The controversy over the sale of Charlie's property became a national issue, however, when Gerard Sweetman of Fine Gael charged that Charlie might have acted improperly by not explaining to the Dáil that he stood to benefit personally from legislation that he had introduced himself. It was suggested that he might have been liable for income tax on the sale of his land, if part of the 1965 Finance Act had not been repealed recently.

Suddenly Charlie's private business dealings became an election issue. 'Because he has impugned my reputation,' Charlie explained, 'I have felt obliged to refer the matter to the revenue commissioners, under whose care and management are placed all taxes and duties imposed by the Finance Act, 1965.'

The revenue commissioners promptly reported 'that no liability to income tax or surtax would have arisen' under any provision of the 1965 act. Although this should have killed the issue, one of his opponents in his Dublin North Central constituency – the Labour party candidate, Conor Cruise O'Brien – raked up the issue repeatedly during the campaign in an effort to expose what he described as 'the Fianna Fáil speculator-orientated oligarchy'. Despite everything, Charlie increased his vote to top the poll, while Cruise O'Brien was a distant second. Although Fianna Fáil's vote dropped by 2% nationally, the party actually gained two seats through the vagaries of proportional representation. Lynch was re-elected as Taoiseach and Charlie was re-appointed as Minister for Finance.

In his three full years in that portfolio, the budget deficit quadrupled. He intended to tell the Dáil in his next budget address that the deficit would be 'substantially higher' in 1970.

'There was a hushed silence as Mr Haughey rose from his usual seat and walked across to the Taoiseach's place on the front bench to open his briefcase,' the *Evening Herald* reported. 'The minister, who began his budget speech earlier than usual because of the small number of queries during question time, started off with a review of the economy in general.'

Over the years Charlie had complained more than once about the unreliability of the media in general and the *Evening Herald* in particular, and this must have been one of the most glaring pieces of irresponsible journalism. Far from starting his budget address early, Charlie was not even in the Dáil. He was in hospital.

Lynch told a stunned gathering that the Minister for Finance had been hospitalised that morning following an accident. As a result the Taoiseach read the budget address himself.

Charlie's injuries resulted from a fall from a horse, but contrary rumours began circulating almost immediately. The garda commissioner informed Peter Berry, the secretary of the Department of Justice, that 'a strange rumour was circulating in North County Dublin that Mr Haughey's accident occurred on a licensed premises on the previous night.' Berry passed on the information to the Taoiseach, who 'was emphatic' that there should be no garda inquiries into the matter.

'Within a couple of days, there were all sorts of rumours in golf clubs, in political circles, etc., as to how the accident occurred with various husbands, fathers, brothers or lovers having struck the blow in any one of dozens of pubs around Dublin', according to Berry.

One unfounded rumour that was later published suggested that Haughey was beaten close to death by the father and brother of a young woman after they supposedly caught him in bed with her, upstairs in the Grasshopper Inn in Clonee, Co. Meath.

Charlie had tried to dismount by hoisting himself out of the saddle by grabbing the guttering above the stable entrance, but it gave way with a large crack, which spooked the horse. Haughey was thrown heavily to the ground, receiving serious injuries that required hospitalisation. The rumours were so persistent that Charlie took the unusual step of having one of his stable hands talk to the press about having witnessed the riding accident.

By then, however, rumours of Charlie's other activities were already rampant and the country found itself in the midst of the arms crisis, which led to his dismissal as Minister for Finance on 6 May 1970.

THE ARMS CRISIS

At about three o'clock in the morning of 6 May 1970 Jack Lynch issued a statement to the press. He announced that he had 'requested the resignation of members of the government, Mr Neil T. Blaney, Minister for Agriculture, and Mr C. J. Haughey, Minister for Finance, because I am satisfied that they do not subscribe fully to government policy in relation to the present situation in the six counties as stated by me at the Fianna Fáil Ard Fheis in January last.' On learning of the Taoiseach's decision, Kevin Boland resigned as Minister for Local Government and Social Welfare in protest, and Paudge Brennan, his parliamentary secretary did likewise. The country was suddenly awash with rumours that the Taoiseach had discovered plans for a *coup d'etat*.

It was not until hours later that Lynch explained to the Dáil that he had acted because security forces had informed him 'about an alleged attempt to unlawfully import arms from the continent'. As these reports involved the two cabinet ministers, he said he asked them to resign on the basis 'that not even the slightest suspicion should attach to any member of the government in a matter of this nature'.

To understand the crisis one must go back to events surrounding serious violence which erupted in Northern Ireland following the Apprentice Boys Parade in Derry City on 12 August 1969. The parade was attacked by Nationalist protesters. The police, supported by Unionist thugs, then besieged the Nationalist area. What became known as the Battle of the Bogside had begun and quickly spread to other Nationalist areas of Northern Ireland, which seemed on the brink of a full-scale civil war.

Amid the escalating violence the cabinet met in Dublin. Lynch had a draft address that he intended to deliver live on television that evening. Several members of the cabinet objected that it was too weak in the circumstances. Charlie, Blaney, and Boland, together with Jim Gibbons, Brian Lenihan and Seán Flanagan all called for something stronger. A new speech was prepared at the cabinet meeting.

'The Stormont government evidently is no longer in control of the situation, which is the inevitable outcome of policies pursued for decades by them,' Lynch told the nation that evening. 'The Government of Ireland can no longer stand by'.

The statement had an electrifying impact on the situation in the north. Besieged Nationalists concluded the Republic was going to intervene militarily, and the Unionist population – blinded by an irrational fear of the south – reacted hysterically. The Dublin government had no intention of invading.

Even Kevin Boland, one of the cabinet's most outspoken proponents of assisting northern Nationalists, believed it would be disastrous for the Irish army to become involved. 'Places contiguous to the border could obviously be assisted effectively,' he contended, 'but to do so would mean the wholesale slaughter of Nationalists (or Catholics) in other areas where there was no defence available. I feel reasonably certain that the others also saw this and that none of them visualised an actual incursion.'

Faced with the irrational frenzy of the heavily armed Unionist community, northern Nationalists were extremely vulnerable. They established defence committees and appealed to Dublin for arms to protect themselves.

Dublin reacted in a number of ways. It launched a propaganda campaign to enlist international sympathy for the Nationalist position, but there was little the government could do in a tangible way. 'There was a feeling among the government, and among the community as a whole, that we could not do a great deal deal to help the people of the north,' Charlie explained. 'We knew that a lot of people were suffering very severe hardship and distress and the government decided to be generous in coming to their aid. I was appointed as the person to see that this aid was given as freely and generously as possible.'

'There was no sum of money specified,' he continued. 'I was instructed by the government to make money available on a generous scale to whatever extent we required.' He was given virtual *carte blanche* to help the Nationalists. 'I have never seen a government decision that was drafted in such wide terms,' Charles H. Murray, the secretary of the Department of Finance, said afterwards.

On 20 August 1969 Peter Berry, the secretary of the Department of Justice, reported that an unidentified cabinet minister had recently told a prominent member of the IRA that the authorities would not interfere with IRA operations planned for Northern Ireland, if the IRA called off all its activities within the twenty-six counties.

'That could have been me,' Charlie told the cabinet. 'I was asked to see someone casually and it transpired to be this person. There was nothing to it, it was entirely casual.'

Berry 'was completely reassured'. Charlie had taken a strong stand against the IRA as Minister for Justice at the beginning of the decade and it seemed inconceivable that he would become involved with them now, but the security people were not reassured. 'They repeated that their sources had proved reliable in the past', Berry noted.

Capt. James J. Kelly happened to be on a visit to in Derry at the time. On returning to Dublin he wrote a report of his impressions of events for his commanding officer, Col Michael Hefferon, the director of military intelligence. Hefferon welcomed this report from Capt. Kelly, an officer with 20 years' army experience, with the last ten years in G2, military intelligence. At the time even G2 had been caught unawares by the ferocity of events in the north.

'I was very glad of any information,' Col Hefferon explained. 'I had to run around and try to find out the people that would give me the most because you had a whole lot of rumours going which had no foundation to them.' He ordered Kelly to maintain his northern contacts. 'It is now necessary to harness all opinion in the state in a concerted drive towards achieving the aim of unification,' Capt. Kelly wrote in his report of 23 August 1969. 'This means accepting the possibility of armed action of some sort, as the ultimate solution.' He added that 'if civil war embracing the area was to result because of unwillingness to accept that war is the continuation of politics by other means, it would be a far greater evil for the Irish nation.'

Col Hefferon was anxious for a first hand report of events in the north, so Capt. Kelly was sent across the border again the following month. This time he accompanied Séamus Brady, a journalist working on the government's propaganda campaign. The people that they met were clamouring for arms to defend themselves, as they felt virtually defenceless against armed Unionist thugs.

Later Haughey invited Col Hefferon to Kinsealy, along with his adjutant, Capt. Kelly. Charlie was looking for advice in order to establish a committee of reputable individuals to oversee the distribution of financial relief in Northern Ireland. Capt. Kelly briefed him on the situation there.

He explained that he was due to meet between fifteen and twenty representatives from the various Defence Committees at a hotel in Bailieboro, Co. Cavan, on the weekend of 4 October. He said he needed money to cover his expenses, and Haughey instructed the Department of Finance to provide him with £500.

The captain's activities had already aroused the suspicion of the garda special branch, which was disturbed that he had been meeting with known members of the IRA. Berry was actually in hospital for tests when he learned that the captain was due to meet with the IRA Chief of Staff Cathal Goulding and other prominent members in Bailieboro, Co. Cavan. Unable to contact either the Minister for Justice or the Taoiseach, Berry telephoned Charlie, who promptly called to the hospital.

'I told him of Capt. Kelly's goings on and of the visit planned for Bailieboro,' Berry noted. 'He did not seem unduly perturbed about Capt. Kelly but was quite inquisitive about what I knew of Goulding. I felt reassured.'

Berry had no idea Charlie had provided money to cover the expenses of the Bailieboro meeting, and Charlie made no effort to enlighten him. This meeting was the genesis of the arms crisis itself. Berry had confided in Charlie, but the latter had not reciprocated.

At the Bailieboro meeting a plan was hatched to provide northern Republicans with guns. Capt. Kelly noted in his report, however, that this was not likely to be enough. 'The defensive aspect of operations is genuinely stressed,' he wrote on 6 October 1969, 'but there is a definite feeling, that in the last analysis, the Defence Forces will have to come to the rescue.'

Haughey did not enlighten Berry who was still in hospital when he learned what happened at Bailieboro. He was again unable to contact the Justice minister Michael Moran, who had a serious drink problem. He therefore contacted Lynch, who called at the hospital on the morning of 18 October, as Berry was undergoing tests.

'I told him of Capt. Kelly's prominent part in the Bailieboro meeting with known members of the IRA, of his possession of a wad of money, of his standing drinks and of the sum of money – £50,000 – that would be available for the purchase of arms,' Berry noted. Lynch later denied Berry's account, but this was apparently one of those occasions on which he was suffering from his infamous forgetfulness. He actually told Gibbons about Berry's report, and the Minister for Defence, in turn, questioned Col Hefferon, but that was apparently the end of the matter. When this information came out a decade later Gibbons stated that as of 'October-November 1969,' he informed the Taoiseach, 'that there were questionable activities on the part of certain members of the government making contact with people they should not make contact with.' This was not a great secret at the time. The *United Irishman*, the mouthpiece for the IRA, accused Charlie and Blaney of promising help to Nationalists in order to undermine the standing of the IRA north of the border. Some people later contended that the two politicians were responsible for the split that led to the establishment of the Provisional IRA.

Despite Berry's warning, Charlie turned to Capt. Kelly for advice and help in the coming weeks. 'I had no hesitation in receiving assistance from Capt. Kelly in briefing me on the situation in the north of Ireland and letting me know who the different groups were and all that sort of thing,' Haughey explained.

Capt. Kelly's suggested the three northern nationalists who were selected to administer the government's financial contributions following the Bailieboro meeting. A bank account under their joint control was opened in Clones, and Haughey personally telephoned the secretary general of the Irish Red Cross to deposit £5,000 in the account.

Thereafter Haughey's personal secretary, Anthony Fagan, would transfer money to the Red Cross with instructions to forward it to the Clones account. The Irish Red Cross was used to launder the money.

Whenever Haughey wanted information or to pass on a message about the north, he would call on the captain. 'Get Kelly to do it,' he would tell Fagan.

When money was needed, Capt. Kelly would go to Fagan, who would forward a note: 'Minister, Kelly wants another £3,500 from the Bank a/c in the usual way. Is this OK please?'

Haughey would then simply write 'OK' on the note. A few times he did balk temporarily. 'This cannot go on for ever', he grumbled. But each time he authorised the payments after discussing them with Capt. Kelly.

The minister to whom Capt. Kelly was closest was Neil Blaney, whom he met just about every week.

There were grounds for believing the conspiracy was much more serious than trying to import arms illegally. Capt. Kelly essentially suggested in his report of 23 August that in order to end partition the state should face the fact that 'war is the continuation of politics by other means.' In his report of the Bailieboro meeting he noted that the northern Republicans were looking for arms for defensive purposes 'but there is a definite feeling, in the last analysis, the defence forces will have to come to the rescue.' The Minister for Defence could authorise the importation of weapons, but no members of the government, not even the whole cabinet, had the right to involve the country in war. Taken to its logical conclusion, this amounted to a conspiracy to subvert the constitution by involving the country in war, contrary to Article 28 of the constitution, which stipulates that 'the state shall not participate in any war save with the assent of Dáil Éireann.'

Kelly sent his reports to Hefferon and they were forwarded to Gibbons. Having been warned by Peter Berry, Lynch questioned Gibbons about Capt. Kelly's activities. If Lynch did not know what was happening, it was because he chose to turn a blind eye. His behaviour, which amounted to disregarding his obligation to uphold and implement the constitution, was both reckless and irresponsible. Of course, he publicly avowed a policy of peaceful intent towards the north, but he seemed prepared to tolerate conflicting views on this vital issue within his cabinet. For instance, Blaney seemed intent on going to war over the north, even though Lynch had been emphasising that government wished to pursue peaceful means. Blaney delivered a speech in Letterkenny, Co. Donegal, on 8 December 1969, at celebration commemorating his twenty-one years in the Dáil. 'The ideal way of ending partition is by peaceful means, but no one has a right to assert that force is irrevocably out,' he said. 'The Fianna Fáil party has never taken a decision to rule out the use of force, if the circumstances in the six counties so demand.'

This was a carefully prepared speech that Blaney took the unusual step of reading, and circulating to the press. It was a challenge to Lynch, but the Taoiseach behaved as if there was no challenge at all.

'While Mr Blaney's feelings on the partition issue are very deeply felt, and he occasionally finds it difficult not to give public expression to them, he knows and endorses government policy on this issue, as he did in his speech in Letterkenny,' Lynch said. Was Lynch saying that the Blaney's speech reflected government policy?

In the last week of December 1969 there was a curious incident following the arrest of some Derrymen with weapons near the border. Berry was told that the Taoiseach wanted 'to throw the book' at those arrested, so charges were preferred against them, much to Charlie's annoyance.

'Twenty-four hours later Mr Haughey was on to me furiously inquiring who had given the gardaí the stupid direction to arrest the men,' Berry wrote. 'I told him that the decision came from the very top.'

If the men recognised the court, Berry said the charges would be thrown out, otherwise they would be committed for contempt. Charlie remained furious. 'His language,' according to Berry, 'was not the usual kind usually heard in church. He said that he would ensure that there would be no contempt.'

At the Fianna Fáil Ard Fheis on 17 January 1970 Blaney appeared to orchestrate an overt challenge to Lynch's leadership. It was the biggest ard fheis in the party's history, because it was the first one held over a weekend, rather than in midweek.

Blaney's supporters made the first four speeches in the debate on the Taoiseach's department. They eulogised Blaney. Then Kevin Boland waded in with a speech denouncing partition. This was a bald attack on Lynch. 'The Taoiseach knew exactly what I was doing,' Boland later wrote. 'I was castigating him in public.'

Lynch confronted this challenge as he departed from his prepared script to declare a policy of peaceful intent in his presidential address to the party. 'If anybody wants this policy to change, this is the place to do it and now is the time,' he said throwing down the gauntlet. 'If people want this traditional Fianna Fáil policy to be pursued by me as leader of the government and the party, now is the time to say it.'

Blaney and Boland were routed. Lynch received a tumultuous ovation. At the end he received a prolonged standing ovation from the gathering as they chanted, 'We back Jack.' But Lynch did nothing about Capt. Kelly's efforts in relation to procuring arms.

As a result of all of this Berry concluded that Lynch did not wish to be informed so that he could turn a blind eye to the planned gunrunning. This assessment – whether right or wrong – was shared by more than one member of the cabinet. Kevin Boland concluded, for instance, that the Taoiseach privately approved.

'As far as I could see,' Boland explained, 'everyone assumed everyone else knew and the matter was spoken of as if it was a case of the government assisting in the only way a government could assist without a diplomatic breach.'

Following a cabinet meeting on 6 February 1970, defence minister Jim Gibbons actually ordered army Chief of Staff Lt Gen. Seán McKeown to prepare for involvement in Northern Ireland. 'I was instructed to direct you to prepare the army for incursions into Northern Ireland,' Gibbons said.

'The Taoiseach and other ministers have met delegations from the north,' he continued. The Nationalist people of Northern Ireland were largely defenceless at the time, and they were terrified that Unionists thugs, who were armed, as many of them were members of so-called gun clubs, would massacre them. Thus, Nationalists visiting Dublin pleaded for weapons that they could use to defend themselves. 'At these meetings urgent demands were made for respirators, weapons and ammunition the provision of which the government agreed,' Gibbons explained. 'Accordingly truck loads of these stores will be put at readiness so that they may be available in a matter of hours.'

In short, Gibbons told the chief of staff that the government had agreed to provide weapons for Nationalist civilians in Northern Ireland. To avoid confusion the army asked for a clarification the following week. 'The military assume that incursion would only be mounted in circumstances where there would be a complete breakdown of law and order in N. Ireland', it was noted. Gibbons confirmed this. Thus, the directive was an order to prepare a contingency plan so that the army could respond 'in a matter of hours'.

During February, Minister for Defence Gibbons secured authorisation for Capt. Kelly to go to Germany to purchase the weapons, which consisted of 200 sub machine guns, 84 light machine guns, 50 general-purpose machine guns, 50 rifles, 200 grenades, 200 pistols and 250,000 rounds of ammunition.

Upon his return he gave the details to Jim Gibbons. Initially it was planned to bring the guns from Belgium to Dublin port on a ship, the *City of Dublin*. In his capacity as Minister for Finance, Charlie instructed customs to clear the cargo without inspecting it, but the cargo had not been loaded because of a problem with the paperwork. British intelligence, which was aware of the scheme, had ensured the paperwork was not in order.

Capt. Kelly went to the continent to have the cargo transferred to Trieste for shipment to Ireland, but while it was en route he had it off-loaded in Vienna so that it could be flown directly to Ireland on a chartered plane.

Plans were made for the weapons to be flown to Dublin on Tuesday, 21 April 1970. But the special branch staked out the airport with the aim of seizing the cargo.

Brian Lenihan, the Minister for Transport, tipped off Col Hefferon. Haughey was then informed, and he telephone Peter Berry, who immediately recognised his voice. 'You know about the cargo that is coming into Dublin airport on Sunday?' Charlie asked.

'Yes, minister.'

'Can it be let through on a guarantee that it will go direct to the north?'

'No.'

'I think that is a bad decision,' Charlie said. 'Does the man from Mayo [the Minister for Justice] know?'

'Yes.'

'What will happen to it when it arrives?'

'It will be grabbed,' replied Berry.

'I had better have it called off,' Charlie said and then hung up.

'I made notes there and then in my personal diary as to what Mr Haughey said,' Berry later explained.

'All this could not have gone on for several months without the knowledge of the Taoiseach unless he was wilfully turning the blind eye,' he concluded. He therefore decided the time had come to get in touch with President de Valera in order to force Lynch's hand.

Berry did not actually give de Valera any details, he just asked him what he should do about some information 'of national concern' when he was not sure the information would get to the Taoiseach by the normal channel. He was not actually looking for advice; he knew the president would tell him to go directly to Lynch. His real aim was simply to involve de Valera in the hope of getting some action from Lynch.

'By consulting the president, and telling the Taoiseach that I had consulted the president,' Berry wrote, 'I would be pushing the Taoiseach towards an enforcement of the rule of law.'

Berry told the Taoiseach on the morning of 20 April 1970. Lynch immediately instructed him to have the whole matter investigated thoroughly and to report again the following morning, when Berry confirmed the involvement of Charlie and Blaney. Lynch decided to interview the two ministers the following day, but that was the day that Charlie went to hospital following his famous 'riding accident'.

'I ultimately got the doctor's permission and I decided to interview Deputy Haughey in hospital on Wednesday 29 April,' Lynch explained to the Dáil. Before the meeting the Taoiseach was very agitated. 'What will I do, what will I do?' he kept muttering as he paced about his office.

'Well, if I were you,' Berry said, 'I'd sack the pair of them and I would tell the British immediately, making a virtue of necessity, as the British are bound to know, anyway, all that is going on.'

But Lynch had not been looking for advice. He was just talking to himself and he abused Berry for having the impertinence to advise him.

The Taoiseach spoke to Blaney first and then went to the hospital to speak to Charlie. Each denied instigating 'in any way the attempted importation of arms,' Lynch told the Dáil. 'They asked me for time to consider their position. I agreed to do so.'

At this point Lynch apparently hoped that the whole thing could be swept under the carpet. He told Berry that the two ministers had assured him there would be no repetition and he therefore considered the matter closed. Berry was stunned. 'Does that mean Mr Haughey remains Minister for Finance?' he asked incredulously. 'What will my position be? He knows that I have told you of his conversation with me on 18 April and of the earlier police information.'

'I will protect you,' Lynch replied.

Next day the Taoiseach told his cabinet that he had decided to accept the denials of the two ministers. But, according to Boland, he warned 'that henceforth no minister should take any action in regard to requests for assistance from the six counties without approval.'

Boland went straight to Charlie and told him the news. Although Boland thought the crisis was over, it was really only beginning. The story had been leaked to Liam Cosgrave, the Fine Gael leader. He tried to interest the *Sunday Independent* and the *Irish Independent* in the story, but their editors thought it too hot to handle.

On 5 May Lynch announced the resignation of Micheál Ó Moráin as Minister for Justice on the grounds of ill-health. Although rumours were already circulating about the arms plot, the Taoiseach managed to skirt questions about further possible resignations. At eight o'clock that evening, however, Cosgrave confronted Lynch with the story. 'I considered it my duty in the national interest to inform the Taoiseach of information I had received which indicates a situation of such gravity for the nation that it is without parallel in this country since the foundation of the state,' Cosgrave told the Dáil.

That night Lynch demanded the resignations of Charlie and Blaney, but both refused. He therefore requested President de Valera to remove them from office in accordance with the constitution. The Taoiseach made his early morning announcement to the press.

At a meeting of the Fianna Fáil parliamentary party the following afternoon, Charlie joined Blaney and the other members of the party in unanimously upholding the Taoiseach's right to remove them. The Dáil then began a continuous sitting that was to last for over 37 hours straight as it debated the crisis. Tension was running so high that scuffles broke out in the lobbies. 'It was not clear who was directly involved, but some deputies had to restrain others,' the *Irish Independent* reported.

Charlie did not take part in the debate but he voted with the government, as did Blaney and Boland. Members of Fianna Fáil seemed pre-occupied with retaining power.

'The necessity to keep the Fianna Fáil government in power at all costs was the overriding consideration,' Berry concluded. 'What was happening in the Lynch regime would have been unthinkable under Mr Lemass or Mr de Valera. The naked face of self-interest in ministerial circles was on exhibition without any attempts at concealment from the serving civil servants.'

Following the Dáil vote, Charlie issued a statement denying having 'taken part in any illegal importation or attempted importation of arms into this country'. He repeated this on 25 May in a further statement in which he endorsed the Taoiseach's view that 'not even the slightest suspicion should attach to any member of the government'.

'I have fully accepted the Taoiseach's decision, as I believe that the unity of the Fianna Fáil party is of greater importance to the welfare of the nation than my political career,' Charlie emphasised. He was facing possible criminal charges and this was a desperate appeal to Fianna Fáil's traditional solidarity. But the appeal was in vain. Three days later he was arrested and taken from home in a police car like a common criminal.

Although the media was slow to question Lynch's motives in dismissing Charlie and Blaney from the cabinet, there could be little doubt that political considerations played a major part in determining the timing of their arrest. As both still enjoyed support within the parliamentary party, there was a danger their supporters might react emotionally and bring down the government in a fit of pique.

The arrests were therefore delayed until Thursday, 28 May 1970. The Dáil broke up early that day for the bank holiday weekend and would not reconvene until the following Wednesday. This afforded deputies an opportunity to get over their initial shock and they had time to ponder the consequences of bringing down the government.

The charge of conspiring to import arms illegally was subsequently dropped against Blaney, but Charlie was returned for trial, along with three others – Capt. James Kelly, John Kelly, a Belfast Republican and a Belgian businessman, Albert Luykx.

The trial began on 22 September 1970. In his opening statement the chief prosecutor appeared to sensationalise the forthcoming testimony for the benefit of the media by quoting what Peter Berry would have to say about his telephone call from Charlie on 18 April. It was obvious, one observer concluded, that the prosecution's tactics were to 'Gut Haughey and gut him fast'.

The defendants stood indicted of having 'conspired together and with other persons unknown to import arms and ammunition illegally into the state' between 1 March and 24 April 1970. To prove the case against Charlie the state was depending on the testimony of three prosecution witnesses, Jim Gibbons, Peter Berry and Anthony Fagan.

Fagan was the first to testify. He told the court that Capt. Kelly came to see Charlie on 19 March. As the minister was engaged, the captain told Fagan that the unspecified cargo, about which he had told Charlie the previous month, would be arriving on the *City of Dublin* on 25 March. He asked if customs could be instructed to admit the consignment without inspecting it. Assured that he had the authority to do so, Charlie gave the necessary instructions.

Berry told the court of his telephone conversation with Charlie on 18 April. He read a verbatim account of the conversation from notes he made in his diary at the time.

Taking the witness stand on the third day of the trial Jim Gibbons testified that he had been uneasy about what Capt. Kelly was doing and so asked Charlie to find another job for him in March 1970. 'We'll make a pig smuggling prevention officer of him,' Charlie suggested.

Gibbons went on to testify that Charlie told him in early April that he was not aware of any conspiracy to import guns. They both agreed at this meeting that collective government action was the only way 'in matters of this kind'.

Later in the month they had a further conversation, according to Gibbons, who was not sure whether the conversation took place on 17 or 20 April.

In his statement in the *Book of Evidence* Gibbons described their discussion as a telephone conversation, but he corrected this on the witness stand. He had telephoned Charlie to arrange an urgent meeting, and they then got together in Charlie's office.

'I told him of certain telephone calls that had come to the Department of Defence concerning the shipment of weapons and ammunition into the country,' Gibbons testified, 'and I asked him if he knew this, and he said, "The dogs in the street are barking it". I asked him if he were in a position to stop it, and he said, "I'll stop it for a month" or words to that effect. I said, "for God's sake, stop it altogether".'

Although the prosecutor had amassed impressive evidence about Charlie's involvement in the whole affair, the state's overall case was already in deep trouble. In order to make the charges stick against any of the accused, the prosecution had to prove beyond a reasonable doubt that Gibbons had not authorised the importation of the arms, because if he had, then the attempt to bring them in was legal and there was no basis for the conspiracy charge.

While on the witness stand, Gibbons admitted that Capt. Kelly had told him at their first private meeting that he intended to help the northern people looking for guns. The captain had given him details of the *City of Dublin* fiasco and the fact that he had another plan to bring in the guns.

'I seem to have a recollection of Capt. Kelly mentioning the possibility of having them shipped through a port in the Adriatic because I suggested to him – would that port possibly be Trieste,' Gibbons testified. He admitted that he did not even suggest that Capt. Kelly should have nothing to do with the planned gun-running.

By the time Gibbons left the stand on the fifth day of the trial, the prosecution's case was clearly in trouble.

In a special *Prime Time* programme on the arms trial in December 2001, RTÉ interviewed some of the jurors, who indicated that the admission by Gibbons that he had not objected when Kelly told him of the plans was vital testimony. 'You could actually sense the reaction in the jury box because that was the turning point for the whole thing,' one of the jurors explained. 'It was the critical moment.'

Gibbons was followed into the witness box by Col Michael Hefferon, who retired from the army just before the arms crisis, after almost eight years as director of military intelligence.

Hefferon's testimony was devastating. He established that Capt. Kelly had not acted independently but with the knowledge and approval of Hefferon himself. Moreover, he added that, as director of military intelligence, he had reported directly to the Minister for Defence on a regular basis and kept Gibbons fully briefed on Capt. Kelly's activities. Indeed he testified that he told Gibbons that the captain was going to Frankfurt in February 1970 to make inquiries about purchasing weapons.

'From what Capt. Kelly said to you, who were these arms to be for?' Hefferon was asked.

'They were to be for the Northern Defence Committees, in the event that a situation would arise where the government would agree to them going to them,' he explained. In order to keep the whole thing as secret as possible he said that he told Capt. Kelly to see Charlie about having the arms cleared through customs without inspection.

On retiring from the army Hefferon admitted he did not inform his successor about what had been happening. 'I felt that the whole project of importing arms was one of very great secrecy in which some government ministers, to my mind acting for the government, were involved, and I felt that it should more properly be communicated to him by the Minister for Defence.'

'Were you satisfied at that time that the Minister for Defence had full knowledge of the activities of Capt. Kelly?'

'Yes,' Hefferon replied emphatically.

Hefferon's testimony caught the prosecution by surprise because there were no references in his statement in the *Book of Evidence* about having told Gibbons about Capt. Kelly's activities. Col Hefferon had actually given the gardaí a detailed eight-page statement explaining his own involvement and making it clear that Capt. Kelly was acting with the full knowledge and approval of the Minister for Defence.

Col Hefferon made some nineteen references to Gibbons in the course of his statement. However, most of those were deleted before the statement was entered into the book of evidence.

The following are some of the passages that were deleted from Col Hefferon's statement:

- It is my opinion that Mr Gibbons knew that Capt. Kelly was involved in assisting the Defence Committee in the north to procure arms.
- I told Mr Gibbons at the time about Capt. Kelly's involvement with the Defence Committee in the north regarding the procuring of arms and ammunition for their defence.
- Around this particular time Capt. Kelly told him [Gibbons] that he might have to go to Germany again in connection with the arms and ammunition for the north and that a lot of snags had developed in connection with them.
- I saw Mr Gibbons again in his office and I told him that Capt. Kelly intended travelling again to the continent in connection with their arms deal.
- Mr Gibbons was prepared to take the necessary steps to have him (Capt. Kelly) relieved of duty in order that he could travel to the continent.
- Capt. Kelly thought he would be required as duty officer at GHQ on the weekend he was going to the continent. I told Mr Gibbons that in the event of he not performing this duty I would have difficulty in explaining his absence, and if he was not relieved of that duty he would be subject to the normal army disciplinary action unless some authority were given to relieve him of the duty. Mr Gibbons was prepared to take the necessary step to have him relieved of duty in order that he could travel to the continent.

Nobody has ever explained why Hefferon's statement was doctored. Des O'Malley subsequently suggested that the evidence was deleted because it would not be admissible in court as it was just hearsay. However, much of the evidence was clearly admissible, because Hefferon gave it in court. His testimony was devastating as it essentially confirmed what Capt. Kelly would say later during the trial in his own defence. Even Conor Cruise O'Brien found the two army officers very credible witnesses. 'No one in Dublin with whom I discussed the case – and I discussed it with many people of widely different views,' Cruise O'Brien wrote in his book, *States of Ireland*, 'had any hesitation in believing Capt. Kelly and Col Hefferon.'

'As the trial went on,' *Private Eye* magazine noted, 'it became clear that if Mr Haughey and his co-defendants were guilty of importing arms into Ireland, so was the entire Irish cabinet.'

The state's case was in shambles by the time Hefferon left the stand next day, but very shortly the whole proceedings were in disarray when the judge, Andreas O'Keefe, the president of the high court, declared a mistrial after being accused of conducting the proceedings in an unfair manner by one of the defence counsels. The latter withdrew the remark and apologised, but it was no good.

Charlie was understandably livid. 'Resign from the Front Bench,' he shouted at the judge.

Outside the court afterwards a member of the jury told Capt. Kelly he 'had the case won'. The various defence teams had not even begun to present their side, but the juror had already made up his own mind. 'It was not a guilty verdict, even at this stage,' he explained.

There was a lot of speculation about O'Keefe's motives in declaring a mistrial. 'Was it that having heard the critical evidence he did not want to have to direct the jury?' Kevin Boland later asked. Many people thought the judge was simply giving the state an opportunity to drop the case without having to suffer the indignity of losing it in open court.

A new trial began on 6 October 1970 with Mr Justice Seamus Henchy presiding. At the outset there was controversy over the status of Hefferon, when the prosecution indicated it would not be calling him as a witness. Counsels for the defendants naturally objected. They were anxious to cross-examine him, so they did not want to call him as their witness. The controversy was eventually resolved by the judge calling Hefferon as his witness so that the state and the defence could cross-examine him. The former director of military intelligence again turned out to be a very effective witness for the defence, as did Capt. Kelly when he elected to take the witness stand in his own defence.

At this point Charlie really did not need to testify at all, but he was anxious to play down his role in the affair. Capt. Kelly's testimony had hardened the evidence of Charlie's involvement, because he testified that he told the Minister for Finance about the plans to bring in guns, which were financed out of the money provided by the Department of Finance for relief of distress in Northern Ireland.

On the stand Charlie gave an added twist to his own defence. Like the others, he contended that what was being done was legal because it had the approval of the Minister for Defence, but he added that he did not actually know that a consignment of arms was involved. He said he authorised customs' clearance without knowing or, for that matter, caring about the actual nature of the cargo, which he assumed was something 'needed by the army to fulfil the contingency plans' to help the people in Northern Ireland. It would have made no difference, he added, if he had been told that guns were involved.

'If you had known that they were intended for possible ultimate distribution to civilians in the north would that have made any difference?' his counsel Niall McCarthy asked.

'No, not really,' he replied, 'provided, of course, that a government decision intervened. I would have regarded it as a very normal part of army preparations in pursuance of the contingency plans that they would provide themselves with, and store here on this side of the border, arms which might ultimately, if the government said so, be distributed to other persons.'

Charlie said he had no reason whatever to suspect Capt. Kelly. He had suggested making him a special customs officer to deal with pig-smuggling because he believed Gibbons was afraid the British might be on to the captain's activities.

'My view of the situation was that Capt. Kelly was a very valuable intelligence officer,' Charlie explained. 'I never heard any suggestion that he did not have Mr Gibbons complete confidence.'

While that seemed plausible enough, Charlie was not as convincing when he said he did not know the exact nature of the shipment. Fagan and Berry had testified that they each talked to Charlie on the telephone about the shipment. They knew it was an arms cargo and each assumed Charlie also knew, but neither actually said that arms were involved.

'Did you ask Mr Fagan any questions as to what this consignment consisted of?' Charlie was asked.

'No,' he replied. 'We were speaking on the phone, and, as far as I can recollect, Mr Fagan told me he had already been in touch with Col Hefferon. I had no doubt in my mind that this was a consignment which was coming in as a result of the direction which we had given in pursuance of the contingency plans.'

'Did you appreciate that it was arms and ammunition?'

'No. I did not appreciate or know at that point of time, and, even when I spoke to Mr Berry, the words "arms and ammunition" were never used.'

In dealing with his telephone conversation of 18 April with Berry,

Charlie tried to give the impression of having a very vivid memory of the discussion. For instance, Berry said that he had answered the telephone himself, whereas Charlie contended that a child answered it first.

To remember a small point like that, which had absolutely no bearing on the subsequent conversation, would indicate a clear recollection of the call. But Berry was later adamant on this point. He had been in the sauna when the telephone began to ring and he hoped somebody else would answer it. When nobody did, he answered it himself in the nude.

Charlie said that Berry had omitted a number of things in his account of the call. For instance, he said that Berry had asked at the outset if Charlie had a scrambler and he mentioned that the consignment weighed 'seven or eight tons'. Berry also said that 'it was the most stupidly handled affair he had ever known in his civil service days'. None of those points were important except that, if true, they would indicate that, even without contemporary notes, Charlie had a better recollection of the conversation than Berry. All this was important because Charlie was categorically contradicting Berry's testimony on two vital points. Firstly, he was contending he had never said anything about guaranteeing that the arms would be sent directly to the north, and secondly, he stated Berry had missed his concluding words. Having said 'it had better be called off', Charlie stated that he added: 'what ever it is'.

He said he called off the shipment in order to avoid bad publicity. 'It was made clear to me,' he explained, 'that the special branch wished this cargo to come, and wished to seize it. I was quite certain in my mind that evening that something had gone wrong, and that army intelligence was clearly at cross-purposes with the special branch, and there was a grave danger of an unfortunate incident occurring at Dublin airport with, as I said, all the attendant publicity.' Yet throughout all this he said that he still did not know that a cargo of arms was actually involved.

Charlie said he did not ask Berry because they were speaking on an unsecured telephone line without a scrambler. Such confusion was understandable under the circumstances, but this would not explain why Charlie did not ask Gibbons what the whole thing was about when they met privately afterwards.

'Do you tell us that a conversation took place with your colleague the Minister for Defence, in the privacy of your office – with nobody else present – and you decided between you to call off the importation of a certain consignment, and that that conversation began and ended without you knowing what the consignment was?' Charlie was asked.

'Yes,' he replied. 'Nor did he mention what the consignment was.'

'Did you not ask him what it was?'

'No. It did not arise. In my mind was present the fact that this was a consignment being brought in by army intelligence in pursuance of their own operations.'

'As a matter of simple curiosity, were you not interested at that stage in finding out what the cargo was that all the hullabaloo was about?'

'No,' Charlie replied. 'The important thing was that the army and special branch were at cross-purposes, and that it had better be stopped. I don't rule out the possibility that it could well have been in my mind that it could have been arms and ammunition – but it could have been a lot of other things.'

'If your evidence is correct,' the prosecutor said, 'I suggest that when Mr Gibbons came to see you on Monday your reaction would have been, "I have already called this off for you but now, please, tell me what it's all about?"'

'That's not what happened,' Charlie maintained. 'It may be what you think should have happened – but it did not happen.'

In his opening address the prosecutor had stated 'that Mr Haughey's involvement – while of a lesser degree, because he was only there briefly – was of a vital nature because it was he who had given directions to Mr Fagan that this consignment was to be cleared without customs examination.' In his closing statement Charlie's counsel contended that the defendant had merely facilitated a legitimate request from army intelligence, seeing that it was actually Col Hefferon who suggested that Capt. Kelly should approach Charlie in the matter in the first place.

Niall McCarthy tried to dismiss the damaging evidence given by Gibbons by contending that the Minister for Defence was posturing as having been opposed to importing the arms even though he never so much as suggested to Capt. Kelly the whole thing should be called off. 'I think,' he continued, 'it is hard to find anywhere – and I mean anywhere – in the evidence of Mr Gibbons anything convincing in his action and in his deeds consistent with what he now says was his view of what was happening at the time.'

'But, Gentlemen,' Charlie's counsel said to the jury, 'if Mr Gibbons' attitude to what was happening was as he now declares it to be, surely he would there and then have said, "Capt. Kelly, you cannot go on with this – this must stop".' But Gibbons did nothing. He left the captain go out of his office without a reprimand, a rebuke or a warning.

Delivering his summation to the jury, the prosecutor challenged Charlie's testimony. 'For the purpose of establishing the case made by Mr Haughey in his defence, it is necessary,' he said, 'to disbelieve the evidence of four other witnesses: Capt. Kelly, Mr Fagan, Mr Berry, and Mr Gibbons.' He then outlined some of the discrepancies.

Capt. Kelly had testified that he told Charlie of the nature of the consignment. Moreover, there was 'one piece of evidence which is crucial to the case, crucial in the sense that a verdict in favour of Mr Haughey cannot be reconciled with this piece of evidence,' the prosecutor continued. 'Mr Berry said that Mr Haughey said on the telephone, could the consignment be let through if a guarantee was given that it would go direct to the north?'

'Gentlemen,' the prosecutor added, 'if it was just Mr Haughey and just Mr Berry, or just Mr Haughey and just Mr Fagan, or just Mr Haughey and just Mr Gibbons, or just Mr Haughey and just Capt. Kelly, nobody could quarrel with the decision that you are not prepared to reject Mr Haughey's account. But I think you have to consider the cumulative effect of the evidence: is he right, and all they wrong? Because you, gentlemen, have got to hold that they are all wrong.'

During an RTÉ interview with Vincent Browne in 1998, Kevin Boland confirmed a story that he had told Browne eighteen years earlier, that he had actually discussed the arms issue with Haughey before the crisis erupted, so there was no doubt he knew that arms were involved. Thus, Haughey was clearly lying when he testified about not knowing about the guns. 'When he denied that he was involved in it,' Boland stated, 'he was not telling the truth.'

In his charge to the jury on the final day of the trial, 23 October 1970, the judge spent some time on the conflict between Charlie's testimony and that of Berry and Gibbons. In each instance, he contended, one of them committed perjury.

In one sense, Gibbons' testimony seemed particularly credible because so much of it was against himself. 'Poor Mr Gibbons was the anti-star of the trial,' reported Sir John Peck, the British ambassador to Ireland. 'From his evidence it is hard to avoid drawing a number of inferences, all unflattering. He seems to have been foolish to the point of idiocy.'

Gibbons, who had earlier denied in the Dáil that he was even aware of the gun-running plans, told a different story at the trial. When he was challenged about this discrepancy, he essentially admitted that he had lied to the Dáil by lamely stating that he was not under oath there. The judge suggested that the jurors would have to decide themselves whether the denials in the Dáil showed 'Mr Gibbons to be a man given to half-truths and lies, and whether, as a result you should treat him as being discredited as a witness.'

Generally, however, the evidence that a witness gives against himself is considered most effective. Haughey's self-serving evidence conflicted with evidence that Gibbons, Capt. Kelly and Anthony Fagan had given against themselves, so there was little doubt in the minds of many people about who had told the truth.

'Either Mr Gibbons concocted this and has come to court and perjured himself, or it happened,' the judge said. 'There does not seem to me to be any way of avoiding a total conflict on this issue between Mr Haughey and Mr Gibbons.' The discrepancies were so great that he did not think they could be attributed to a simple memory failing of one of the participants. 'I would like to be able to suggest some way you can avoid holding there is perjury in this case,' Henchy continued. 'You have a solemn and serious responsibility to decide in this case, firstly, whether Mr Gibbons' conversation took place or not, and, secondly, whether Mr Berry's conversation took place or not. I shall not give any opinion on these crucial matters because, were I to do so, I might be thought to be constituting myself the jury.'

As far as the conspiracy charge went, however, all this would be important only if Capt. Kelly was found guilty. If Charlie's testimony was believed he could be found not guilty while all the others could be convicted. Thus the crucial issue was whether Gibbons had authorised the importation. If he had, then the operation was legal. Henchy told the jury that they could conclude that when the Minister for Defence was informed about the planned importation and 'did not say No, in categorical terms, Capt. Kelly was entitled to presume that Mr Gibbons was saying Yes. That is a view that is open to you.'

'Did the accused come to an agreement to import arms and ammunition into the state without the authority of the Minister for Defence?' was the main question that the jury had to answer, according to one of the jurors. They found the answer simple. 'It was a completely unanimous verdict,' he explained. 'It didn't take an awful lot of time actually.'

Another juror explained that he had concluded that 'the cabinet had decided to get these arms in and get them up to the north, and at some stage they changed their mind, or some of them changed their minds. For me, it was a big charade from the beginning.'

The verdict was a foregone conclusion. The Taoiseach had conveniently gone to New York for a meeting of the United Nations. Everyone who attended the final session of the trial had clearly 'come to cheer the inevitable result', Kevin Boland wrote.

It took the jury less than a hour to reach a verdict. 'Not Guilty' on all counts.

The court immediately erupted into a wild scene of cheering and shaking hands. Outside in the foyer Charlie's supporters were ecstatic.

'We want Charlie,' they shouted. 'Lynch must go.'

'I was never in any doubt that it was a political trial,' Charlie declared at a press conference immediately afterwards. 'I think those who were responsible for this debacle have no alternative but to take the honourable course that is open to them.'

'What is that?'

'I think that is pretty evident,' he replied. 'There is some dissatisfaction with the Taoiseach at the moment.'

When asked if he would be a candidate for Taoiseach himself, he said he was 'not ruling out anything'.

His remarks were unanimously interpreted as a challenge to the Taoiseach. But Lynch was confident of coping with any challenge to his leadership.

'If the issue is raised,' he told newsmen in New York, 'I look forward to the outcome with confidence.'

Lynch's supporters were ready for a showdown. As a test of strength they called on all members of the parliamentary party to show their loyalty to the Taoiseach by going to Dublin airport to welcome him home from the United States. 'Everyone had to be there unless he or she had a doctor's cert', according to Boland. As a result an overwhelming majority turned out, and Charlie's challenge promptly evaporated.

There was little doubt that Haughey lied about his knowledge of the whole affair, but then so did Lynch. One of the jurors later raised serious questions about Lynch's relationship with Gibbons. 'Either Jack Lynch wasn't aware of what went on in the Four Courts, or he ignored what went on in the Four Courts,' the juror argued. There is no doubt that Lynch did follow the trial.

The British ambassador reported, for instance, that Lynch 'told me privately that he was furious with Mr Gibbons for his performance as a witness, and that he seems to be getting into an impossible position. I thought it very likely that his resignation would be ready to be put in the Taoiseach's hand when he returned.'

Lynch refused to reinstate Charles Haughey and Neil Blaney to cabinet, even though they had been cleared in court. He justified this on the grounds that they knew of the plans to import the arms but had not informed him. Gibbons admitted in court that he also knew of the plans, so why did Lynch retain him?

Surely, it was because Gibbons had actually informed the Taoiseach about the plans. In late 1969, Gibbons told Hefferon that Lynch had been asking questions about Capt. Kelly's activities as a result of a warning from Peter Berry. Gibbons later stated that he 'did pass on information to the Taoiseach at that time in 1969 that there was questionable activities on the part of certain members of the government making contract with people they should not make contact with, certainly without the sanction of the government and the Taoiseach.'

Yet nobody questioned Lynch, or pressed people like Gibbons, Moran, or Berry to say what they told the Taoiseach. It was like investigating Watergate without ever asking what Richard Nixon knew.

Had Haughey not testified, he could later have explained his behaviour on the grounds of trying to help the people of the north. But with the benefit of more than a quarter of a century of hindsight, there are no medals for realising that it was a crazy scheme. The arms consignment consisted of more than 330 machine guns of various types and 200 grenades, Those would not normally be considered defensive weapons.

'The giving of arms to untrained people is a most serious matter,' Hefferon successor, Col Patrick Delaney warned Gibbons on 22 April 1970. 'John Hume expressed the view that such action would be "suicide".'

Haughey had never shown any real sympathy for the IRA, so why was he prepared to supply weapons? The most likely explanation was that it was part of the ongoing power struggle within Fianna Fáil. Charlie had sympathy for the plight of the Nationalist people, but his prime motivation in becoming involved in the whole affair was to ensure that Neil Blaney did not gain unchallenged control of the green wing of the party.

Although Charlie was acquitted by the jury, he still had some questions to answer. During the trial it came out that the controversial arms shipment was purchased with public money and the Dáil decided that the committee of public accounts should investigate the whole affair in order to determine whether money allocated for relief of distress in the north had been misappropriated.

Legislation was passed setting up a select twelve-man committee to investigate. It was given power to subpoena witnesses to testify under oath. Members of the committee included Ray MacSharry, Jim Tunney, Ben Briscoe and Sylvester Barrett of Fianna Fáil, Garret FitzGerald, Dick Burke and Eddie Collins of Fine Gael, as well as Justin Keating and Seán Tracy of the Labour party.

Most of the witnesses at the Arms Trial were called and the hearings inevitably covered much of the same grounds. Some witnesses were actually cross-examined on testimony given at the trial. As court rules did not apply during the committee hearings, witnesses were able to give hearsay testimony that would have been inadmissible in court.

Chief Superintendent John P. Fleming of the special branch admitted at the outset that all his pertinent information was second-hand 'from confidential sources' whom he was not at liberty to name. He made some sensational disclosures.

'I know,' Fleming declared at one point, 'that Mr Haughey had a meeting with one of the leading members of the IRA' and promised him £50,000.

'For what purpose?' the committee chairman asked.

'For the IRA, for the north.'

When asked for further details of the alleged meeting, however, he said he was 'not sure of the date or the place'. All he could say was it took place somewhere in Dublin in either August or September 1969. He was then asked if he thought Charlie had any more meetings.

'I am not sure,' the chief superintendent replied. 'I know his brother, Pádraig was deeply involved.'

A striking feature of Fleming's evidence was how much the security people knew about Pádraig Haughey's activities. This was not material gathered in hindsight. Capt. James Kelly related details of his own involvement later in his book *Thimble Riggers*, which suggested that even at the time there were grounds for suspecting that they were under intense security surveillance. During November John Kelly learned that arms were available in London, and he went there in an attempt to purchase them. 'John, accompanied by a Dublin man, Paddy, headed for London,' Capt. Kelly recalled. 'John briefed me on what was afoot on the night before their departure.' The Paddy referred to was Pádraig (Jock) Haughey, younger brother of Charles J. Haughey, the Minister for Finance. The two men were kept under surveillance by British intelligence. They were photographed coming out of Oxford Street tube station. Kelly noticed a man standing on his tip toes at a bus stop looking at them with a radio to his ear. Further down the street he noticed a woman take a radio from her handbag after they passed her. This was before the era of mobile phones. They met Capt. Peter J. Markham-Randall, a small swarthy man with a goatee. He said that he was half-Arab and had served in the British army. Many Irishmen had served in the British army over the years, he noted, and they remained just as Irish. In the same way he had strong Arab sympathies.

John Kelly was deeply suspicious. They had already made arrangements with the bank in Dublin to arrange to cash a cheque drawn on the account of George Dixon at a bank in Piccadilly next day, but they had obviously become so spooked that they flew back to Dublin separately instead.

John Kelly told Capt. Kelly what had happened. He then telephoned London to say that he had been called back to Ireland urgently, and he asked that Markham-Randall come to Dublin to conclude the negotiations. Markham-Randall was supposed to fly to Dublin, but Capt. Kelly monitored all the London planes, and the man was not on any of them. When the captain went to tell John Kelly at the Gresham Hotel, however, Markham-Randall was already there. They concluded that he must have come via Belfast, which only made them more suspicious.

'There are many Irish and many Arabs who do not like the English,' Markham-Randall said. 'I am here to help you.'

He seemed particularly well informed as he made numerous references to Capt. Kelly and referred to cabinet ministers Charles Haughey, Neil Blaney, Kevin Boland and Jim Gibbons as having strong northern Nationalist sympathies. 'I could be a big help to your people,' he told John Kelly. 'If I visited one or other of your training camps I would be very useful: small arms, fire and movement, tactics and that sort of thing.'

'It's arms we are interested in at the moment,' John Kelly insisted.

Markham-Randall indicated that he could provide automatic weapons and grenades, and he even offered to provide them at a bargain price. This convinced Kelly that he was not a real dealer, because he was too eager to help, rather than make money for himself.

When Kelly confronted him, Markham-Randall said he was just trying to get access to the training camps. Kelly could have the weapons and keep the money for himself. In effect, he was trying to recruit John Kelly. Throughout the meeting Randall had a small flat top case in front of him. He may have been recording, or even filming their conversation. Downstairs Capt. Jim Kelly waited with three northern Republicans. When John Kelly told them what happened, some of the men wished to kill Markham-Randall on the spot, like Michael Collins would have done. 'He shot the British spies and saved the day,' one of the men said.

But this was too much for Capt. Kelly. He warned that it would be too embarrassing for the Dublin government, which had been so cooperative up to this point. They therefore agreed not to kill Markham-Randall, who remained in Dublin for a few days, during which he telephoned Jock Haughey, who had already told him that his home was under special branch surveillance. Fleming believed he was George Dixon.

Markham-Randall wrote a note to G. Dixon in care of the manager of the Munster and Leinster Bank in Baggot Street, Dublin. George Dixon was the name on the account into which the government money was transferred to purchase weapons that were later at the centre of the arms crisis. The account had only been opened two weeks earlier, but by then it was obvious that outsiders were on to what was happening.

When Colonel Hefferon made inquiries through his British contacts, he was informed that Markham-Randall was a disreputable underworld type who would involve himself in activities like arms dealing. Of course, if he was one of their agents, the British would say that!

In February Capt. Kelly was shown a garda file on attempted arms purchases, which included a photograph of John Kelly and Jock Haughey alighting from the Oxford Street tube station. The gardaí apparently did not recognise John Kelly, but they did know that the man that the northerners referred to as Paddy 'Dublin' was Jock Haughey. John Kelly had been interned in the north during the border campaign of the 1950s, so the British intelligence was undoubtedly aware of his identity. Yet Capt. Kelly continued to work with John Kelly in the attempt to acquire arms, even travelling to the continent together, and they continued to use the Dixon account to fund the operation, even though Markham-Randall was obviously aware of that account. In the light of Capt. Kelly's recounting of the events, it would be ridiculous to depict the whole affair as some kind of sophisticated conspiracy. He was the main functionary in arranging the gun-running, but his own account also exposed him as the virtual personification of the classic oxymoron 'Military Intelligence'.

On the day following Fleming's testimony before the Public Accounts Committee the *Irish Times* carried an extraordinary article by Dick Walsh on Jock Haughey's activities, which was obviously based on leaked information. It recounted Jock's visit to London, with extraordinary details such as the meeting held in the sixth floor office of Hyman Godfrey at 299 Oxford Street. Godfrey, who had a company called Savoy Finance, was reputedly the intermediary who contacted Markham-Randall, who gave the prices for various weapons such as Sten guns, rifles, and Browning machine guns. Walsh even mentioned that Haughey and his colleague had lunch at the Irish Club in Eaton Square, where they 'had salad and beef and potatoes'.

Of course, those details were irrelevant, except to suggest that Jock and his colleague were being closely watched. The article went on to relate how Markham-Randall came over to Dublin and stayed at the Gresham Hotel. He telephoned Jock, who told him that he was under special branch surveillance. If this was true, it would suggest that Jock's telephone was being tapped, and Walsh's story was planted to soften him up. Walsh went on to say that even though some of those involved wished to go ahead with the gun-running plans, Jock 'refused to have any more to do with it.' He added that Jock was unlikely to have known the people he was involved with in advance and that 'at best, they would have made uneasy partners'.

Although there were a number of apparent discrepancies in the account, those could have been included by whoever leaked the information in order to cover his own tracks, but there could be little doubt that the article would have bolstered Fleming's evidence in the public arena. When Jock Haughey appeared before the committee the following week, he made a statement at the outset.

'I wish to state that I never, directly or indirectly, got in touch or sought to get in touch with Mr C. J. Haughey in order that he would authorise customs clearance for any guns, ammunition or materials of any nature or description, nor did he ever indicate to me what his attitude would be if such requests were made to him as the matter never arose between us.

'I definitely state I never received or gave any cheque, or any valuable security in the name of George Dixon; nor did I ever use the name of George Dixon in any connection with any financial or banking dealings,' Jock added. Neither did he ever discuss with his brother, Charles, anything about the money voted for relief of distress, prior to receiving the subpoena to appear before the committee. He then announced he would not answer any questions because he would not have any immunity for his testimony. 'I am advised,' he said, 'that by giving evidence before this committee I might be liable in civil law and under the laws of the land for any answer I might make.' He added, rather pointedly, that his own lawyers were considering legal action in relation to supposed evidence given to the committee about him.

The committee subsequently cited him for contempt. but this is getting ahead of the story. Charlie was suddenly back in the eye of the storm. He vehemently denied either meeting the IRA leader, or promising him money. 'No such meeting ever took place, and no such promise was ever made by me,' Charlie protested in an open letter to the committee chairman.

'Chief Superintendent Fleming's evidence, if one may properly so call it,' he wrote, 'included such phrases as – "I had other confidential information" – "I take it that" – "I am not sure but" – "I would imagine" – "as far as my impression goes" – "as far as I am aware" all, plainly, indications that his "evidence" was based on rumour, reports, and other hearsay. No court would ever permit such an abuse of privilege quite apart from the fact that such "evidence" would be inadmissible.'

Testifying before the committee on 2 March 1971, Charlie said it was impossible to give a full and proper accounting for the expenditures. 'None of us ever envisaged that any such accountability would ever be required,' he explained. 'We administered this particular money more or less along the same lines as we would administer the secret service vote.'

When the Dáil formally authorised the expenditure in March 1970, it did so without comment. 'Nobody asked me questions,' Charlie said, 'and it went through without any discussion whatsoever.'

The money was intended for relief of distress in Northern Ireland. A valid case could have been made for arguing that certain propaganda activities or providing arms were indeed means of relieving mental distress, but Charlie did not argue on these lines. Instead, he accepted that using money for such purposes was 'absolutely' out of order and irregular.

'Public funds were misappropriated,' he declared. 'That is a criminal offence.'

There were doubts about the validity of expenditures in relation to: (1) a visit of Jock Haughey and others to London in August, 1969; (2) Capt. Kelly's meeting in Bailieboro in October 1969; (3) funds used to finance *The Voice of the North*; and (4) the money used to purchase the arms.

Charlie admitted that his brother and three others were selected to go to Britain by himself. 'The purpose of the visits,' he explained, 'was to mobilise assistance over there for relief of distress in the north'. He added that he knew nothing of Fleming's allegations that his brother had engaged in arms talks.

'If the evidence which Chief Superintendent Fleming gave to this committee about my brother is as false and misleading as it is about me,' Charlie said, 'then I think the committee should throw it into the waste paper basket.'

The money used by Capt. Kelly for the Bailieboro meeting had actually been paid to Col Hefferon by the Department of Finance. The captain had asked for the money; so the two army officers believed the £500 was for the Bailieboro meeting, but Charlie – who instructed the department to give the money to Hefferon – said he believed the funds was just part of payments made to Col Hefferon to fund an office to help northern refugees.

The circumstances surrounding the financing of *The Voice of the North*, however, were more complicated. Séamus Brady, the editor, had submitted a bill to the Bureau of Information which was forwarded to the Department of Finance. Charlie thought the Taoiseach's Department should look after the bill, so he instructed Fagan to enquire into the matter. But the Taoiseach's Department, under which the bureau of information functioned, refused to have anything to do with the bill.

'I felt Mr Brady was unfairly treated,' Charlie told the committee. 'Mr Brady understood that the Government Information Bureau wished him to publish this newspaper. Whether he was right or wrong, or did not understand it, I cannot say.

'He came to me and indicated that he had put £650 of his own money into the publication and he was now in difficulty with the

Government Information Bureau because they were not prepared to pay up,' Charlie continued. 'I went to the Taoiseach on the matter. The Taoiseach gave me a direction and a ruling that public moneys were not to be used for the publication.'

Although there was no hope of Lynch agreeing to spend public money on the project, Charlie indicated he would personally make sure Brady would not be out of pocket on what had already been spent but he said it might be necessary to suspend publication for the time being. 'You had better hold it,' Charlie told him. 'I myself will see you all right with what you have spent if it come to that.'

Brady told Capt. Kelly that *The Voice of the North* would have 'to fold as no money was coming in for it'. But within a couple of days Capt. Kelly came back to him with financial support in the form of a cheque drawn on a private account. Brady said that he had no idea that this was government money. Fagan told the committee that shortly afterwards he saw Brady's original bill on Charlie's desk. 'What is being done about this?' Fagan asked.

'Oh, that is being looked after,' Charlie replied. 'Ask Kelly how Brady's affairs stand?'

The captain told Fagan to 'tell the minister he is OK'. Thus, contrary to the specific direction of the Taoiseach, government funds were used to support *The Voice of the North*, but Charlie swore that he did not know who helped Brady out. He also testified that he knew nothing about four private bank accounts used to secretly channel the money. The first he heard of them, he said, was during the arms trial.

Two of the witnesses felt Charlie must have known about one of accounts, but neither was definite. Capt. Kelly testified that he 'certainly' told Fagan about this account. 'And,' he added, 'I should imagine Mr Haughey would know too. I cannot see any reason why not.' Fagan thought it 'inconceivable' that he would not have told the minister but added that he could 'not honestly recall' mentioning it on any specific occasion.

Charlie explained that he had selected three northern Nationalists to distribute the relief money in Northern Ireland when it became apparent that the Irish Red Cross could not operate there. He was not aware of the bank accounts opened in false names. As far as he was concerned these were none of his business; they were operated by the northern Nationalists.

'If they nominated someone else to administer the fund, that was not really any particular concern of mine,' he argued. 'We were not concerned with the mechanics of the payments.'

He forcefully denied knowing that any of the relief money had been spent on buying weapons. 'I have no knowledge whatever,' he emphasised, 'that any of these moneys, any halfpenny of these moneys, went for the procurement of arms.'

As a result of his refusal to testify before the Dáil's Public Accounts Committee Jock Haughey was sentenced to six months in jail by the high court, but this was overturned on constitutional grounds, when he appealed the conviction to the supreme court. In a unanimous judgment, announced on 24 June 1971, Chief Justice Cearbhall Ó Daláigh concluded that the high court had acted unconstitutionally in not according Jock a jury trial.

'This judgment deprived the committee,' in the estimation of its own members, 'of any effective powers in the event of a witness refusing to attend, to produce documents or to answer questions.' Opposition members of the committee wanted to ask the Oireachtas for the necessary powers, but this was blocked by Fianna Fáil members, with the result that the hearings spluttered to a rather ineffective conclusion with the presentation of the committee's final report on 13 July 1972.

The report was incomplete; the committee was only able to conclude 'definitely' that a little over £29,000 was 'expended on or in connection with the relief of distress' in Northern Ireland. It found that a further £31,150 may have been spent in the same way, but over £39,000 had, in effect, been misappropriated.

There was no definitive conclusion on who was directly responsible for the misappropriations, but the committee was specifically critical of Charlie on two counts. Firstly, it concluded that 'the misappropriation of part of the money which is now known to have been spent on arms might have been avoided' if either Charlie, Blaney or Gibbons had 'passed on to the Taoiseach their suspicion or knowledge of the proposed arms importation.' The committee came to that conclusion without even asking any of the witnesses what they had told Lynch.

Garret FitzGerald, one of the opposition members of the committee, later explained to Justin O'Brien that the threat posed by the likes of Neil Blaney was considered so serious, that even the opposition did not want to destabilise Lynch's leadership. He explained 'the committee's hearings were designed specifically by government and opposition alike not to ascertain the truth but "to buttress the state against the greatest threat to its security since partition".'

But there was no such reluctance to be critical of Haughey. The committee concluded that it was 'not satisfied' that Charlie's actions in connection with the £500 given to Capt. Kelly for the Bailieboro meeting 'was justified under the terms of the fund'.

Following the dismissal of Charlie and Blaney in May, the Taoiseach had said that there could not be 'even the slightest suspicion' about the activities of a minister, but he then seemed to apply a different standard to Jim Gibbons. If the latter's testimony about not having approved the importation of arms had been accepted by the jury, it is difficult to see how all the defendants could have been acquitted. This at least raised the spectre of doubt about his role in the controversial events. Moreover, during the trial Gibbons essentially admitted that he had deliberately deceived the Dáil back in May when he denied any knowledge of an attempt by Capt. Kelly to import arms. 'I wish emphatically to deny any such knowledge,' he told the Dáil at the time. Yet in court he admitted that Capt. Kelly had already informed him, and he lamely tried to excuse deceiving the Dáil by implying that a different degree of veracity was required in Leinster House.

Surely deceiving the Dáil in such a blatant manner was valid grounds for his removal; so why did Lynch promote him to Agriculture rather than drop him from the cabinet? Was it because Gibbons knew too much? It may have been significant that after Lynch's retirement from politics, Gibbons admitted that he had told him what was going on before the arms crisis.

Rather than vote confidence in the Minister for Agriculture or side with the opposition, Kevin Boland resigned from the Dáil. In the circumstances all eyes were on Charlie, but he dutifully voted with the government, thereby affording his critics another opportunity of slating him.

'Whatever charisma attached to the name of C. J. Haughey,' *Hibernia* noted, 'was very seriously, perhaps irrevocably tarnished by his decision to vote with the government on the Gibbons censure. For a man who so terribly badly wanted to be leader, his epitaph may well read that he tried too hard.'

Boland went on to found a new party, *Aontacht Éireann*. 'I went to Haughey and tried to persuade him that even if he did succeed in taking over Fianna Fáil, he would be dealing with people who were incompetent, inadequate and unreliable,' Boland recalled. 'But he didn't see it that way.'

Charlie decided to re-establish himself within Fianna Fáil instead. At the party's Ard Fheis in February 1972 he was elected as one of the party's five vice-presidents. His supporters were ecstatic as he arrived on the platform to be greeted by many of the party hierarchy, but there were some determined exceptions. Erskine Childers sat silently reading his newspaper. Dismayed at the prospect of Haughey's return to prominence, he repeatedly urged Lynch not to restore Charlie to the front bench of the parliamentary party.

Childers had already departed the political scene to succeed de Valera as president of the country when a general election was called in 1973. The Tánaiste, Frank Aiken, one of the principal founders of Fianna Fáil in 1926, urged Jack Lynch to block Charlie's nomination as a party candidate, but Lynch rejected the idea. Aiken was so annoyed that he decided to retired from politics himself. Initially he threatened to give the press his reasons for quitting, but under pressure from President de Valera and others, he relented and allowed Lynch to announce that he was retiring 'on doctor's orders'. It was a sad end to a long political career of a particularly courageous man, and it was all the sadder that he should leave politics quietly while the truth about his principled stand was distorted.

A couple of years later Charlie was returned to the front bench of the party, much to the indignation of the widow of President Childers, who had died some weeks earlier. When she was invited to a Mass arranged by the party, she declined with an open letter.

'The late president would not benefit from the prayers of such a party,' she wrote. 'Happily for him he is now closer to God and will be able to ask His intercession that his much loved country will never again be governed by these people.' It was an extraordinary outburst, but Fianna Fáil was returned to power at the next general election in 1977 with a record twenty-seat majority.

Haughey was offered a cabinet position as Minister for Health and Social Welfare. Health was essentially a poison chalice. Only Noel Browne had ever made a name for himself in the post, but he got into bishop trouble and never got another government job. One of Charlie's greatest tasks was to do something about the political unrest surrounding the public demand for the legalised sale of contraceptives, which had plagued Liam Cosgrave's outgoing government. Charlie was going to have to tackle this thorny question as an essential outsider within the cabinet.

Lynch surrounded himself with an inner cabinet consisting of George Colley, Des O'Malley and Martin O'Donoghue, who all despised Haughey. But if they thought they were going to bury him in the Department of Health, they were badly mistaken, because he had real administrative ability.

During his two and a half years as Minister for Health, Charlie generated a considerable amount of publicity to enhance his own political image. He used his administrative and legislative experience to telling effect in securing funding for a wide range of programmes that he had the skill and drive to get off the ground. He also implemented some legislative measures that received enormous, if not always favourable, publicity.

'His greatest coup,' according to the *Irish Medical Times*, 'was bought for the modest expenditure of £1 million – the cost of dramatically expanding the role of the new Health Education Bureau', which had been set up by his predecessor in 1975. Through this bureau, Haughey launched imaginative publicity campaigns aimed at promoting better standards of fitness and hygiene. He was credited with bombarding the public with exhortations to walk rather than drive, to jog, to dance, to play games, to quit smoking and to cut down on alcohol.

He introduced legislation to deal with the promotion and advertising of tobacco products. He banned cigarette companies from sponsoring a wide range of events and made it illegal for competitors in certain events to carry the name of a tobacco company, or its products. He had the imagination and drive to introduce legislation to ban tobacco advertising more than twenty years before the Americans or the British.

The groundwork had already been done for a new hospital programme by the previous government, and Charlie implemented it by cutting through reams of red tape. He took the design of Cork Regional Hospital and had it used for the Beaumont Hospital in Dublin, thereby speeding up the construction of the new building. He secured funds for a £5 million development at Mullingar General Hospital, authorised an extension doubling the size of Sligo General Hospital, and got funds for a new general hospital in Tralee.

In July 1978, Charlie announced a new scheme providing free hospitalisation for all those earning under £5,500 per year. His predecessor had been anxious to introduce free hospitalisation and the Department of Health had drawn up a scheme, but consultant doctors refused to implement it. Haughey compromised with the consultants and got cabinet approval for the scheme, which was a real political achievement, because free hospitalisation had not been part of the 1977 election manifesto.

In November 1978 hundreds of uniformed nurses descended on Leinster House, looking for salary increases. Charlie has some 300 of them invited into the Dáil. Fine Gael proposed 'to set up a commission of inquiry on nurses' pay and conditions', and Haughey stole the initiative by establishing such a commission of inquiry. By the time the nurses left Leinster House, they were being called 'Charlie's Angels'.

In 1979, he took on the Catholic hierarchy in forcing through the first law providing for the sale of artificial contraceptives. A provision of the legislation required that condoms could only be sold on a doctor's prescription for bona fide family planning purposes. When Kevin Moore of the *Irish Independent* suggested that the Irish Medical Association would balk at doctors writing such prescriptions, Charlie was dismissive. 'Listen Kevin,' he said, 'those fuckers will do anything for money.'

This was his idea of 'an Irish solution to an Irish problem'. It paved the way for others to pass amending legislation. One cynical commentator contended at the time that Haughey's plans were not for health but to fulfil his own ambition of becoming Taoiseach. 'What he's done,' he said, 'is to keep ten balls in the air at the same time and protect his own'. He had taken a political poison chalice and not only survived but made a success of it.

On the night of general elections returns in June 1977 Haughey was at the count centre at the Royal Dublin Society when the news came through that Jack Lynch had led Fianna Fáil to a 20-seat majority, the greatest margin of victory since independence. Geraldine Kennedy of the *Irish Times* was standing next to Charlie and she remarked that his chances of every becoming Taoiseach were now dead.

'No,' Haughey replied. 'Those are all my men,' he explained, referring the many new deputies elected for the first time. 'Now I know I will be Taoiseach.' He seemed so confident that she asked if he would give her his first interview as Taoiseach. He agreed.

'Is that a promise?' she asked.

'Yes,' he replied emphatically. It was a promise.

When Jack Lynch announced his decision to step down as Taoiseach in December 1979 following his return from a short tour of the United States, there was no suggestion that Charlie was in any way involved in the decision, but the charge would later be made that he was behind what amounted to Lynch's ousting. It would virtually become an accepted fact that Charlie orchestrated a sneaky, sordid campaign to destroy Lynch, and this would do as much damage to him politically as many of the earlier controversies.

In the circumstances it is necessary here to evaluate what actually happened in the run up to Lynch's resignation. The first real signs of trouble occurred in April when it came to voting on the bill introduced by Charlie to legalise the sale of contraceptive in certain restricted circumstances. Four Fianna Fáil deputies defied their party's three line whip by refusing to vote on the measure. Three of them later apologised but the fourth, Charlie's Arms Trial adversary, Jim Gibbons, was unapologetic.

As Minister for Agriculture, Gibbons could easily have arranged to be away on business, and his absence would not have been noticed because his vote was not needed. Instead, he stayed around the Dáil until just before the vote was due to take place and then he left. Afterwards he announced defiantly that he would not be supporting any stage of the bill.

The whole thing was seen as a clear challenge to Lynch's authority, but the Taoiseach took no action. Relations between Lynch and Gibbons had been 'distinctly chilly, even glacial', according to press secretary Frank Dunlop. This led many to conclude that Gibbons had something damaging, possibly in relation to the arms crisis, that Lynch dared not drop him from the cabinet. Even now he dared not move against Gibbons. It was the first time since the foundation of the state that any minister had publicly defied his own government in such a blatant manner. The first nail had been driven into Lynch's political coffin, and the man responsible was not Charlie, but his implacable critic, Jim Gibbons.

A public opinion poll conducted during the controversy found that Charlie had the most favourable rating of all the members of the government, including the Taoiseach. Some 75% expressed the opinion that Charlie had done well or very well in his ministry. Only 20% were not favourably impressed with the job he was doing. On the other hand, George Colley had a dismal approval rating of just 38%, with 53% feeling that he had been doing a poor job as Minister for Finance. Indeed, he had the poorest rating of all, with the exception of Pádraig Faulkner, the Minister for Posts and Telegraphs, who was plagued at the time by a protracted postal strike.

Public disillusionment with the government became apparent in June when Fianna Fáil's vote dropped to 34.6% in the European elections. Down from the 50.6% of two years earlier, it was the worst showing in the party's 53 year history. As a result nervous backbenchers began to look for a change of leadership.

The record twenty-seat majority which Fianna Fáil won in 1977 really sowed the seeds of instability, because the party was left holding many marginal seats. Backbench deputies from those marginal constituencies became noticeably uneasy as things began to go wrong for the government. Fearing for their seats, they became restless for change.

Five deputies stood out in the movement for change. Dubbed 'the gang of five', they were, Albert Reynolds, Seán Doherty, Tom McEllistrim, Jackie Fahey and Mark Killilea. Beginning with a slow, relentless campaign to secure Charlie's election as Lynch's successor, they soon found enthusiastic supporters in deputies like Paddy Power, Síle de Valera, Charlie McCreevy, Seán Calleary and Bill Loughnane. They started sniping openly at Lynch's leadership.

During a speech outside Fermoy on 9 September 1979 Síle de Valera delivered a veiled attack on Lynch's Northern Ireland policy. She was basically accusing him of deviating from the core values of Fianna Fáil. This was followed a month later by Tom McEllistrim making an issue of allowing the British military to overfly Irish territory.

79

In November Lynch suffered the humiliation of having Fianna Fáil lose two by-elections in his native Cork – including one in Cork city, his own backyard, after he had campaigned there personally. His electoral magic seemed to have deserted him.

The Cork setbacks were quickly followed by a further political attack by another of the party's backbenchers, Bill Loughnane, who accused him of lying to the Dáil about the government's security co-operation with the British. Lynch was in the United States at the time, and he called on Colley to have Loughnane expelled from the parliamentary party, but Colley had to settle for a compromise in which the deputy from Clare merely withdrew the accusation.

The dissidents next began circulating a petition calling for Lynch to step down. Deputies were asked to sign without being allowed to see the other names on the list unless they first signed. Although more than twenty signed, they were still well short of a majority.

Had Lynch wished to stay on as Taoiseach, there was little doubt he could have continued, but he intended to go in a few weeks anyway. He no longer had much stomach for the party in-fighting and he was persuaded by Colley and Martin O'Donoghue that the time was opportune to retire, because Colley would be elected to succeed him.

Colley should, of course, have seen the writing on the wall for himself when he failed to secure the expulsion of Loughnane, but he would later contend that he had been misled by some deputies who offered him their support while secretly intending to vote for Charlie. George was not the most perceptive of politicians.

On Wednesday, 5 December 1979, Lynch announced his impending resignation as Taoiseach. In a blatant effort to prevent Charlie organising a proper campaign, the meeting to select a successor was called with just two days notice. Hence the campaign was very short.

Colley's people apparently thought that Charlie would be caught on the hop, but Charlie had been preparing for the day ever since he withdrew from the leadership contest back in 1966. He was supremely confident, as there were few people on the backbenches for whom he had not done favours. Now he expected their backing in return. Sitting in his office he totted up his likely support and concluded that he would get 58 votes to Colley's 24.

'Do you know,' Seán Doherty exclaimed, 'you're the worst fucking judge of people I ever met.'

The contest was going to be much closer than Charlie expected. Most members of the cabinet supported Colley, but the backbench deputies were terrified lest his low standing in the polls would lead to a repetition of the party's poor showing during both the European elections and the recent Cork by-elections. Charlie, on the other hand, was riding high in the polls. He had been excluded from the government's major economic decisions but, as those had recently turned sour, it was a distinct advantage to him to be seen as an outsider within the cabinet.

Charlie's people cleverly set his bandwagon rolling with some announcements timed to give him a boost at the right psychological moments. First of all there was the announcement that Colley's parliamentary secretary, Ray MacSharry, would be proposing Charlie. This was followed at the eleventh hour by an announcement that the Minister for Foreign Affairs, Michael O'Kennedy (who was regarded as a likely compromise candidate), would be voting for Charlie. Suddenly Colley's supporters realised they were in trouble. Ministerial colleagues made frantic efforts to persuade deputies to support Colley by threatening to cut off funds already allocated for local projects. The campaign threatened to get dirty.

Garret FitzGerald related an extraordinary story in his memoirs about some backbench deputies who said they were being intimidated by Charlie's supporters and wished to know if Fine Gael could 'do anything to ensure a genuine secret ballot'. He learned, however, that booths were provided so that deputies could vote in private.

One Fianna Fáil deputy later told FitzGerald that 'despite the polling booth arrangement some deputies had not felt that the privacy of the ballot had been ensured, because the voting papers when marked at either end of the room had to be deposited in a box near the centre of the room. Some deputies claimed they had been told that unless as they walked back to deposit their votes in the box they showed them to members of the Haughey camp they would be assumed to have voted for Colley and would subsequently be treated accordingly.'

No doubt FitzGerald was telling the truth; a member of Fianna Fáil had told him the story, but it sounded like so much sour grapes. Colley's supporters controlled the party mechanism at that stage and if this could have happened without them being forewarned, then they were even more out of touch with the rest of the party than anyone could have imagined. Colley had really outmanoeuvred himself by rushing the election.

The whole thing turned into a contest between the government and its backbenchers. 'They were voting to save their jobs and we were voting to save our seats', was how one backbench member summed up the division. When the votes were counted Charlie had won by 44 votes to 38.

The ballot papers were immediately burned, and the resulting smoke set off the fire alarm in Leinster House. This was seen by his critics as a portent of things to come, but his supporters were absolutely jubilant.

'Nixon's comeback may have been the greatest since Lazarus,' one of them said. 'But there is only one resurrection that beats Charlie's'.

At the press conference following Charlie's election as leader of Fianna Fáil, members of the cabinet were conspicuously absent, as he surrounded himself with backbenchers. Reporters sought to question him on issues on which his silence over the years was interpreted as a sign of ambivalence. In particular, they were interested in his attitude towards the Provisional IRA.

He had not spoken out before, he said, because he had no authority from the party to speak on the Northern Ireland question. Now he was unequivocal. 'I condemn the Provisional IRA and all their activities,' he declared.

Another reporter asked about the arms crisis, but this was a wound he had no intention of re-opening. 'This is very much now a matter for history,' he replied. 'I am leaving it to the historians'.

Would he help the historians? John Bowman asked.

'I will write my own.'

While Fianna Fáil had a comfortable majority in the Dáil, the divisions within the party were so great and the bitterness between Charlie and Colley so intense that the new leader's election as Taoiseach could not be taken as a foregone conclusion. There were still some doubts about whether he could actually win the necessary confidence of the Dáil.

'There were rumours of a split in Fianna Fáil,' Garret FitzGerald noted in his memoirs. 'Possibly because of the rumours of a split that might prevent Charles Haughey's election by the Dáil', the Fine Gael leader did not begin to write his speech until the eleventh hour. He found the task a very difficult one.

'Charles Haughey and I had known each other since the autumn of 1943, when we had met while studying several first arts and commerce subjects together in UCD,' FitzGerald noted. 'Our personal relationship had always been friendly, although not close.'

FitzGerald's ensuing speech following Charlie's formal nomination for the post of Taoiseach on 11 December, should be seen partly as a play for the support of disillusioned Fianna Fáil deputies. 'I must speak not only for the opposition but for many in Fianna Fáil who may not be free to say what they believe or to express their deep fears for the future of this country under the proposed leadership, people who are not free to reveal what they know and what led them to oppose this man with a commitment far beyond the normal,' the Fine Gael leader declared. 'He comes with a flawed pedigree. His motives can be judged ultimately only by God but we cannot ignore the fact that he differs from all his predecessors in that those motives have been and are widely impugned, most notably but by no means exclusively, by people within his own party, people close to him who have observed his actions for many years and who have made their human, interim judgment on him. They and others, both in and out of public life, have attributed to him an over-weening ambition which they do not see as a simple emanation of a desire to serve but rather as a wish to dominate, even to own the state.'

Nowhere in the speech did FitzGerald make any specific charges as to why Charlie was unsuitable for office. All he made were vague insinuations and then cloaked those with the pretence that he could not be more specific 'for reasons that all in this House understand'. But, of course, all remarks made in the Dáil are privileged, so there was no justification whatever for his underhanded approach. If, as he implied, he had reasons for saying what he did, then he should have had the gumption to substantiate his charges.

'It will be for the historians to judge whether placing my views bluntly on the record at that point was counter-productive, or whether it may have contributed to my opponent's failure to secure an overall majority at any of the five subsequent general elections', Fitz-Gerald argued years later.

Whatever about the years ahead, his 'flawed pedigree' speech certainly set the tone for the opposition that day. Others like John Kelly and Richie Ryan of Fine Gael also made caustic comments, as did the long time maverick Noel Browne, who described Charlie as a dreadful cross between former President Richard Nixon and the late Portuguese dictator, Antonio Salazar. 'He has used his position unscrupulously in order to get where he is as a politician,' Browne told the Dáil. 'He has done anything to get power; does anybody believe that he will not do anything to keep power?'

Even back in 1932 when the political climate was still poisoned by civil war bitterness, Eamon de Valera had not been subjected to such abuse. Throughout most of the invective, Charlie sat alone on the government benches, treating his tormentors with contempt by refusing to reply, and restraining others from replying on his behalf. His actions were a silent assertion that the charges were so ludicrous as not to merit a reply.

Since Charlie's family, including his seventy-nine year old mother were in the public gallery, the attacks were seen as most ungracious and were resented by the general public. FitzGerald's own genial image was tarnished, and there was a lot of sympathy for Charlie – even among people who had serious reservations about him. Some of them might have agreed with the sentiments expressed, but they thought the occasion most inappropriate.

Following his election as Taoiseach Charlie went to great lengths to bind up the wounds within Fianna Fáil by reappointing most of the outgoing cabinet, even though only one of them, Michael O'Kennedy had supported him openly. Ray MacSharry, the minister of state who had nominated Charlie, was also rewarded by being elevated to the cabinet.

Albert Reynolds was the only member of 'the gang of five' who had orchestrated Charlie's campaign, to be given a cabinet post, but the others were all appointed ministers of state.

Four ministers were dropped – Jim Gibbons, Martin O'Donoghue and Bobby Molloy were the most notable. Although Colley was appointed Tánaiste and was given a virtual veto over the appointments of the Ministers for Defence and Justice, he was still far from placated.

On 19 December 1979 Colley told Bruce Arnold of the *Irish Independent* that he and his colleagues believed that Charlie was 'dangerous, should have been blocked from the leadership, and should be got out as fast as possible.' Arnold later contended that Haughey began subverting the country's constitution from the moment he took over as Taoiseach, but Arnold's own biography of Charlie would seem to indicate that it was Colley who was guilty of this behaviour. He had extracted unprecedented concessions from the Taoiseach for his support, but then, even though he was constitutionally pledged to the concept of collective cabinet responsibility, he essentially began conspiring against the government.

Earlier that day, the Tánaiste had told a cabinet meeting that Charlie had misrepresented him when he told the press conference after his election, that Colley had pledged loyalty and support. In view of the campaign that Haughey's supporters had waged against Lynch, Colley indicated that he no longer felt bound to give loyalty to the Taoiseach.

'Must you?' Haughey asked.

'Yes,' Colley replied.

If Colley was telling Arnold the truth about this exchange in cabinet, it was a clear breach of cabinet confidentiality. 'Since Haughey had been campaigning, or supporting campaigns on his own behalf, for the previous five months,' Arnold argued, 'it was Haughey, not Colley, who had changed the rule about party loyalty within

Fianna Fáil.' No evidence has ever been produced that Haughey was actively engaged in the campaign against Lynch.

At worst, he was guilty of canvassing for the leadership of the party among members of the parliamentary party who elected the leader, whereas Colley went outside the party and sought to enlist the help of the press. He went public next day disavowing what Haughey had said.

'In my speech at the party meeting,' Colley explained, 'I referred to Mr Haughey's ability, capacity and flair and I wished him well in the enormous tasks he was taking on. I did not, however, use the words "loyalty" or "support" which he attributed to me.' Colley fully understood how, 'in the excitement and euphoria' of victory, Charlie had misunderstood him, but now the Tánaiste was setting the record straight. As far as he was concerned the traditional loyalty normally given to the leader of the party had been withheld from Lynch, and it was now legitimate to withhold 'loyalty to, and support for the elected leader'.

He made these views clear to Charlie before the cabinet was formed, he said. Since then he told him that he intended to set the record straight publicly. As far as he was concerned the rule henceforth would be that 'the Taoiseach is entitled to our conscientious and diligent support in all his efforts in the national interest'.

When Geraldine Kennedy of the *Irish Times* asked if he expected the Taoiseach to seek his resignation, Colley responded rather indifferently. 'I couldn't say what I would expect,' he replied. 'Obviously, if I were asked to resign, it would be a matter for the Taoiseach. It is not for me to say.'

These were most extraordinary speeches for any deputy leader to make barely a week into the life of a new government. Naturally they provoked an immediate political crisis. Next day Charlie called Colley into his office.

'Before he agreed to join the government the Tánaiste expressed to me the views which he has now stated publicly,' Charlie explained in a statement to the press. 'Following our discussion, he has assured me of his full support and loyalty in his office as Tánaiste and as a member of the government.' And that was the end of that.

But the perception was born that Charlie had led the campaign against Jack Lynch. This would be widely accepted by elements of the media, even though no evidence was ever produced to show that he played any part.

'It is untrue to say that Charlie Haughey orchestrated an undermining campaign against Jack Lynch,' Charlie McCreevy admitted in

January 1992, shortly after Haughey had announced his impending retirement. 'It is correct that it was pro-Haughey people who participated, but the man himself neither orchestrated nor encouraged it – of course, neither did he do anything to halt it.'

Tom McEllistrim, one of the gang of four who orchestrated the campaign to replace Lynch, was adamant that Charlie was not behind the whole thing. They informed him about what they were doing, but they were acting in their own political interest. McEllistrim's assessment would seem to have been confirmed by subsequent events. Two of the gang – Albert Reynolds and Seán Doherty – led the moves to oust Charlie in 1992, and by then Jackie Fahey had already broken with Haughey.

'George and his followers sincerely believed Haughey's treachery in the demise of Jack Lynch, but in this they were wrong,' McCreevy continued. 'An unfortunate consequence of that period was that the pro-Lynch/Colley axis of the party believed the orchestration theory when their favourite did not succeed. This was the basis of many party troubles in the early 1980s.'

On the night of the election count in 1977 Haughey had promised his first interview as Taoiseach to Geraldine Kennedy. She told government press secretary Frank Dunlop of the promise and asked him to arrange the interview, but Charlie obviously regretted his rash promise. He decided to explain the situation to Geraldine personally.

Dunlop called her to arrange this meeting and forewarned her of what was going to happen so that she would not be too disappointed. Haughey explained that he could not fulfil his promise, because giving her an exclusive interview would offend other journalists. She thanked him for the courtesy of telling her to her face and added that she was not really surprised. It was what she had come to expect from what colleagues had been telling her.

'What are they saying?' Haughey asked.

'That you're a liar,' she replied.

Haughey was taken aback. He was not about to confirm what his critics in the press thought of him, so he immediately reversed himself and again agreed to give her his first formal interview as Taoiseach. For all his combativeness over the years, it would become apparent in the following months and years that he was a classic bully. When confronted he frequently backed down, as he demonstrated with both Colley and Geraldine Kennedy.

The promised interview turned sour when Geraldine asked questions about the arms crisis. He actually threatened to terminate the proceedings, if she persisted with her line of questioning. She wrote about this in her report, but her editor excised that material. The seeds of future discord had been sown.

She had seen Haughey close up and was not impressed, while his distrust of journalists was probably strengthened by what, in his eyes, would have amounted to the hostility of a journalist he had facilitated. In the following weeks he repeatedly put off requests for interviews without actually refusing them. As a result the requests built up to the point where there were over 250 applications from journalists to interview him.

Frank Dunlop was summoned to Haughey's office one Monday morning. 'Were the fuck were you yesterday?' Haughey asked.

'Yesterday – Sunday – I was at home in the bosom of my family,' Dunlop replied.

'We're making some progress – the fucker knows yesterday was Sunday', Haughey remarked to his aide Pádraig Ó hAnnracháin.

'With that my reserve broke,' Dunlop noted. 'I stood up and approached his desk. 'Don't you ever speak to me like that again,' I said, and made for the door.

Haughey shouted after me to come back, but I kept going. Ó hAnnracháin later admonised Dunlop for speaking like that to the Taoiseach.

'Pádraig, you are missing the point,' Dunlop replied. 'He can't speak to me like that!'

Haughey did not speak to him for the rest of the week, but the following Monday had called Dunlop to ask his opinion on some subject. It was his way of apologising.

To mark the tenth anniversary of the arms crisis in May 1980, Vincent Browne of *Magill* began a series of articles that re-opened the whole controversy. Based largely on the reminiscences of Peter Berry, the late secretary of the Department of Justice who had died in 1975, they provided an extraordinary insight into the controversial events. A number of people tried to block publication by threatening to sue the publisher, distributors and sellers of the magazine. Although publication was temporarily delayed, the controversy helped to generate public curiosity and the issues carrying the Berry story were in great demand. As a result Haughey's role in the whole crisis became the focus of public attention and the Dáil held another debate on the arms crisis, some ten years after the traumatic events.

Although the *Magill* articles raised serious questions about Charlie's conduct, the disclosures were probably even more damaging to some of his critics within Fianna Fáil, because Berry had already told the court virtually all he knew about Haughey's involvement in the affair during the two arms trials. Thus, his most startling posthumous disclosures related to others.

Browne concluded that Haughey 'could easily and justifiably defend what he did at the time' but was so anxious to put the whole affair behind him that he glided over the facts. 'While Mr Haughey certainly behaved improperly,' Browne concluded, 'he was and has been innocent of the more colourful charges that have been laid against him concerning the crisis. It can be argued with some force that he was more a victim of the arms crisis than anything else.'

The *Magill* articles were dragged out over four different issues of the monthly magazine. Browne wrote that Kevin Boland had tried to persuade Haughey to secure cabinet approval for the planned importation of the arms in March 1970. If this conversation took place, there was no way that it could be squared with Haughey's arms trial testimony both about believing the importation was totally proper and not knowing that guns were involved.

When the Dáil conducted a debate on the arms crisis revelations the following autumn, George Colley approached Fine Gael with an extraordinary proposal. Through an emissary, he suggested that if Fine Gael amended its motion in order to highlight the conflict of testimony between Gibbons and Haughey at the arms trial a number of Fianna Fáil deputies would abstain rather than support Haughey.

'On 19 November I met George Colley at a party and he confirmed the proposal, saying that about twenty members would abstain,' FitzGerald noted in his autobiography. This would be enough to bring down the government. In the circumstances, the Fine Gael leader was naturally interested, but Colley got cold feet.

'When I put the matter to the test by inviting George Colley to draft the amendment himself – which seemed to me the best way of ensuring that the abstentions would in fact occur,' Garret wrote, 'he backed away from the proposal.' The idea that Colley ever suggested such a proposal was an extraordinary reflection on his sense of loyalty and collective responsibility. Yet, ironically, he was the main person questioning Charlie's integrity in such matters.

On 10 January 1980, less than a month after his election as Taoiseach, Charlie addressed the nation. 'We have been living at a rate which is simply not justified by the amounts of goods and services we have been producing,' he said. 'To make up the difference we have been borrowing enormous amounts of money, borrowing at a rate which just cannot continue.' It was ironic that Charlie Haughey of all people should have lectured the Irish people about living beyond their means, when he had been spending at a rate that bore little relationship to his income. For the past decade, the Allied Irish Banks (AIB) had been trying to rein in his personal spending.

In September 1971 he owed the bank £244,000. At the time, he was only backbencher. On the kind of money politicians earned, he would never be able to pay off that debt. He agreed to pay off £101,000 by selling £23,000 worth of shares in Tara Mines and Whim Creek, along with £20,000 worth of cattle and his interest in Simmonstown Stud, which was expected to raise £48,000. He would raise the other £10,000 by selling 'other odds and ends.' He told the bank that he was trying to sell the farm he owned in Ashbourne, Co. Meath, for £100,000.

He had the assets to cover his bank debts, so he really viewed his financial difficulties as a mere cash flow problem. The bank fixed his credit limit at £250,000 subject to him halving that debt in three months and clearing it altogether in six months. In June 1972 he got a further loan of £100,000 from another bank by putting up the farm in Co. Meath as security, but this only brought his debt down to £153,000, and by December 1973 he owed AIB £283,000.

'Mr Haughey is quite irresponsible in money matters,' J. J. McAuliffe, the AIB regional manager wrote the following month. 'He cannot be controlled on a running account. His affairs can only deteriorate further.' In 1973, he had paid £20,000 for the island of Innisvicillaun off the Kerry coast, where he planned to build a summer home.

By that September, his bank manager, Michael Phelan, was calling on the bank to take action on the account. 'Despite the unattractiveness of the proposition, Mr Phelan recommends sanctions, bearing in mind the likelihood of Mr Haughey being a man of influence in the future,' one internal bank memorandum read. A year later, the bank was noting that Haughey 'mentioned that the bank did not make use of his influential position and he indicated that he would be more than willing to assist the bank in directing new business, etc.'

On 1 October 1976, Charlie met Phelan and James Denvir, the area manager of AIB. They said that he would have to surrender his cheque book. 'Haughey became quite vicious and told Mr Denvir that "he would not give up his cheque book as he had to live," and "that we were dealing with an adult and no banker would talk to him in this manner",' according to a bank report. The bank officials had talked tough until the client showed his teeth, and then they turned chicken. They were afraid to bounce his cheques as they would do to most other customers in his circumstances. He not only became aggressive and shirty when they asked for his cheque book, he had the audacity to ask for more money. They offered him £10,000 a year for the next two years on the understanding that he would sell 150 acres of Abbeville. When the meeting ended, 'he departed having been left in no doubt as to the seriousness of the situation and the bank's firm intentions once and for all to free the debt and obtain payment in full in the short ter', the report continued.

Of course, this was a piece of fatuous delusion. They had capitulated in the face of his ire. They not only backed off in their demand for his cheque book but also had extended him even more credit for the next two years, and they had cheek to suggest that they were insisting on a short-term solution. They really put him in his place, didn't they!

By the following April he was being warned, according to bank records, that 'if he failed to honour his undertaking we would be forced to dishonour his cheques.' But again, the bank did not have the guts to act. Liam St John Devlin, the chief executive of AIB, concluded that it would be impractical to bounce Haughey's cheques because 'he was a popular and powerful leader and a potential Taoiseach'.

The most senior people in AIB already had doubts as to whether the bank would ever get its money back. As of 1976, the interest that Haughey owed was being recorded in a suspense account, which meant that the officials suspected it would never be paid.

Once he was back in government in 1977 things got even worse. He began building his holiday home on Innisvicillaun at enormous expense, seeing that most the building material had to be ferried to the island by helicopter. But that did not deter Charlie; he was content to leave his accountant, Des Traynor, to worry about the money. 'I just decided to go ahead with the building, leaving it up to Mr Traynor to fund the operation,' he later explained.

He was being charged penal interest in the hope that he would seek better terms from another bank and clear off his debt with AIB. In July 1979 Michael Phelan, concluded that Haughey obviously 'does not believe the bank will force a confrontation with him because of his position.'

Haughey even sought to exploit his position when he suggested he could put some business the way of the AIB and he offered £400,000 as a final settlement of his debt. He had recently returned from Iraq, which he had visited as a result of the Aer Lingus subsidiary PARC taking over the running of a Bagdad hospital, and he suggested the possibility of getting the Iraqi Rafidain Bank, which was controlled by Saddam Hussein, to deposit £10 millions with AIB. The offer was not taken up.

'The account appears to be out of control,' Phelan wrote in August 1979. Charlie owed £913,279 and this was due to rise a further £100,000 when the interest became due. At the time the interest rate was 26%. On 18 September, Des Traynor began some protracted negotiations with the bank on Haughey's behalf to clear his debt.

Barely three months later Charlie became Taoiseach and suddenly Phelan adopted an almost sycophantic approach. 'It gives me great pleasure to convey to you my warmest congratulations on your election to the high offices of leader of Fianna Fáil and Taoiseach and to offer you my sincere good wishes for success in both,' Phelan wrote to him. 'To say the task you have taken on is daunting is an understatement but I have every faith in your ability to succeed in restoring confidence in this little nation.'

AIB had already virtually despaired of Haughey's ability to handle his indebtedness, which had proved intractable over the past decade. Now that he had finally achieved power, however, he was able to resolve the problems with the help of Traynor within a matter of weeks.

Charlie personally sought help from Patrick Gallagher, whose father, Matt, had helped to make Haughey a rich man by advising him to buy the house and lands in Raheny in 1957. After Matt Gallagher died in 1974, Patrick took over the business and was more than willing to help finance Charlie. He provided at least £15,000 to him in political donations during the next five years.

As soon as Haughey had achieved his ambition of becoming Taoiseach, he turned for financial help to young Patrick Gallagher, then still in his twenties. On Sunday afternoon, 7 December 1979, he invited Gallagher to Abbeville to ask him for financial help.

'What is the mess?' the 26-year-old Patrick asked.

'£750,000,' replied Haughey.

'Can you get someone to raise half of it?' Gallagher asked.

Haughey affirmed.

'Say no more, I'll sort it out with Des Traynor,' Gallagher said. He had his own selfish motives. 'I was naive enough,' he later admitted, 'to think I could get a favour. But not a thing. You might be introduced to people who could help, but he was not slow to tell you to go and sort out your own business.'

Anybody who thinks that they could buy favours from Haughey does not know the man, according to his long-time mistress Terry Keane. 'They don't understand Charlie's character,' she later emphasised. Haughey would think the money was his by right. 'It would be like the three wise men putting gold, frankincense and myrrh in front of the saviour and that he would have no obligation because of a gift,' she argued.

Even if he had intended to do favours for some of his building and property friends, Colley was determined to frustrate any effort to help those people. John Byrne, a Kerry man who had made his money in construction and Irish dance halls in Britain following the Second World War, was persuaded to return to Ireland in the Lemass era like Matt Gallagher. Byrne built a number of prominent buildings in Dublin, like O'Connell Bridge House, D'Olier House and Parnell House. He leased office space to the state, but as Minister for Finance, Colley blocked any further deals with Byrne, and he enlisted the help of Garret FitzGerald, the leader of Fine Gael, to get Dublin County Council to block planning permission for any development on what had been Baldoyle Race Course, which had been bought by Byrne in the 1970s. In that instance, Byrne's friendship with Haughey was a distinct handicap.

Gallagher's company provided the promised £300,000, as a non-refundable deposit on 35 acres of land at the Kinsealy estate that he would buy for £1.225m. This was subject to a provision that he would find a suitable stud farm that would be purchased for the Haugheys out of the price of the land and the whole deal had to be finalised by 1986. (It seemed like a crazy way of doing business and within a couple of years the Gallagher Group and its Merchant Bank, worth an estimated £70 million, went into liquidation. The receiver deemed any claim on the lands at Kinsealy unrecoverable, and Patrick Gallagher's ties to Haughey were of little value to him, because he went to jail anyway in Northern Ireland over his business dealings.)

In talks between AIB and Des Traynor, it was agreed that the only way to deal with Charlie's borrowings 'was to clear the debt totally'. Traynor made a deal with the bank that Haughey would pay £750,000 by mid February 1980 and that he would promise to pay £110,000 at some time, while the remainder of the debt would be written off. The three-quarters of a million amounted to all the money he had actually borrowed and a little of the interest, while the £110,000 covered only interest and it was to be cleared as a matter of honour without any further interest.

There were rumours of that AIB had written off a large chunk of a loan for Charlie, but nobody was prepared to go on the record with the story, so the media were not in a position to report what had happened for almost 20 years. The opposition attacks on Haughey on the day of his election as Taoiseach had backfired badly and generated sympathy for him in the press. For the next two months, he enjoyed a virtual honeymoon with the media.

While some of Haughey's old enemies were more implacable than ever, he was enjoying good media coverage. His victory was clearly welcomed by prestigious editors like Douglas Gageby of the *Irish Times*, Tim Pat Coogan of the *Irish Press*, and Michael Hand of the *Sunday Independent* and Vincent Browne of *Magill* magazine, though the latter did persist in asking how Haughey had apparently become so fabulously wealthy.

Addressing the Fianna Fáil Ard Fheis on 16 February 1980 Charlie said that his government's 'first political priority' was to end partition. To further his aim he intended to enlist international help in order to put diplomatic pressure on Britain. As far as the Taoiseach was concerned, Northern Ireland was failed as a political entity; so a new beginning was needed. But it was noteworthy that he did not call on the British to announce their intention to withdraw from the area. Rather, he asked them to declare 'their interest in encouraging the unity of Ireland by agreement and in peace'.

When Charlie went to London to meet Prime Minister Margaret Thatcher in May, his chances of securing any kind of advance seemed remote because, on the eve of their meeting, she told the House of Commons that the constitutional affairs of Northern Ireland were 'a matter for the people of Northern Ireland, this government and this parliament and no one else.' In short, the Northern Ireland question was none of Charlie's business.

The two of them got on surprisingly well next day. He brought her a silver Georgian teapot as a present, and she was apparently charmed by him. One member of her cabinet later told friends 'he was sure he detected a "sexual" attraction for the smallish, rather worse-for-wear Irishman'.

After their meeting the two leaders issued a joint communique emphasising that they had decided to have regular meetings in order to develop 'new and closer political co-operation between our two countries'. The most significant aspect of the communique was their agreement that 'any change in the constitutional status of Northern Ireland would only come about with the consent of a majority of the people of Northern Ireland'.

In the following weeks there was a controversy over the proposed appointment of a new Irish ambassador to the United States that was played out largely behind the scenes. Part of Haughey's overall plans for the north was to enlist diplomatic pressure on the British government to work for a settlement. Traditionally Irish-Americans were the Dublin government's most influential supporters, but they were usually faction-ridden. In 1980 they were divided on the Northern Ireland question, with a large, vocal and well-organised minority supporting the campaign of the Provisional IRA. Ever since his appointment as Irish ambassador to the United States in 1978 Seán Donlon had sought to isolate those militants and in the process he ran foul of the organisations they controlled – Noraid, the Irish National Caucus and the Ancient Order of Hibernians. Charlie decided to replace Donlon with someone acceptable to a broader spectrum of Irish-Americans so that their voice could be consolidated behind Haughey's own settlement plans. He decided to transfer Donlon to the United Nations, but word of this leaked and some powerful voices were raised in Washington, where Donlon was held in high esteem by influential Irish-American political figures like Thomas 'Tip' O'Neill, Speaker of the House of Representatives, Senators Edward Kennedy of Massachusetts and Daniel Patrick Moynihan of New York, as well Governor Hugh Carey of New York and the former California Governor Ronald Reagan, then engaged in his successful bid for the presidency. Faced with such opposition, Haughey backed off and left Donlon at his post in Washington.

As his first year in the Taoiseach's office was coming to a close, Charlie desperately needed some kind of real achievement. He was obviously indebted for his reinstatement within Fianna Fáil to the so-called green wing of the party, which wanted the government to take a more active part in seeking a solution to the northern problem. The whole question took on added significance on 26 October 1980 when seven Republican prisoners went on hunger-strike for what amounted to political status. A week later Charlie was in Letterkenny, Co. Donegal, for a by-election rally. He watched aghast from the platform as Síle de Valera denounced 'Mrs Thatcher's lack of compassion' and her 'callous, unfeeling and self-righteous statements'. Síle's controversial address revived memories of her speech outside Fermoy, which marked the public beginning of the push to secure the removal of Jack Lynch as Taoiseach.

Although Charlie made no reference to Síle's speech during his own address moments later, he was obviously taken aback. Immediately after the rally he and some senior colleagues retired to a local hotel to discuss the situation. About an hour later Ray MacSharry issued a statement to the press as director of elections. He emphasised that neither the Taoiseach nor any member of the government had seen Síle's script in advance. He added that her remarks had not reflected the views of the government.

She expressed surprise at the statement disassociating the party from her remarks. Lynch had banned her from making any public comments on the northern situation following her speech in September 1979, but Charlie lifted the ban when he became Taoiseach. 'Mr Haughey told me when he assumed office that the ban no longer applied,' she explained. 'I was working under the assumption that there was no ban when I spoke in Letterkenny.'

Privately Charlie may well have agreed with Síle's sentiments, but he clearly did not like her timing. He was anxious lest the incident would impair his relations with the British prime minister before their next meeting, which was due to take place in Dublin Castle on 8 December 1980. Since he had been sitting beside Síle on the platform when she made the remarks, it would appear that he was openly endorsing her comments, unless some kind of repudiation were issued.

Thatcher was accompanied to the Dublin Castle summit by chancellor of the exchequer Geoffrey Howe, foreign secretary Lord Carrington and Humphrey Atkins, the secretary of state for Northern Ireland. The inclusion of Carrington gave rise to speculation because he had recently played a major role in changing the direction of British policy in regard to the Rhodesian question. Prompted by the foreign secretary, Thatcher had radically altered her Rhodesian policy and agreed to a settlement which brought one of the guerrilla leaders to power.

Charlie, with his almost Messianic belief in his own capability, seemed to think he had a real chance of persuading the British to settle the Irish question for once and for all. He was accompanied by Brian Lenihan and Michael O'Kennedy, his respective ministers for Foreign Affairs and Finance. They were included in most of the day-long discussions, though not in the private meeting lasting an hour and a quarter between the two leaders.

Afterwards a joint communique was issued describing their talks as 'extremely constructive and significant'. Both sides 'accepted the need to bring forward policies and proposals to achieve peace, reconciliation and stability' in Northern Ireland. To further these aims they agreed to promote 'the further development of the unique relationship between the two countries' by commissioning 'joint studies covering a range of issues including possible new institutional structures, citizenship rights, security matters, economic co-operation and measures to encourage mutual understanding'.

Around a hundred reporters from different parts of the globe were present at a press conference afterwards when Charlie explained that there had been 'an historic breakthrough'. He was not prepared to elaborate publicly, but he was more forthcoming immediately afterwards in an 'off-the-record' briefing for Irish political correspondents. He indicated 'by implication and innuendo' that the British leader had agreed that the joint studies could reconsider Northern Ireland's whole constitutional position, according to Bruce Arnold. The Taoiseach anticipated an early end to partition during this briefing, and Lenihan declared in a RTÉ interview that the Northern Ireland question was on the verge of resolution.

Margaret Thatcher promptly denied there was any intention of altering the constitutional position of the six counties, but Ian Paisley exploited Unionist uneasiness by taking to what he called the 'Carson Trail' in order to demonstrate the intensity of Unionist opposition to constitutional change. A whole series of demonstrations were organised throughout Northern Ireland to rail against the joint studies.

Intense spleen was vented at Charlie, a long-standing hate figure in the eyes of Unionists. Paisley talked about their ancestors cutting 'civilisation out of the bogs and meadows of this country while Mr Haughey's ancestors were wearing pig skins and living in caves'. At a Newtownards rally he conjured up a picture of the Taoiseach with 'a green baton dripping with blood' in one hand and 'a noose specially prepared for the Protestants of Ulster in the other'.

The bitterness with which Paisley and his followers reacted to the outcome of the Dublin Castle summit no doubt encouraged optimism in Nationalist circles. The H-Block hunger-strike was called off within ten days. Whether the exaggerated significance attached to the Dublin Castle summit had encouraged those advising the hunger-strikers to engage in some wishful thinking is a matter for speculation, but in time it would become apparent that Charlie and company had – either wittingly or unwittingly – grossly oversold the significance of the summit.

Opposition leaders criticised him for not being more specific about his talks. Garret FitzGerald complained that the government seemed to be trying to bring about Irish unity without the prior consent of the northern majority, which he believed was a recipe for civil war.

Yet Charlie made no apologies for the secrecy surrounding the joint studies. 'To suggest that permanent officials engaged in such studies should try to carry out their task in the full glare of publicity is nonsense,' he later declared. 'We were accused of trying to settle matters over the heads of the people of Northern Ireland when in fact we were seeking to set up a political framework in which they could participate without prejudice to their principles.'

At the time, however, he allowed his own people to encourage the belief that he was close to a settlement that would end partition. As the summit had taken place on 8 December, the feast of the Immaculate Conception, Haughey's handling of the subsequent publicity was dubbed 'Charlie's Immaculate Deception'. He was apparently looking towards an early general election, even though the existing Dáil still had eighteen months to run. In January 1981, for instance, the government introduced what amounted to an election budget which did not reflect the country's real economic situation. He apparently intended to call the election immediately after the Fianna Fáil Ard Fheis in mid-February, but these plans went awry on the first night of the party conference when disaster struck in the form of the Stardust tragedy.

Forty-eight young people were killed in a discotheque fire in Charlie's own constituency. Given the magnitude of the disaster, the remainder of the Ard Fheis was postponed. When it was reconvened in April, Charlie was still talking in terms of an early end to partition. 'A year from this Ard Fheis if we persevere faithfully,' he declared, 'we may begin to see in a clearer light the end of the road on which we have set out.'

By this time, however, the political climate had already been poisoned by the start of another H-Block hunger-strike on 1 March 1981. This one received massive international publicity, following the election to Westminster of one of the men, Bobby Sands. The hunger-strikers vowed to fast to death and others pledged to replace them on the fast until their demands were met. Sands expected that Charlie would be compelled to support their demands publicly, but the Taoiseach refused to be pressurised, even after Sands and his colleagues began to die.

When Haughey called a general election for 11 June 1981. Fianna Fáil's private polls were indicating that the party was in good standing with the rather volatile electorate.

With the 'don't knows' excluded, the poll estimated that Fianna Fáil would get 52% of the vote, which would be an even higher percentage than that which gave the party its record landslide victory in 1977. At the outset of the campaign, therefore, things were looking well for Charlie personally and for Fianna Fáil generally, but the electorate had little idea of what was actually going on. The country had already spent most of its budget for the whole year. The financial position was just as illusory as the promises on partition.

DESPERATION POLITICS

When Charlie warned in his first national broadcast on 10 January 1980 that the country was living beyond its means, he did not say how he hoped to cope with the economic problems that night, but in the following weeks his government indicated it would be restricting the free bus service to rural school children and limiting wage increases in the public sector. It was also announced that a resource tax would be introduced in order to get farmers to bear a fairer share of the tax burden. These were bold proposals, but Charlie lost his nerve.

Tackling the country's financial difficulties by cutting back on services, or else increasing taxes, would have risked short-term unpopularity with the electorate, and that was a chance that Charlie was not prepared to take. His leadership was under continuous pressure within Fianna Fáil as he had never really been accepted by the Colley clique, and he had worked too hard to get to the top to risk it all. Consequently, he succumbed to the pressure and abandoned the various proposals; his government borrowed and spent money as if there were no tomorrow. It capitulated to public service pay demands by conceding a staggering 34% increase.

Some of Charlie's more prominent supporters, like ministers of state Tom McEllistrim and Pádraig Flynn were allowed to announce extravagant schemes. McEllistrim, who was Charlie's self-styled campaign manager, made so many announcements in his own constituency that he was dubbed 'MacMillions' by a local newspaper. Flynn, as minister of state for Transport, announced the building of a major airport near Knock in his own Mayo constituency. The local airport company was only asked to put up £100 for the multi-million pound project. As a result of these and other extravagant policies the budget deficit ended up more than 50% over target for the year. Having identified the grave financial predicament facing the country back in January, Charlie and his government merely compounded the problems with their profligate economic policies.

The budget figures presented to the Dáil for 1981 really bore little relationship to the country's economic position. It was obviously an election budget designed to deceived people by painting an unrealistic economic picture. Had Charlie been able to exploit the apparent success of the Dublin Castle summit with a good party Ard Fheis and an early general election, he may well have won a majority, seeing that he came so close under much less favourable circumstances some months later. Events seemed to conspire against him, when the Stardust disaster forced the postponement of the Ard Fheis and then the H-Block hunger-strikes poisoned the atmosphere generated by the Dublin Castle summit.

At the beginning of 1980 Charlie had been the darling of the media. But the political correspondents gradually came to the conclusion that Charlie had used them in overplaying the significance of the Dublin Castle summit and they resented being used in that fashion.

By the time a general election was held in June 1981 a considerable amount of the money allocated for 1981 had already been spent and it was necessary for the new government of Garret FitzGerald to introduce legislation to secure supplementary funding for the remainder of the year by way of increased taxes.

Charlie was critical of the new government's economic policies. 'Our approach is positive and theirs is negative,' he contended. 'We are development-investment minded, and they are committed to monetarism and deflation.'

People like Colley, O'Donoghue, O'Malley were quietly critical, but Charlie McCreevy, one of Haughey's more ardent backbench supporters in 1979, spoke out publicly. In an interview with Geraldine Kennedy of the *Sunday Tribune*, he was particularly critical of Fianna Fáil's performance in opposition. 'We seem to be against everything and for nothing,' he said. When asked if he was disillusioned with the party leader, he pointedly refused to comment, thereby leaving little doubt about his own disenchantment with Haughey.

On 11 January 1982 he spoke out again in a similar vein. He complained that general elections were 'developing into an auction in promises' with scant regard for the national interest. 'We are so hell bent in assuming power that we are prepared to do anything for it,' he declared.

Bristling under the criticism, which he considered a challenge to his own leadership, Haughey asked the parliamentary party to expel McCreevy. The latter allowed the matter to be brought to the brink of a vote before announcing that he would spare colleagues the necessity of a divisive vote by withdrawing from the whip voluntarily. Before the end of the month, however, Haughey would invite him back after the coalition government collapsed following the defeat of the budget introduced by Minister of Finance John Bruton on the night of 27 January 1982.

Garret FitzGerald announced that he was going to Áras an Uachtaráin to tender his resignation and to ask President Patrick Hillery to call a general election. The outcome of such a meeting would normally be a mere formality, but it was different this time. While the constitution stipulated that the Dáil is 'summoned and dissolved by the president on the advice of the Taoiseach', this was one instance in which the president had discretionary powers, because it also states clearly that 'the president may in his absolute discretion refuse to dissolve Dáil Éireann on the advice of a Taoiseach who has ceased to retain the support of a majority in Dáil Éireann'. As FitzGerald had just lost the vote on the budget, the president was therefore free to refuse to grant a dissolution.

Neil Blaney apprised Charlie of the situation and suggested that he notify the president of Fianna Fáil's readiness to form a government. This was a real chance for the president to exercise one of his few discretionary powers because of the numerical situation in the Dáil. If those who had voted against the budget were prepared to support Fianna Fáil, Charlie would be able to form a government. Even if it did not last very long, the party would, at least, have the advantage of fighting the next election as the government party with all that this entailed. It was therefore worth a try.

Although there were precedents for this in Canada in the 1920s and Australia in 1975, it was an unprecedented situation in Ireland. The big question was whether the president would use his discretionary power. Brian Lenihan, who had sat next to Paddy Hillery at the cabinet table for eight years, was asked for his opinion.

'We wouldn't get anywhere with Hillery,' he replied.

The Fianna Fáil front bench decided, nevertheless, that a statement be issued highlighting the availability of the Fianna Fáil leader.

'It is a matter for the president to consider the situation which has arisen now that the Taoiseach has ceased to retain the support of the majority in Dáil Éireann,' Charlie declared. 'I am available for consultation by the president should he so wish.'

Charlie suggested someone telephone the president to apprise him of this statement. 'He nodded at me,' Lenihan recalled. 'He has a habit of making requests by nodding his head instead of actually saying anything. I shook my head.'

'I am not the man for the job,' Lenihan said. It was not that he saw anything wrong with calling, but he felt it would be a waste of time.

Charlie then nodded to Sylvester Barrett, who, as a fellow Clare-man, was on particularly good terms with the president. Barrett left the room to telephone, but the duty officer manning the telephone switchboard at the Aras told him that the president was not available.

If this was just a courtesy call to inform the president of Charlie's statement, Barrett could have accomplished this by merely leaving a message without bombarding the Aras with further calls. Barrett tried again later and so did another Fianna Fáil deputy, Brian Hillery, a cousin of the president, but none of them got through. Independent deputies Blaney and Seán Dublin Bay Loftus also tried. Charlie called himself in apparent exasperation and he is alleged to have become quite abusive when the duty officer, Capt. Ollie Barbour, refused to put him through.

Garret FitzGerald had not gone straight to the president, but had given a press conference and was then delayed for a time. It was not until around ten o'clock – about an hour and three-quarters after the vote – that he reached Aras an Uachtaráin.

'I was ushered in to a disturbed and indeed quite angry President Hillery,' he later wrote. 'The Aras had apparently been besieged with phone calls.' The president 'was so upset by what had happened,' according to FitzGerald, 'that he kept me there for three-quarters of an hour, thus leading many back in Leinster House to speculate that he might in fact be exercising his prerogative, the inappropriateness of which in current circumstances he was so vigorously propounding to me.'

Next day the president in his capacity as commander-in-chief of the army ordered that the Chief of Staff, Lt Gen. Hogan, should ensure that Capt. Barbour's military record was in no way compromised by his failure to facilitate Charlie on the telephone the previous evening. The captain had simply been following the instructions, the president explained.

Later it would be suggested that Charlie had actually threatened the officer. 'I intend to roast your fucking arse, if you don't put me through immediately,' he reportedly warned. But Charlie vehemently denied this.

The whole affair was really a storm in a tea cup that was of practically no significance at the time. The fact that phone calls were made was leaked to the press, but these did not actually become an election issue until nearly nine years later when they almost brought down Charlie's fourth government and played a key role undermining Fianna Fáil's bid to have Brian Lenihan succeed Paddy Hillery as president.

Of course, that is getting ahead of the story.

While Fine Gael people were despondent at the defeat of the budget on 27 January 1982, FitzGerald was strangely buoyant from the time his government's defeat was announced. 'I experienced a moment of total exhilaration,' he later wrote. 'This was it. We were going into battle on a budget that we could defend with conviction and enthusiasm, both on social and financial grounds. We would be able to contrast our vigorous tackling of the financial crisis and the honesty with which we had prepared the budget against Fianna Fáil's appalling four-year record of extravagance and the dishonest budget they had produced a year earlier, in which spending figures had been arbitrarily slashed without any policy decision being taken to implement these nominal cuts.'

Haughey intended to make the rejected budget the central issue of the election campaign. At a press conference next morning he placed a very high priority on the need to dispose of 'most of the provisions of yesterday's budget'. He was deliberately vague about his own plans, and he became irritated when journalists pressed him for specific details of how he would handle the economy.

He blamed government policies for allowing 5,000 vacancies to develop in the public sector and he intimated he would have those vacancies filled. He also indicated that he would retain food subsidies that the coalition government had planned to abandon.

Fianna Fáil's newly appointed spokesman on finance, Martin O'Donoghue, was furious that Charlie had ignored a front bench decision to accept the government's proposed ceiling on spending and its projected deficit. It was therefore intimated strongly to Charlie that if he continued to campaign as he had begun, then O'Donoghue, Colley and O'Malley would repudiate his policies. He therefore agreed to adopt the economic approach advocated by O'Donoghue, who was invited to prepare a speech in which Charlie accepted the government's targeted deficit.

'We would stick to the same levels of borrowing and the current budget deficit,' he told a party rally, 'because it would not be sensible, wise or prudent to depart too much.' He contended, however, that some of the harsher aspects of the defeated budget could easily be eliminated.

If Charlie hoped that taking this line would unite the dissidents behind him, he must have been sorely disappointed. Interviewed on RTÉ radio's *This Week* programme next day, O'Donoghue beat around the proverbial bush rather than answer when asked four different times if he thought Charlie was fit to be Taoiseach. In another RTÉ interview later in the campaign, Colley similarly refused to say that he hoped Charlie would be the next Taoiseach.

When Charlie tried to explain how the government's budget targets could be met without adopting the harsher measures proposed, he and his economic advisers were accused of 'creative accounting' because their figures simply did not add up. The shortfall was referred to as 'Fianna Fáil's funny money'.

Charlie's credibility on such matters was further questioned at the height of the campaign when *Magill* magazine published a leaked Department of Finance document showing that his government had deliberately underestimated expenditure in the run up to the 1981 general election.

The Fianna Fáil leader's image had clearly become an electoral liability as he trailed FitzGerald by more than twenty points in the public opinion polls. By the time of the last such survey before election day, Charlie was only the choice for Taoiseach of only 33% of the electorate as against 56% for FitzGerald.

Albert Reynolds, Fianna Fáil's national director of elections, accused Fine Gael of conducting a smear campaign against Charlie. There could be no doubt he was being treated unfairly. This was acknowledged by some of his most outspoken critics.

'There was a lot of personal sniping against Charlie Haughey which was unfair,' Geraldine Kennedy admitted. 'It could just as equally have been done on Garret FitzGerald, and it wasn't.'

Fianna Fáil dissidents had been hinting that their leader was an unsuitable person to lead the country, and the media reflected this even though no specific evidence was cited to justify the unstated reservations about him. 'Because they were unstated and therefore unsubstantiated, they were unfair,' conceded Seán Duignan, RTÉ's political correspondent.

On election day there was a sensational development when Charlie's election agent, Pat O'Connor, was arrested on a charge of double voting. He and his family had inadvertently been registered to vote at two different polling stations. There was evidence that he and his daughter had requested ballot papers at both places, but to secure a conviction it was necessary to prove not only that they had deposited two ballot papers each but also that they had actually voted correctly on each. If they had deliberately or inadvertently spoiled their voting papers, they would not be deemed to have voted under the existing law. As there was no way of identifying the ballot papers to prove that either of them had voted properly once, much less twice, they were acquitted of the charges.

Of course, Charlie was not personally involved in any of this, but his name was immediately dragged into the affair, because it involved his election agent, who was also his solicitor and a close personal friend. Charlie's opponents predictably exploited the affair against him.

One of those elected, after a seven-month absence from the Dáil, was Jim Gibbons, who lost no time in raising the spectre of an impending challenge to Charlie. 'I expect the question of the leadership will be raised at the first meeting of the parliamentary party,' he told reporters following his victory. This was immediately interpreted as the first move in a bid to get rid of Charlie. As the count continued the *Evening Herald* went on sale with a bold front page headline: 'Leadership Fight Facing Haughey'.

Some hours later it became apparent that Fianna Fáil were going to be three votes short of an overall majority in the Dáil. Disgruntled members of the party openly contended that Charlie had been a distinct electoral liability.

The outgoing chairman of the parliamentary party, William Kenneally, who had just lost his seat in Waterford, made no secret of his disillusionment. He told Geraldine Kennedy that the party would have fared much better under a more popular leader, with the result that he 'would not be surprised' if the leadership became an issue in the very near future. She reported that 'a movement seemed to be brewing' within Fianna Fáil to overthrow the 'leader as he struggles to form the next government without an overall majority'.

Charlie was obviously stung by the story, which he described as 'rubbish' during an interview that afternoon on RTÉ's lunchtime news programme. 'If I were in the *Sunday Tribune,*' he said, 'I would be inclined to look after my own future.'

Speculation about the leadership was certainly not helping his chances of regaining power. He needed the active support of at least two deputies from outside his own party and the abstention of another, in order to replace FitzGerald. This was likely to prove difficult when there was uncertainty about his own hold on the leadership of Fianna Fáil. He therefore had a meeting of the new parliamentary party called for Thursday, 25 February, with a view to selecting the party's nominee for Taoiseach.

If only to remove the uncertainty, his desire to have the issue resolved speedily was understandable. Of course, his opponents felt he was simply trying to deny them time to organise properly. They went into action and held a series of backroom meetings at which Colley threw his support to O'Malley, who then became the front-runner among the potential challengers.

O'Malley began canvassing for support with the help of Colley, Seamus Brennan, Martin O'Donoghue and others. Although many deputies had reservations about the timing of a challenge when there was a real chance of getting into power, O'Malley's people were encouraged by the response. At one point they were convinced they had the support of a majority of deputies, and their optimistic predictions were reflected by the media.

Vincent Browne published a list of 30 Fianna Fáil deputies who he believed would probably vote against Charlie, while he could only count 17 probable supporters. On the eve of the party meeting, the *Irish Independent* had a front page article by Bruce Arnold with a headline running right across the top of the page: 'My score so far Haughey 20, O'Malley 46, Unknowns 15'.

The headline was an example of sloppy proof-reading. Arnold had only referred to 36 deputies, whom he listed as being prepared to support O'Malley – not the 46 stated in the headline, probably written by a sub-editor. However, the newspaper made no effort to correct the mistake, which was particularly significant because the figure cited would have been a clear majority of Fianna Fáil deputies, while Arnold's list was five short of the vital number. Suddenly O'Malley became a money-on favourite with bookmakers to replace Charlie.

It was even rumoured that the latter was going to resign that day. Stephen Collins, a young reporter with the *Irish Press* group, was sent to Leinster House to find out, but when he asked Charlie he was not prepared for the reaction.

Charlie made a drive at him. 'Would you fuck off,' he shouted, backing him against a wall and spelling out his message. 'That's F-U-C-K-O-F-F.'

A photographer colleague came to the rescue by pointing out that Collins was only doing his job. Charlie promptly regained his composure. 'What is your question again?' he asked.

Collins repeated it, this time with an explanation that his news desk had a tip that Charlie was about to resign. 'That's complete nonsense,' the Fianna Fáil leader replied quite calmly. 'I have no intention of resigning.' And with that he walked away.

His people were clearly running scared. Throughout the day and into the early hours of the following morning they bombarded dissident and wavering deputies with telephone calls to support Charlie. At around midnight O'Malley formally announced that he would be challenging for the party's nomination next morning.

Arnold's list actually hurt O'Malley's chances, because it had the dual effect of shocking Charlie's people into action and providing them with the names of deputies on whom to concentrate their pressure. But Charlie could feel justifiably aggrieved about the way the *Irish Independent* was covering the story, especially the reports emanating from dissident sources. What those people had to say was newsworthy, even when inaccurate, but inaccurate charges should have been identified as such and not credulously reported.

On the morning of the parliamentary party meeting, for instance, there was a front page article in which Raymond Smith not only repeated a dissident prediction that O'Malley had 'sufficient votes to oust Mr Haughey', but also quoted one of the dissidents as saying that 'what's happening now is an exact carbon copy of how Mr Lynch was forced out of the Fianna Fáil leadership through a sequence of events'.

The implications were unmistakable – Charlie and his supporters had brought down Lynch and they were now receiving some of their own medicine. But Lynch had retired voluntarily. While there had been sniping against him in 1979, it was Gibbons, one of Charlie's bitterest critics and the one who set the ball rolling in this latest challenge, who was the first to break party discipline by refusing to support the government's contraception bill that April, and it was one of O'Malley's strongest backers, George Colley, who had persuaded Lynch to retire early in the belief that the time was opportune for him to win the leadership. Consequently it was unfair of the press not to question the scenario then being painted by the dissidents.

Aspects of the press coverage were undoubtedly biased against Charlie, but it should be noted that the *Irish Times* and *Irish Press* leaned heavily towards him in their editorial comments. *The Cork Examiner* was more detached, but it predicted he would win. The *Irish Independent* was the only national daily which carried an editorial leaning towards O'Malley.

There was a great air of expectation about Leinster House that morning. Photographers and a television camera were allowed into the meeting room beforehand. Charlie's entrance was stage-managed for the television camera. He was ceremoniously announced so that his supporters could greet him with one of those spontaneous bursts of applause. The press were then ushered out.

Pádraig Faulkner was one of the first deputies to speak. He had opposed Charlie in the past but he said was supporting him this time, and he urged O'Malley not to go through with the challenge, because such a contest would be too divisive and would rip the party asunder. Jim Tunney, Rory O'Hanlon, and Liam Lawlor – all of whom had been listed as anti-Haughey by both Vincent Browne and Bruce Arnold – spoke in a similar vein. But it was Martin O'Donoghue who delivered the most devastating blow of all when he urged that there should be no contest. Suddenly it seemed that O'Malley's support had evaporated. He announced he would not allow his name to go forward, and Charlie was chosen by acclamation. The whole meeting was over in little less than an hour.

Afterwards Charlie was triumphant. 'You got it wrong!' he crowed to a reporter on his way into a press conference.

He was particularly annoyed at the *Irish Independent*. When Raymond Smith asked a question without first identifying himself, Charlie pretended not to recognise him.

'Who is this man?' he asked.

'You can call me Mr Smith, or Raymond, or Ray, but you don't have to ask who I am.'

'To me,' Charlie said contemptuously, 'you are just a face in the crowd. Now what is your question?'

It was a bad start to the press conference at which Charlie's annoyance at the *Irish Independent* would surface repeatedly. He interrupted in the middle of one question as Smith was saying that 'certain names have been mentioned in the papers as who might vote against you –'

'I am *delighted* you mentioned that,' Charlie interjected, 'because your particular newspaper published perhaps the falsest list of names in Irish journalism.' He emphasised *ad nauseam* that he had been selected unanimously and he complained repeatedly that media speculation about the O'Malley challenge had turned out to be just 'so much rubbish'.

To regain power Charlie's best chance seemed to lie with securing the support of independents, who included his arms crisis colleague Neil Blaney. John O'Connell, the sitting Speaker could be neutralised by being re-appointed, which meant that all Fianna Fáil needed was the support of the newly elected Dublin Independent, Tony Gregory, who seemed to share Charlie's strong Nationalistic views. Gregory obviously held the key to power.

'I have 78 seats, plus Blaney, and O'Connell will be Ceann Comhairle,' Charlie told Gregory on Tuesday, 23 February. 'I need your vote to become Taoiseach. What do you want?'

Intermittent negotiations were conducted during the next two weeks. But this was not the only thing Charlie was working on. He also had approaches made to the Fine Gael deputy, Richard Burke, to see if he would be interested in being appointed Irish commissioner to the EEC. This would necessitate his resignation from the Dáil and would mean that Fianna Fáil would need one vote less to gain power. But Burke killed the speculation with a statement emphasising that there was 'no possibility' that he would fail to vote for Garret FitzGerald for Taoiseach when the Dáil reconvened on 9 March 1982.

Having successfully staved off the O'Malley challenge, Charlie returned to the task of winning the support of Gregory. Although Charlie had never tired of expressing his admiration of his father-in-law's political acumen, he seemed curiously oblivious to the example set by Seán Lemass under comparatively similar circumstances back in 1961. Fianna Fáil lacked a majority then, but Lemass refused to deal with anyone. Before the Dáil voted on his renomination as Taoiseach, he proudly proclaimed that he had not and would not ask for support from outside Fianna Fáil. He had made no deals, but he was re-elected anyway.

When Charlie went to Gregory, however, the latter came up with a long list of specific demands in matters relating to employment, housing, health and education in Dublin, especially in the inner city area. Throughout the discussions, which were held at Gregory's headquarters, Charlie seemed highly amenable. He personally agreed with most of the demands.

'You're pushing an open door,' was his stock response.

'It was clear he wasn't interested in the other independents,'

Gregory said afterwards. 'He believed I could accommodate him.'

FitzGerald also tried to win over Gregory with lavish promises but the Fine Gael leader was in a weaker position because, in addition to Gregory, he needed the support of the Workers' party and at least one other Independent, so he could not offer as much to Gregory. Charlie won out in this auction for power by agreeing to have £4 million allocated to employ 500 extra men in the inner city, have 3,746 new jobs created in the same area within the next three years, have Industrial Development Authority grants raised to attract new industries to the city, acquire a 27 acre port and docks site, provide government money to build 440 new houses in the inner city and another 1,600 in the rest of Dublin, have free medical cards provided for all pensioners, to have the supplementary welfare system over-hauled, increase the number of remedial teachers in the inner city, and to nationalise Clondalkin Paper Mills, if no other option could be agreed upon within three months. Those were only some of the features outlined in the agreement, which both Charlie and Gregory signed as principals. The document was then witnessed by Michael Mullen, the general secretary of the Irish Transport and General Workers Union.

'As the Mafia say,' Charlie exclaimed on shaking hands with Gregory following the signing, 'it is a pleasure to do business with you.'

Had Charlie held out as Seán Lemass had done in 1961, he would probably have been elected anyway, because the three Workers' party deputies voted for him. In all likelihood he did not need Gregory's vote.

Following his elections as Taoiseach, Charlie went back to Burke with his offer of the European commissionership. Burke agreed to take the appointment, but then backed off when a storm erupted within Fine Gael, only to change his mind again and accept the position. As a result he resigned from the Dáil, leaving a vacancy in the Dublin West constituency, where he had won the seat by a narrow margin over Charlie's wife's sister-in-law, Eileen Lemass.

The *Irish Times* and *Irish Press* praised Burke's appointment to the EEC, but *The Cork Examiner*, which generally adopted a rather bland, non-partisan editorial policy, came out with a blistering condemnation of Charlie's assertion that the appointment was made purely in the national interest. 'The Taoiseach must be entirely contemptuous of the intelligence of the Irish people to insult them with this sort of hypocrisy,' the editorial contended.

The subsequent by-election was held at the height of the Falkland's

War* during which the Fianna Fáil leader was accused of 'playing the green card for all that it is worth'. But Fine Gael retained the seat. Suddenly what had been called 'one of the most extraordinary political strokes' of Charlie's career turned sour; he had given a 'plum job' to someone outside his party and received nothing in return.

* *Falkland islands are also known as the Malvinas*

Charlie's relations with Margaret Thatcher were already strained as a result of events following the Dublin Castle Summit of December 1980, coupled with what the British believed were Charlie's efforts to exploit the partition issue in order to paper over his serious economic difficulties at home.

The Haughey government, on the other hand, was annoyed at the extortionist tactics being employed by the British in vetoing new farm prices within the EEC in order to get Britain's budgetary contribution lowered. Things were further complicated as relations reached a new low during the international crisis over Argentina's invasion of the Falkland Islands.

When the invasion began on 2 April 1982, most Irish people did not even know where the islands were. Britain had seized them from Argentina in 1833 but now the overwhelming majority of inhabitants wished to remain British, so Britain protested against the seizure to the Security Council of the United Nations (UN), which passed Resolution 502 calling for an immediate Argentinean withdrawal.

Ireland was a member of the security council at the time, and the Irish representative voted for the resolution, but the Dublin government only reluctantly supported a British request for an EEC embargo on trade with Argentina. Charlie was personally 'very cool' towards the proposed sanctions, but eventually went along with the other EEC countries in unanimously implementing an embargo.

Irish trade with Argentina was comparatively small anyway. In fact, the total value in 1981 amounted to little over IR£15 million. While the trade balance was in Ireland's favour, the Irish Meat Marketing Board predicted the embargo would be even more in the country's favour, because Irish beef would be able to replace imports from Argentina on the British market.

For almost three weeks there was little hint of any real dissatisfaction with the position taken by the Dublin government until Síle de Valera issued a statement to the press on 22 April criticising the handling of the crisis on the grounds that it eroded the country's supposed traditional policy of neutrality. She had lost her seat in the Dáil so her intervention was not all that significant, but Charlie had to take notice a couple of days later when Neil Blaney spoke out.

'We should support Argentina,' Blaney declared, 'for both political and economic reasons – politically because of the continued British occupation of the six counties of Northern Ireland, and economically because Argentina is one of the few countries with which we have a credit trade balance.'

As Blaney was one of the independent deputies on whose support the government was dependent, there were grounds for believing that his remarks prompted Charlie to reverse his policy on the Falkland's dispute, but this was probably an over-simplification. For one thing, the Taoiseach had already got some room for manoeuvre with the resignation of Dick Burke to take up his appointment to the European commission. As a result the government needed one less vote to maintain its majority support until the by-election.

Charlie's policy change probably had more to do with his own philosophy. After all he had been reluctant to implement sanctions against Argentina in the first place.

He had reversed his policy following the sinking of the Argentinean battleship, *General Belgrano*, which went down with the loss of several hundred lives. This marked the real beginning of the Falkland's war.

The Irish government announced it would be calling on the UN security council to bring about an immediate end to hostilities and would also be seeking the withdrawal of the EEC's economic sanctions against Argentina on the grounds that those were 'no longer appropriate'.

'We were never very enthusiastic about the imposition of sanctions,' Charlie told a press conference on 6 May, 'but the argument was persuasive that they could be instrumental in applying pressure to achieve the implementation of Resolution 502 and so lead to a diplomatic solution.' He was ready to accept sanctions supporting the UN resolution, but added 'sanctions complementing military action are not acceptable to a neutral country'.

The Irish announcement was bitterly resented by the British, who saw Charlie's attitude as a blatant attempt to undermine their support within the security council and EEC. 'It appeared that he was going out of his way to make Britain's position difficult,' said Jim Prior, the secretary for Northern Ireland.

The stand on the EEC sanctions was largely symbolic, seeing that most of the Irish imports from Argentina were trans-shipped through Britain, so the decision was unlikely to have any practical effect on trade. It was the Irish moves in the security council that provoked the wrath of the British, because no reference was made to implementing Resolution 502. If the Irish proposal were accepted, Argentinean forces would be able to remain on the Falkland Islands, pending a diplomatic settlement. Argentina would therefore undoubtedly enjoy an advantage as a result of her invasion, which was a blatant violation of her obligations under the UN charter.

Charlie made no apologies for his government's behaviour. As an elected member of the security council, Ireland had a particular responsibility to do what the country could to secure a peaceful settlement. 'It would be easier to stay quiet and do nothing but that would be an abnegation of responsibility in this appalling situation,' he contended. 'Undoubtedly, when there is an emotional situation over the Falklands in Britain and elsewhere there will be misunderstanding. What we must do is keep our heads, act responsibly, act as a peace-loving nation.'

The Taoiseach deplored the escalation of the war in the South Atlantic. 'Inbuilt into any war is escalation of this sort,' he said. 'We went along with sanctions when they were in support of diplomatic political pressure. Once it became clear that they could be seen to support military activity, we had as a neutral state, no alternative but to withdraw from the sanctions position and hope that our stand will be understood by the British government.'

What was not generally known at the time was that the British had sunk the *General Belgrano* even though it was well outside the exclusion zone proclaimed by Britain and had been moving further away for some hours. The sinking was apparently a deliberate attempt to provoke the actual war.

While the Irish media was generally supportive of the Dublin government's stance, it did report some strong criticism from abroad. The British prime minister was reported to be furious with Charlie. 'If he was to turn up tomorrow with a silver coffee pot,' one British government source said, 'she'd likely crown him with it.'

Gerry Fitt was even more forthright in his condemnation of the Dublin government. 'The bellicose and belligerent statements emanating from the extremely anti-British government are not representative of the Irish people,' he said. British forces were already gaining the upperhand in the Falklands, with the result that the Irish cease fire request at the security council was regarded as most unhelpful by the British. 'It is not seen as humanitarian,' Fitt continued, 'but as an attempt to help the Argentineans and stop the British now they are on the islands. Ireland is not seen as neutral but as having come down in favour of the Argentineans.'

In the midst of the chauvinistic fervour that swept Britain there was a considerable wave of anti-Irish sentiment and some virulent anti-Irish propaganda. 'It is tempting to yearn for a return of the Vikings to plunder Ireland's coastal area and rape her nuns so that we, too, can have an opportunity to declare high-minded neutrality and demand a diplomatic solution,' Auberon Waugh wrote in the *Sunday Telegraph*.

The Argentinean regime, which was a military dictatorship that seized power from a democratically elected government in the mid 1970s, had been particularly tyrannical and had shown scant regard for human rights, with the result that it had little international support. Charlie was was accused of 'playing the green card for all that it is worth' in an attempt to win the Dublin West by-election to fill the seat vacated by Burke.

If this was his aim, then he must have been sorely disappointed because the Fine Gael candidate won with a couple of thousand votes to spare.

'Strokes and deals have surely had their day,' Vincent Jennings, the editor of the *Sunday Press* declared. His signed editorial, coming in a newspaper that had traditionally been seen as a Fianna Fáil organ, was almost like *Osservatore Romano* criticising the pope. The editorial may well have provided the impetus for George Colley to make a particularly forceful denunciation of what he described as 'a new style of politics and politicians' the following weekend. 'The idea seems to be spreading that in politics success is all important no matter how achieved, that any deal or "stroke" or promise is justified if it results in the achievement or the retention of power,' he contended. 'This is, of course, not so, and I think it is time the whole idea was challenged.' His outburst was reminiscent of his remarks about 'low standards in high places' a decade and a half earlier, and just as he did on that occasion he rather disingenuously denied that he was referring to Charlie.

'I am not as naive to think that there have not always been people in politics who have believed that any price is worth paying to stay in office or to get into office,' Colley explained. 'The big difference now is that while these people always existed in politics and always will, in the last three years there has been a tendency for this to be accepted at the top in politics rather than just among certain individuals who were not at the top.' By referring to the last three years and specifically mentioning Burke's appointment, it was obvious that Colley was indeed referring to Charlie, notwithstanding his own disingenuous denial.

In June 1982 Charlie was faced with another and much more crucial by-election following the death of Fianna Fáil's John Callanan. In the run up to the summer recess the government had survived only on the vote of the speaker of the Dáil on several occasions. Consequently victory in the Galway East by-election was now crucial to his survival.

Fine Gael pulled out all the stops. On 22 June the former Minister for Justice, Jim Mitchell, caused a sensation by disclosing that telephones which Charlie had installed in his own office shortly after his election as Taoiseach in December 1979 were capable of listening-in undetected on all telephones in Leinster House and the adjoining Government Buildings. The implication of his charge was that Haughey's previous government had tapped the telephones of all members of the government, the Dáil, the Senate and their aides.

Within a week of becoming Taoiseach, Charlie had requested that the Private Automatic Branch Exchange system, which he had used as Minister for Health and Social Welfare, be installed in his new office. This contained a telephone console with a loudspeaker and an executive over-ride button that could be used by a secretary to listen in to a call or by the minister to issue instructions to a secretary over the telephone without terminating a call. While the over-ride was being used there was supposed to be a bleep on the line every six seconds, but the consoles installed in Charlie's office and later in other offices were programmed so that a user could listen into a conversation undetected by using the over-ride with the console's loudspeaker. It was possible to listen undetected into any conversation on any telephone served by the Leinster House exchange by dialling the number, turning on the loudspeaker, replacing the telephone in its cradle, and then pressing the over-ride button.

The telephones had already been reprogrammed since the previous year to eliminate the extraordinary over-ride capabilities, so the media realised that Mitchell's timing was dictated by political considerations. Almost all of the national newspapers off-handedly dismissed the idea that Charlie knew about the over-ride capabilities. Even the *Irish Independent,* the one newspaper that tended to take the Fine Gael charges seriously, warned that those had 'to be kept in perspective if we are not to get bogged down in a Watergate-style scenario'. Some facetious allusions were made to the Nixon White House. When

Charlie invited the press into his office to explain the affair an extractor fan on the ceiling suddenly kicked on.

'The tape recorder is running'! a reporter exclaimed.

'No,' cried Charlie defensively, 'they are for the smell.' There were two extractor fans in white casings on the ceiling to deal with odours from the kitchen beneath. The *Irish Times* published a cartoon of Charlie showing his console with a massive tape apparatus overhead and a depiction of Nixon in the background. There was actually a comparatively similar occurrence during the presidency of Richard Nixon. He had 'hot-lines' installed in the offices of state governors so they could contact the White House directly in an emergency. One governor had his 'hot line' checked to find that it remained live to the White House even when the telephone was in its cradle. As a result the 'hot-line' amounted to an electronic bug capable of over-hearing all conversations in the governor's office. When the telephones of other governors were checked some thirty were found to have the same 'fault', which was attributed to the telephone company.

Although Geraldine Kennedy stopped short of accusing Charlie of wittingly having the over-ride installed with its extraordinary capabilities, she nevertheless wrote that a majority of Dáil deputies thought he 'would, at least, be capable of such an act'.

Charlie dismissed the idea as 'absolutely ludicrous' and preposterous. 'I never asked for an over-ride facility and I didn't even know the facility was there,' he explained.

'I handed over those telephone consoles to the incoming Taoiseach, Dr FitzGerald, and I think that speaks for itself,' Charlie contended. In other words, if there had been anything sinister, he would not have been so foolish as to leave the evidence behind him.

Fine Gael was not really in a strong position to exploit Charlie's expressed ignorance about the capabilities of the over-ride button, because two consoles – ordered while Fianna Fáil were still in power – were actually installed with FitzGerald's approval after he took over as Taoiseach in July 1981. Like Charlie, the Fine Gael leader stated he was totally unaware of the significance of the equipment at the time. No one thought for a moment that FitzGerald might not be telling the truth, but some media people seemed to question Charlie's statement.

When the Minister for Justice, Seán Doherty, left the country on holidays in August 1982, Charlie took over his portfolio temporarily and soon found himself in the midst of one of the most bizarre scandals in the country's history.

A man being sought by the gardaí in connection with two recent murders was arrested in the apartment of the attorney-general, Patrick Connolly. The man, Malcolm MacArthur, had been staying with the attorney-general for the past nine days during which he travelled in Connolly's state car and accompanied the attorney-general to a hurling match at which he was actually introduced to the garda commissioner, Patrick McLoughlin. At one point he even asked the commissioner about the investigation of 'that dreadful' murder that he had committed himself. It was like the script of some far-fetched murder movie.

The garda press office and government information service initially refused to confirm that MacArthur had been arrested in the attorney-general's apartment. As a result the press only reported that the arrest had taken place in the complex in which Connolly was living, rather than in his actual apartment. Nevertheless wild rumours began circulating almost immediately.

The following day the *Evening Herald* reported that MacArthur was being investigated for the murder of Charles Self, an RTÉ producer who had been bludgeoned to death earlier in the year. That murder had received extensive publicity over the months because of protests of police harassment from the gay community. It was widely believed that Self, who had been active in gay circles had been killed by another homosexual.

Having made a statement to the police, Connolly left the country on a pre-arranged holiday. Charlie did telephone him in London and suggested that it might be best if he returned, but the attorney-general decided to go on to New York. The full story had not broken yet, and they were both obviously hoping it could be contained until the trial, at any rate.

Rumours were fuelled when the *Sunday Tribune* broke the news that MacArthur had actually been arrested in Connolly's apartment. This gave rise to inevitable speculation about a possible homosexual relationship between Connolly and MacArthur. Suddenly Dublin was awash with 'an endless stream of rumours, innuendoes, and lurid tales,' according to a report in *The Guardian*.

The media had to be very careful, of course, about reporting such rumours because of the libel laws, but an official denial could easily have been used as the basis for a story about the rumours. In fact, there was no homosexual connection between Connolly and MacArthur; the rumours were without foundation. MacArthur was not involved in the murder of Self, and Connolly was not a homosexual, but one can easily imagine the public reaction to a headline such as 'Government Spokesman Denies the Attorney-General is Queer'.

'We were dealing with a situation where an innocent man was being made the victim of some scurrilous rumours, and we felt any denials should come from him,' Frank Ryan, the deputy director of the Government Information Service, explained. 'We knew that any denials from us would be taken as giving greater weight to the rumours.'

But this did not excuse the evasiveness about MacArthur's arrest in Connolly's apartment. 'Surely,' the *Irish Times* declared, 'nearly two days did not lapse before the Taoiseach or some other cabinet member woke up to the fact that rumour thrives when news concerning prominent people can be construed by the public as seeming to be played down.'

Charlie came in for intense criticism as a result of some ham-fisted efforts by the authorities to conceal MacArthur's connection with the attorney-general. He excused his own initial dithering on the grounds that the whole affair was grotesque, unbelievable, bizarre and unprecedented. Those words prompted Cruise O'Brien to coin the acronym GUBU.

Charlie requested the attorney-general to return home from New York and accepted his resignation upon his return. Connolly issued a statement explaining that he had been a longtime friend of MacArthur's girlfriend and had invited him to stay in his apartment during a visit to Dublin without any idea that MacArthur was wanted for questioning in connection with any crime. There was little else he could say as the case was *sub judice*. The media spotlight was then turned on Charlie himself. He gave a press conference at which he had to face some particularly thorny questions. He was under intense pressure and the strain showed as he slipped up when he was asked why nobody had complimented the gardaí on their handling of the investigation.

It was known that the police had set up a surveillance outside

Connolly's apartment some days before the arrest. They might therefore have saved the attorney-general and the government considerable embarrassment if they had arrested MacArthur outside the apartment. Thus, asking why nobody had complimented the police was really a loaded question.

'It was a very good piece of police work', Charlie replied, praising the gardaí for their painstaking efforts in 'putting the whole thing together and eventually finding the right man'.

By alluding to MacArthur as the 'right man', the Taoiseach was clearly prejudging his guilt, but the remark was unintentional. Faced with television lights, cameras and the army of reporters, he did not appreciate the implications of what he had said until told afterwards by an aide. Reporters were then asked to withhold the remark as it had been inadvertent.

Some segments of the British media – relishing in the Taoiseach's embarrassment following what was seen as his unhelpful attitude during the Falkland's war – seemed to take a keen delight in highlighting the gaffe. Irish reporters had to be more circumspect, however, because of the *sub judice* situation. They could not report what Charlie had said, but the fact that the Taoiseach had made a prejudicial comment was highlighted. The *Sunday Tribune* described the remark as 'a gaffe for which the greenest junior reporter would be sacked out of hand'.

This was unfair on a couple of counts. First of all it made the unspecified comment seem much worse. And secondly, it should be noted that reporters have a chance of reading over their stories to correct them, while the politician answering questions at a press conference has no such opportunity. In delicate circumstances politicians usually confine themselves to written statements. On this occasion the Taoiseach facilitated the journalists by answering their questions personally, and he could feel understandably aggrieved at the way in which his gaffe was highlighted.

Much of the whole affair could be put down to bad luck in Charlie's case. There was no question of any misconduct by the attorney-general. He was 'entirely innocent', Garret FitzGerald later wrote in his memoirs, yet Connolly and the Taoiseach found themselves in the eye of an unprecedented political storm.

'If Charlie had ducks, they'd drown on him,' John Healy concluded in his *Irish Times* column.

On Friday, 1 October 1982, Charlie McCreevy dropped a political bombshell by placing a motion of no confidence in Charlie's leadership on the agenda of the Fianna Fáil parliamentary party meeting the following Wednesday. Having tried to dismiss the previous challenge to his leadership in February by pretending the whole thing had been dreamed up by the media, Haughey met the challenge head on this time.

Interviewed on RTÉ's *This Week* programme on Sunday afternoon, he indicated he was going to demand a roll call vote on the issue so the dissidents could be identified, as the party was fed up with 'the small section of deputies' continually sniping at him.

'The Fianna Fáil organisation wants to get back to a situation where we have the strength that derives from discipline,' Haughey said, 'and I will ensure that discipline will be enforced.' He added he was going to begin by insisting that all members of his government should pledge their loyalty to him as the elected leader of Fianna Fáil. 'I will insist,' he declared, 'that the cabinet stand four square behind me with no shilly-shallying.' He had no doubt he would be victorious. 'I am,' he said, 'absolutely confident of the outcome. As Seán MacEntee said: "Go dance on somebody else's grave".'

There was a certain amount of manoeuvring by both sides prior to the parliamentary party meeting. The Taoiseach secured the support of the party's national executive, while Colley announced that O'Malley and O'Donoghue would be resigning from the cabinet rather than support Haughey. The two men then waited until the morning of the meeting to submit their letters of resignation, thereby ensuring the dissidents received positive publicity right up to the start of the meeting.

From early on it was clear that there would be a vital test of strength between the two sides on whether the vote should be taken openly or in secret. Rule 83 of the Fianna Fáil *Coru* (constitution) specifically stated that 'every ballot throughout the organisation should be held by secret ballot', but the dissident position was really not all that strong, because the parliamentary party was traditionally free to make its own decisions without outside dictation from the party itself. Moreover in the aftermath of the arms crisis Jack Lynch had demanded and secured an open vote of confidence. Now some of his supporters were demanding his successor should agree to a secret vote, and they were being undermined by the precedent they had set themselves.

The parliamentary party meeting began at 11 am on 6 October with 80 of the 81 Fianna Fáil TDs present, as well as 27 Senators, and 5 members of the European parliament. Though the atmosphere was tense, the proceedings were conducted in an orderly manner.

It was decided to discuss McCreevy's motion and the method of voting simultaneously. McCreevy explained he was objecting to Haughey's leadership because there had been a lowering of political standards, mishandling of the economy, as well as the party's failure to secure a majority in two successive general elections. People wanted to be governed not bought, he said, emphasising it was time 'to get decency back into the party'.

Haughey was obviously nervous when he spoke. He paused frequently to choose the right words, or to rummage through notes. He defended himself and his government on the grounds that they had been facing unprecedented difficulties in the deepest recession since the 1930s. Having worked hard to prepare a new plan to tackle the economic situation, he said they should be given a chance to let it work. Under the circumstances he felt the motion was not only divisive but also badly timed.

This time the dissidents were determined that there would be no repetition of the debacle surrounding the abortive challenge in February. They had arranged for people to speak in favour of the motion in order to prevent a precipitate collapse of their challenge as had happened earlier. Thus the meeting dragged on throughout the day and into the night, with adjournments for lunch and tea.

Some senior deputies like Pádraig Faulkner and Michael O'Kennedy called for a secret ballot, but the dissidents had again overestimated their support for this crucial test of strength. On a role call vote, only 27 favoured a secret ballot on the actual motion with 53 preferring an open vote. The subsequent vote on the McCreevy motion was then defeated by 58 votes to 22.

Haughey had won and some of his supporters were anything but magnanimous in victory. 'These people have been flushed out now, once, finally and for all,' was how one supporter put it. 'The situation after tonight is that they had better be ready to kiss Haughey's ass or get out of the party.'

The mood was so ugly that gardaí tried to persuade McCreevy to leave Leinster House by a side entrance, but he refused. As he emerged by the front door, surrounded by six gardaí, he was met by a jeering group of Haughey supporters, many of whom had been drinking throughout the day as they waited for the outcome of the meeting.

When Jim Gibbons left the building shortly afterwards, he was not only jeered loudly but also jostled about by the unruly crowd. It was one of the ugliest scenes witnessed in Irish politics for many years. One of the hecklers tried to attack him and actually landed a glancing blow. These incidents, which were captured on television, were probably more damaging to the government than anything that happened during the day.

The next IMS poll, published on 23 October 1982, showed Haughey's popularity slumping even further, and his party dropped to its lowest rating since the poll began in 1974. Only 23% of those sampled were satisfied with the way the government was running the country, and his personal popularity dropped to 32%.

As it was his government was already in trouble as a result of the death on 18 October of Bill Loughnane, and the hospitalisation next day of Jim Gibbons, following a heart attack. Without their votes the government was in deep trouble.

The publication of Fianna Fáil's new economic programme, *The Way Forward*, virtually killed any chance of survival. Tony Gregory and the three Workers' party's deputies joined with the opposition to bring down the government.

Fianna Fáil was out of office barely a week when the public received the first indication of the coming political storm. Peter Murtagh, the security correspondent of the *Irish Times,* reported that the telephones of Bruce Arnold and Geraldine Kennedy had been tapped 'officially' with the full knowledge and approval of the last Minister for Justice, Seán Doherty.

Charlie promptly denied any involvement. 'I wouldn't countenance such action,' he declared on RTÉ next day. He called for a judicial inquiry to investigate the matter fully. 'The capacity to listen in to phone conversations is one which must be kept under the very closest, rigid scrutiny,' he said.

Back in 1964 he had assured the Dáil that there were safeguards to ensure that telephone-tapping could not be abused for political purposes. The request for a tap had to come from the garda commissioner or a deputy commissioner, who had to be satisfied that the person to be tapped was involved with a subversive organisation or engaged in organised criminal activities. Moreover, an officer of the Justice Department had then to advise the minister on the application.

'The Minister for Justice cannot initiate the procedure,' Charlie assured the Dáil as Minister for Justice himself. 'He can act only when a written request comes to him from a responsible authority and when he is satisfied and when his Departmental advisers are satisfied that the information concerned can be obtained in no other way.' It would therefore be necessary to have 'the connivance of a whole group of people,' he contended, 'before there could be the slightest possible abuse of power.'

'I don't think any politician himself should ever initiate because that would be an abuse,' Charlie explained eighteen years later when he was asked in an RTÉ interview on 19 December 1982 about the reported taps on the telephones of Bruce Arnold and Geraldine Kennedy. 'There's a very limited number of reasons which justify the issue of warrants and it's to combat crime or subversion,' he explained. 'Now I don't think either of the two journalists whose names have been mentioned would come within that category.'

Over nine years later Seán Doherty complained that Charlie made this statement before he had a chance to comment himself. Charlie had been aware of the tappings, according to Doherty, who decided not to contradict him at the time. 'I felt pressured to support Mr Haughey's stated position,' Doherty explained in a sensational announcement on the evening of 21 January 1992. 'Not only did I take the blame,' he continued, 'but when Mr Haughey claimed not to have been aware of the tapping while it was in progress, I did not correct this claim, and indeed supported it.'

Although Charlie expressed concern about the allegations in the RTÉ interview of 19 December 1982, he took his time in questioning Seán Doherty about them. It was not until two days later that he even broached him on the subject. Then, assured by Doherty that there was nothing to worry about, he did not bother to pursue the matter further.

As Minister for Justice, Doherty had asked deputy commissioner Joe Ainsworth of the garda síochána to have a tap placed on Arnold's telephone. Commissioner Patrick McLoughlin duly authorised this request on Ainsworth's recommendation.

When the Justice Department official, who was charged with vetting the application, asked for the reason for the tap, Ainsworth explained that Arnold was 'anti-national in outlook' and 'might be obtaining information from sources of a similar disposition'. There was no question of Arnold being involved with criminal or paramilitary organisations, so the official recommended against the tap, but Doherty signed the necessary warrant anyway. In the following weeks the tap produced nothing of value, so it was discontinued in the immediate aftermath of the over-ride controversy.

By then Geraldine Kennedy had replaced Arnold as the greatest thorn in the side of the Taoiseach. She had the confidence of someone privy to what was happening within the cabinet. On 11 July 1982, for instance, she quoted some cabinet exchanges and disclosed that the government had decided to reverse its economic policies and adopt an approach of fiscal rectitude. In another article she disclosed that Charlie had been having some secret talks in an effort to come to a political arrangement with the Labour party, but any hope of this was killed when she broke the news of the discussions.

Charlie complained to Hugh McLoughlin, the publisher of the *Sunday Tribune*, about Kennedy's articles. McLoughlin in turn told Conor Brady, the newspaper's editor, to keep a tighter control of Kennedy and to go easy on Charlie. He explained that the Taoiseach was 'desperately worried about the Kennedy woman' and wondered who in Fianna Fáil was talking to her. A few days later Doherty asked for and then formally authorised a tap on Kennedy's telephone for reasons of 'national security'.

Charlie said afterwards that he knew nothing about the tap. In fact, even the garda commissioner who formally requested it was not aware that it applied to Geraldine Kennedy's telephone, because it was actually in the name of a previous tenant of the apartment in which she was living.

Among her calls intercepted was a conversation in which she forewarned Peter Prendergast, the general secretary of Fine Gael, of the McCreevy motion. Seán Doherty was so interested in this intercept that he requested a transcript on the eve of the parliamentary party meeting at which McCreevy's motion was considered.

Immediately after this meeting there was a curious incident when the Taoiseach's son, Ciarán, walked up to Geraldine Kennedy. 'I want to tell you one thing,' young Haughey said. 'You'll be hearing from us.'

She asked if this was a threat.

'You can take it as such,' he replied.

She thought at the time he must have been annoyed at some remarks she had made on television the previous night. Of course, she never suspected there was a tap on her telephone.

The political storm surrounding this tap did not break until 20 January 1983 when Michael Noonan, the new Minister for Justice, confirmed that the telephones of Arnold and Kennedy had indeed been tapped and that the procedures outlined by various Ministers for Justice had not been followed in either case. He also disclosed that Ray MacSharry had borrowed sophisticated garda equipment and had secretly recorded a conversation he had with Martin O'Donoghue on 21 October 1982.

Charlie initially accepted responsibility for what had happened but at the same time he tried to distance himself from the abuses. 'Any head of government must take responsibility for anything that happens during his administration,' he said. 'But I want to make it crystal clear that the government as such and I, as Taoiseach, knew absolutely nothing about any activities of this sort and would not countenance any such abuse.' He was particularly dismissive of the suggestion that the taps were connected with his own leadership problems within Fianna Fáil.

'I wouldn't need any such secret information from any such sources,' he said. 'I know as a politician and leader of the party exactly what is going on in the party and who was saying what. The idea of resorting to telephone-tapping or any other devices to get that sort of information is ludicrous.'

But, if it was ludicrous, why had he been so interested in learning Geraldine Kennedy's sources only days before the tap was placed on her telephone? In a front page article in the *Sunday Press*, where she had taken over as political correspondent following the collapse of the *Sunday Tribune*, she disclosed that Haughey had asked her publisher about her sources back in July. This story, which raised some serious questions, hurt Charlie politically.

Within Fianna Fáil he appointed a four man committee to investigate the whole affair. It was headed by Jim Tunney, the new chairman of the parliamentary party. From the very outset Tunney was sceptical that Charlie might have been responsible for any misconduct. 'All the evidence shows that Mr Haughey knew absolutely nothing about it,' he declared on the day the committee was set up.

When the parliamentary party next met, Charlie was clearly on the defensive. Although he had already publicly stated there was no justification for the taps, he now sought to justify Doherty's actions on the grounds that 'national security' had been endangered by 'cabinet leaks'.

'What leaks?' Pearse Wyse asked.

'The Fianna Fáil farm plan had appeared for instance in the *Farmer's Journal,*' Charlie replied to a chorus of incredulous laughter.

'Isn't it strange then that you would tap the telephones of journalists working in the *Tribune* and the *Independent?*' rejoined Wyse.

This use of the 'national security' cloak was the exact same one used by Richard Nixon to defend the misdeeds of his people during the Watergate scandal in the United States almost a decade earlier. And this latest Irish scandal was rapidly beginning to look like a repetition of Watergate.

'The parallels to the Nixon White House are uncomfortably close and to the point,' thundered Vincent Jennings in a signed editorial in the *Sunday Press*. 'Wall-to-wall distrust and paranoia; anyone who disagrees with the leadership is an enemy, or worse – anti-national. Get them, the expletive deleted.' There were a number of distinct parallels, but there was also an enormous difference. Watergate had been the subject of a thorough, exhaustive investigation in which congressional leaders were careful to avoid any taint of engaging in a political vendetta. The Democratic leadership went to great pains to ensure their Republican counterparts were satisfied the investigation was being conducted in an impartial manner. In the end Nixon was brought down, not because of any involvement in the initial crimes, but because he impeded the investigation by engaging in a cover up.

There was, however, only a superficial investigation into the so-called Liffeygate scandal. Some of the things which had happened while Charlie was Taoiseach could well have been more serious than anything involved in Watergate.

Was it just a coincidence that Charlie was asking questions about Geraldine Kennedy's sources just before Doherty asked for the tap to be placed on her telephone? Was there any justification for basing the request for the tap on grounds of national security? Why did Doherty ask for copies of the transcripts of the tap intercepts on the eve of the crucial parliamentary party meeting in October? Did he show this material to anyone? Why did Ciarán Haughey single out Geraldine Kennedy after that meeting? Did he know the dissidents had taken her into their confidence? If so, how did he know?

Such questions had enormous potential ramifications. The answers might possibly have cleared the people involved of all suspicion of any wrong doing.

After all Doherty contended there was a sinister plot to bribe politicians. 'We had information,' he later stated, 'that large sums of money were on offer to sway politicians, that a foreign intelligence service was operating in the country and that information from within the cabinet was being made available in an unauthorised manner.

'That was the security background to the 1982 situation,' he explained. In the aftermath of the Falkland's war, it was not beyond the bounds of possibility that Britain's MI 6 would pay a few hundred thousand pounds to oust Charlie, especially in the light of efforts already made by that organisation to oust its own Prime Minister, Harold Wilson in the 1970s.

'I myself was offered £50,000 in cash to help oust C. J. Haughey as Taoiseach,' Doherty continued. Even people within Fianna Fáil – who were quite critical of Doherty and convinced that he was the victim of his own over-active imagination – accepted that he genuinely believed there was a sinister plot against the government.

If, for argument sake, one were to accept that foreign money was being used as he suggested, it would throw a new light on events. The matter should therefore have been investigated. Charlie called for a judicial inquiry, which was certainly justified by all the unanswered questions.

In Irish society people are supposed to be presumed innocent until proven guilty, but in Charlie's case his opponents automatically assumed he was guilty. The coalition government was so intent on securing his removal that it decided against holding a judicial inquiry for fear that the delay involved in setting up the tribunal might afford him an opportunity of regrouping his forces and holding on to the leadership of Fianna Fáil. In short, he might survive in spite of the guilt they so readily assumed. Consequently the government left further investigation of the whole affair to the media, which was not equipped for the task. The issues involved were much too serious to leave any room for suspicion that they were being used to score political points in order to skewer a few politicians and roast them on a spit over inflamed public opinion. In comparison with the Watergate investigation, Charlie was being railroaded.

He was indeed responsible for appointing Doherty, who left himself wide open to the charge of having abused his official powers on a whole series of matters, but it should be emphasised that he broke no law by initially suggesting a tap be placed on a telephone. He merely ignored guidelines set by his predecessors. If they had the power to set such guidelines, then he had the power to change them.

If Michael Noonan and the members of Garret FitzGerald's government really believed his actions were so terrible in this matter, why was no serious attempt made to change the law?

Doherty's contention that his actions were justified left the two journalists in an invidious position. He should have had to substantiate his charge, but he could not be expected to do so without a judicial inquiry because the matter was covered by the Official Secrets Act.

The media allowed itself to be stampeded by the coalition government after Noonan highlighted the whole affair by forcing the early retirement of the two senior gardaí. The only public accusation levelled against Commissioner Patrick McLoughlin or Deputy Commissioner Joe Ainsworth was of having carried out the instructions of the Minister for Justice. It could hardly have been in the public interest that servants of the state should appear to be so unfairly treated. The media were stampeded by the suggestion that Haughey's government had done the unthinkable in tapping journalists, which was depicted as totally unacceptable in a democracy. Charlie's call for a judicial inquiry into the whole affair was ignored. Michael Noonan later explained to John Bruton that this was because it would have come out that a previous Fine Gael-Labour coalition had tapped Tim Pat Coogan of the *Irish Press* and Vincent Browne of *Magill* Magazine. When Browne later asked Garret FitzGerald why he was tapped, Garret explained that it was because he had been in touch with a certain Republican, but Browne noted that he had broken off contact at that stage. 'Yes,' Garret said, 'but we thought you might get back in touch with him.'

If the coalition thought it was justifiable to tap Browne on the off chance that an individual might call him, would the tapping of journalists who were privy to cabinet leaks not be even more justifiable? Against that backdrop it was easy to understand why the coalition was so reluctant to hold a judicial inquiry. Of course, transcripts of telephone conversations were printed up that had no relevance to cabinet leaks and the high court later concluded that the tapping of the journalists was wrong. It was noteworthy that Browne was awarded almost twice as much money as either Geraldine Kennedy or Bruce Arnold. In allowing itself to be manipulated the media missed the broader issues and became pre-occupied instead with Charlie's political fate.

He certainly seemed to be in a precarious position with his party dispirited and leaking like a sieve. Within a week Michael O'Kennedy had already begun canvassing openly for the party leadership, and he was quickly followed by O'Malley. There were rumours that Charlie had written a letter of resignation and would formally announce his decision at a meeting of the parliamentary party on Thursday, 27 January, by which time all four national daily newspapers had carried editorials depicting his position as party leader as untenable.

There was general agreement in the media that Charlie was all but finished politically that morning as the parliamentary party gathered for its weekly meeting. This was reflected both in the editorials and opinion columns as well as in news reports predicting his demise. But those predictions were made on the basis of incomplete calculations.

Each of the newspapers published lists of deputies who were supposed to be opposed to Charlie, but when the names in all of those lists were compiled in one master list, they still did not add up to a majority of Fianna Fáil deputies. Most deputies were apparently keeping their views to themselves. The reporters simply jumped to the wrong conclusion. And the *Irish Press* took the extraordinary step of publishing what amounted to Charlie's political obituary reviewing his whole career.

The media had written him off again, but he refused to be stampeded. When Ben Briscoe proposed the standing orders of the parliamentary party meeting be suspended so the leadership issue could be discussed, Charlie objected but was not able to prevent a debate. He was adamant, however, that he was not going to be driven out of office by a 'vindictive press'.

'I will take my own decision in my own time,' he declared.

This was generally understood by those present to mean he intended to step down within a few days. Even Mark Killilea, one of the original 'gang of five' who had spearheaded Charlie's drive for the leadership, admitted to the press that he believed the leader was indicating his intentions of resigning. Eileen Lemass was actually reported as saying Charlie was finished and should recognise it.

Some people believed he would have been forced out at this meeting if the issue had been put to a vote, but there was widespread agreement within the party that the press had been unfair to him; so there was no desire to force the issue when he seemed prepared to step down. A number of deputies at the meeting were close to tears.

'I love you, Charlie Haughey,' Briscoe blurted out at one point.

'I love you, too, Ben,' Charlie replied.

'I hope the papers don't hear about this,' David Andrews was heard to groan at the back of the room.

Of course they did within minutes. The confidentiality of the meeting was a shambles as reporters were given *verbatim* details of what had been said, including Charlie's charge that the media were conducting a campaign of vilification against him.

It all seemed reminiscent of Nixon's final hours in the White House. One enterprising *Irish Times* columnist actually contacted Carl Bernstein, the famous Watergate reporter, for his views on the Irish situation.

It is doubtful that Charlie had any intention of resigning, but he did encourage Brian Lenihan and Gerard Collins to sound out their prospects for the leadership. He was apparently encouraging people to run in order to confuse the contest before he began his fight back over the weekend. A massive campaign was undertaken on his behalf at grass roots level with a large demonstration by supporters outside Fianna Fáil's general headquarters in Dublin. He and his people sought middle ground support to allow him to stay on for a few weeks until the party's Ard Fheis, at which he could enlist his greatest support within the party.

Those wishing to get rid of him, however, began to react to his survival efforts on Monday, 31 January. Preparations were made to draw up a petition of deputies calling on him to stand down at the next parliamentary party meeting, which was due to be held on Wednesday, 2 February. Suddenly fate seemed to come to Charlie's rescue.

Clem Coughlan, one of the deputies who had already called publicly for his resignation, was killed in a car accident on Tuesday morning. In the circumstances it was inappropriate for the parliamentary party to discuss the leadership issue next day. In such circumstances party meetings were always adjourned as a mark of respect. But the dissidents were determined that another meeting should be called for Friday, the day after the funeral.

At the outset of the Wednesday meeting Charlie delivered a short tribute to the deceased deputy. The chairman, Jim Tunney, then spoke of the tragic death and called for a minute's silence. Immediately afterwards, as Mary Harney was on her feet calling to be recognised, Tunney announced in Irish that the meeting was adjourned until the following week. He then bolted out the door.

'Dammit!' exclaimed one disgruntled deputy. 'He just ran out of the room.'

Forty-one deputies and seven senators signed a petition calling for a parliamentary party meeting to be held on Friday, 4 February. They seemed determined that the leadership issue should be settled before the following Wednesday when the coalition government was due to bring in its first budget. This would be a golden opportunity for Fianna Fáil to score political points, especially as a harsh budget was expected.

The chance would be lost, however, if the party was still embroiled in a leadership wrangle, because this would undoubtedly divert media attention from the budget. As a compromise it was agreed to hold the meeting on Monday. This would allow the leadership issue to be resolved before the budget and also afford the Tunney committee time to complete its report.

Some of the 41 deputies who signed the petition were supporters of Charlie. They did so in order to learn what the dissidents were planning, but the media mistakenly assumed all 41 were likely to call for the leader's resignation. The press therefore concluded he would definitely be toppled as only 37 were needed for an overall majority. He seemed to increase the tension himself on Thursday afternoon when he issued a controversial statement.

'Despite everything that a largely hostile media and political opponents at home and abroad could do to damage not only me but the great party and traditions of Fianna Fáil,' he contended that a large number of members and supporters had called on him 'to stay on' as leader. Consequently, he continued, 'having calmly and objectively considered the situation in all its aspects I have decided that it is my duty in the best interest of the party to which I have devoted all my political life to stay and lead it forward out of these present difficulties. I am now, therefore, calling on all members of the party to rally behind me as their democratically elected leader and give me that total support that I need to restore unity and stability, to re-organise the party, to give it a new sense of purpose, to restate our policies, to re-establish and implement the traditional code of party discipline, and to make it clear that those who bring the party into disrepute, cause dissension or refuse to accept decisions democratically arrived at can no longer remain in the party.'

On the two previous occasions when Charlie's leadership had been challenged, his supporters contended that the dissidents did not have the right to remove him even with the support of a majority of the parliamentary party. Back in February 1982, for instance, when O'Malley was challenging for the leadership the circumstances had been somewhat different, but the argument was comparatively similar. On the eve of that parliamentary party meeting Brian Lenihan emphasised on a *Today Tonight* programme that the challenge was not for the leadership because Charlie was already the leader. The contest was only for the party's nomination for Taoiseach. Charlie would remain as party leader regardless of the outcome, because even though he had initially been elected leader by the parliamentary party, his selection had subsequently been confirmed by the party's Ard Fheis, the supreme body within the organisation. Thus, from a *de jure* standpoint he could be removed only by an Ard Fheis, or by his own resignation.

In October after McCreevy introduced his motion of no confidence, it was said that Charlie would remain on as Taoiseach regardless of the outcome of the vote. He had been elected to the office by the Dáil so by law – irrespective of whether he had the majority support of his own party – he would remained as Taoiseach until replaced by the Dáil. In view of the earlier arguments, many people believed that Charlie was implying in his latest statement that the parliamentary party did not have the authority to remove him, though he did not specifically put forward this argument.

'It was a most dreadful statement from a party leader,' Briscoe declared in a RTÉ interview. 'If you examine it line by line you could only come to the conclusion that Mr Haughey no longer recognises the right of the parliamentary party which elected him to remove him from office.'

Briscoe therefore decided to force the issue by formally proposing a motion for Monday's meeting calling for 'the resignation of Mr Charles J. Haughey as party leader now'.

Amid the furore Charlie issued a further statement on Saturday, 4 February, emphasising he would accept the decision of the party meeting. 'I want it stated publicly and clearly,' he declared, 'that any decision of the parliamentary party will be fully accepted by me'.

Interviewed on a RTÉ lunchtime news next day, he stressed that his statement on Thursday had been misinterpreted. He would, he said, 'with honour and dignity accept any decision of the parliamentary party'.

If somebody else should be elected to succeed him next day, Charlie said that person would be accepted as president of the whole Fianna Fáil organisation. 'That's the way it's been done in the past,' he added. 'That's the way it will be done in the future'.

The odds seemed very much against him. Having initially excluded the possibility of his survival the bookmakers listed him only in joint fourth place with O'Kennedy behind Collins, O'Malley and John Wilson. 'Even paying exaggerated respect to Mr Haughey's recuperative power and ability to survive,' the *Cork Examiner* declared, 'today should see the end of the Haughey era'.

The meeting, which lasted throughout the day and late into the night, began with skirmishes over whether to discuss the leadership issue first or the report of the Tunney committee set up to investigate the whole tapping controversy. O'Malley's supporters wanted to discuss the leadership, but this was beaten on a vote. All of those present, including Senators and members of the European parliament were able to vote in this contest, so the outcome was not necessarily indicative of the feelings of Dáil deputies. Still Charlie had clearly won the first round.

He got a further boost when the Tunney committee reported that there was no evidence to link him directly to the telephone-tapping. There followed a four-and-a-half hour discussion of matters relating to the Tunney report before Briscoe formally proposed his motion calling for Charlie's resignation. Briscoe had obviously done little to secure support for his motion, because he did not even have a seconder lined up. For a moment it looked as if the motion would fail for a lack of a seconder, until McCreevy filled the void. Deputies then spoke for and against the motion.

Charlie's supporters depicted their man as having been crucified by a hostile media which, they said, should not be allowed to dictate how Fianna Fáil should be run. His backers also exploited the idea that certain monied interests wanted to get rid of him. If they were allowed to have their way, this would be tantamount to admitting that Fianna Fáil was for sale.

Charlie's opponents, on the other hand, accused him of presiding over a succession of scandals which had done enormous damage to the party. He was depicted as a distinct electoral liability, and it was emphasised he had failed to secure a majority in three consecutive elections. These people and the media in general conveniently forgot that Eamon de Valera had also failed to secure such a majority in his first three general elections as party leader.

Most of those at the parliamentary party meeting on 7 February 1983 felt the media had been unfair to Charlie. His critics, both inside and outside the party, had in recent days been trying to get rid of him with almost indecent haste. They did not even want to wait for the Tunney report. All this rebounded to Charlie's advantage in securing the support of many middle-ground deputies at this critical point. People like the fighter who battles against the odds, and he seemed to be battling against enormous odds for the past several days. Even individuals who despised him were heard to express a begrudging admiration of his tenacity.

This time Charlie agreed to a secret vote. In all probability it was to his advantage, because opponents who had found their ambitions for the leadership thwarted for the present could now back him, as he was likely to be more vulnerable than a new leader. In addition, there were those who, according to one reporter, had been 'kissing Charlie on all four cheeks in October' but had recently found it necessary to express public reservations about him. Under the cloak of secrecy they were quietly able to return to his fold.

When the votes were counted Charlie survived by seven votes. He had, in fact, increased the majority by which he had first won the leadership over George Colley in the last secret vote in December 1979.

'I saw at least two of my colleagues in the media turn visibly pale, total disbelief showing on their countenances,' Raymond Smith wrote about hearing the news outside. 'We did not believe our ears'.

In late 1983 the publication of the book, *The Boss* caused a major political stir. Written by two journalists, Joe Joyce and Peter Murtagh, it was probably the most interesting and provocative book ever published on contemporary Irish politics.

Despite its subtitle, 'Charles J. Haughey in Government', the book was not so much about Charlie in government, as it was about the events which occurred while he was in power during 1982. In some cases he had no connection with the events under discussion and the authors might have taken a more dispassionate look at his actual role in the instances where he was involved.

Like so many others, the authors seemed inclined to presume Charlie's guilt, despite his right to be presumed innocent until proven guilty. Easons, one of the major book distributors in the country, refused to handle *The Boss* for fear of being sued for libel. But this did not prevent it becoming a runaway bestseller, setting unprecedented sales records in the country for a book on a political topic. In a sense it was almost like another GUBU.

While readers would undoubtedly have been familiar with much of the material in the book because of the media's extensive coverage within the past couple of years, the authors still brought out new information on virtually every facet of the story. They had the advantage of being able to provide a broader picture than the media had been able to give in the midst of the events. There was detailed coverage of the dismissed charge of double voting against Charlie's election agent, and a thorough account of events leading to the O'Malley heave, the Gregory Deal, and Burke's appointment to the European commission. There was also fresh material on the MacArthur affair, and the Dowra case in which Seán Doherty's brother-in-law had the charges against him for assault dismissed after his victim failed to turn up in court. He had been 'lifted' by the police in Northern Ireland in an obvious attempt to prevent him testifying. He later won damages against both the police who detained him and the man who assaulted him.

The Boss was particularly good on the politicisation of the police, and the wire-tapping of the journalists. It went a long way to conveying the impression of fear that permeated opposition circles in 1982, when leading politicians, like Garret FitzGerald and Dick Spring, actually suspected that their telephones were being tapped. Frequently the authors did not actually give their own conclusions, they just led the reader to a point where conclusions seemed inescapable. But when they did come to conclusions, they seemed to judge Charlie by one set of standards and his critics by a very different criterion.

Charlie was depicted in a most unfavourable light over the Gregory Deal, while FitzGerald came off lightly even though he had also tried to make a deal. Burke's appointment to the European commission was depicted as a piece of cynical opportunism, even though the reaction of Fine Gael was even more cynical, because, with the experience already gained in the past, Burke was obviously better qualified for the position when Charlie appointed him, than he had been when first appointed by the coalition government in 1976. Short term party considerations were paramount within Fine Gael, so it was unfair to depict Charlie as if he was the only one putting his own or his party's considerations first.

The authors went even further in relation to the Charlie's slip of the tongue in referring to Malcolm MacArthur as 'the right man' at the press conference following the resignation of the attorney-general. Charlie was 'clearly in contempt of court', Joyce and Murtagh wrote. 'His aides pleaded with reporters not to publish or broadcast this remark. Those working for the Irish media were unable to in any event because if they did, they would have been as guilty as Haughey.' This insinuated that Charlie's remark had been premeditated, which was grossly unfair. When MacArthur's lawyers tried to have Charlie cited for contempt of court, the judge accepted that he had made a genuine mistake. But the authors seemed to question the judge's decision.

'It did not stop some people thinking that the remark was part of a huge conspiracy to keep the case out of the courts and thus protect certain unnamed people, politicians and lawyers,' they wrote. 'Haughey, acting justice minister at the time and indeed himself a former justice minister, knew exactly what he was doing,' they claimed. Of course, some foolish people will believe anything. It was wrong, however, to give credence to such distorted views by repeating them without identifying them as nonsense.

Still, Charlie could not escape responsibility for the activities of his Minister for Justice. He had selected him. The book documented some outrageous behaviour on the part of a number of individuals, but Malcolm MacArthur was the only person convicted of wrong doing. Whose fault was that?

The various accusations certainly warranted a thorough investigation, but the authors never tried to analyse why Charlie's call for a judicial inquiry had been ignored. Was it because the other side was as guilty of some of the more colourful charges?

Charlie and members of his family came under intense public pressure following the publication of the book. His own frustration became apparent during a session of the New Ireland Forum, when he became involved in a confrontation with Dick Spring, who was infuriated by leaks to the media. Spring blamed Charlie, who replied that it was despicable to suggest that he would leak to the press. 'No one has suffered more than I have from journalists,' he emphasised. At that point, to the amazement of everyone, he burst into tears and he was led from the room sobbing. This was a human side of the political machine that Spring had never seen before.

Later that afternoon Charlie told Dick that his family had been greatly upset by *The Boss*. All their lives his children had to put up with abuse from people just because he was their father. On one occasion he recalled his daughter had to come home early from a gymkhana because she could not take any more abuse. This was understandably hard for any father to take. While Dick Spring appreciated the situation, he had little reason to feel sorry for Charlie.

Back in January 1982 when Dick was recovering from serious back injuries sustained in a car accident, Charlie had refused to allow anyone to pair with him on the forthcoming vote on the budget. As a result Dick had to make the arduous journey from his home in Tralee while in considerable pain. To make things worse, it was a wasted journey, seeing that the government was defeated on the budget anyway. Yet now, possibly for the first time, Dick had genuine sympathy for Charlie.

'Immediately after the afternoon session,' FitzGerald noted in his autobiography, 'Dick and I were discussing Haughey's breakdown together when we both suddenly realised that in response to queries from the *Sunday Tribune* about our likely Christmas reading we had each mentioned *The Boss* as a book that we would want to read during the break.' Both felt so sorry for Charlie that Garret asked Vincent Browne, the editor of the *Sunday Tribune*, to replace *The Boss* with other works in the lists supplied by Dick and himself. Browne, who actually felt that *The Boss* was unfair to Charlie in many respects, readily agreed. Having had a tap of his own telephone authorised by Fine Gael ministers in two different governments, he had more reason than most to know that many of the insinuations being made against Charlie, could just as easily have been directed against his opponents.

The nickname the 'Boss' had an historical Irish connection. William Marcy Tweed, or 'Boss Tweed' as he was called, was the son of an Irish father. He built up the infamous influence of Tammany Hall to control New York politics from 1863 to 1871, when he was brought down in the midst of an enormous scandal over the misappropriation of funds. It was estimated that he had taken at least $6m for himself. His closest henchmen were Irish-Americans Peter Sweeney and Richard B. Connolly. The so-called Tweed Ring was accused of misappropriating up to $300m. Tweed was eventually convicted in 1873 on 204 counts of fraud, forgery and embezzlement. He was sentence to twelve years in jail, where he died in 1878.

Boss Richard Croker, was born in Clonakilty, Co. Cork, but reared in New York. He was a minor functionary in the Tweed Ring. Croker rose through the Tammany machine to gain control of New York politics during the late 1880s and early 1890s, but he fled to England in 1894 when Tammany was being investigated. He returned in 1897 to regain control. The opportunities for corruption flourish until 1902 when another investigation was held. Croker again retired to England and eventually to Ireland. In his later years, he dabbled in horse-racing, and one of his horses won the Epson Derby in 1907.

Haughey was so well read that he was undoubtedly aware of the historical significance of the name, the Boss, but he obviously did not care, because because he was apparently content to be called 'the boss'.

Charlie continued to live beyond his means and quickly got back into debt, especially while he was out of power from December 1982 to February 1987. At the start of this period in opposition, he borrowed £400,000 from Guinness & Mahon, where he would have four different bank accounts, which he said that Des Traynor opened without reference to him. But he had to accept that he applied for the loan. He tried to give the impression that Traynor ran his finances essentially without consulting him, but there is ample evidence to suggest that his own involvement was much more extensive than he tried to let on.

The Guinness & Mahon loan was to be repaid by 31 January 1985, but this was extended. Even £400,000 was not enough to fund Charlie's life-style. In May of 1983, there were unexplained deposits in his account of £240,000, and he got a further £120,000 the following month when hotelier P.V. Doyle took out a loan for him that he promised to pay back. Doyle obtained another loan of £50,000 for Charlie in 1985. Haughey also received £50,000 from the billionaire Arab, Mahmud Fustok, supposedly for a horse that he had purchased. He gave the money to the independent deputy Dr John O'Connell, who paid with a cheque of his own. Nobody was able to provide any details about the mysterious horse.

By way of explanation, Charlie said that he had tried to interest Fustok in establishing some bloodstock business in Ireland. 'I feel sure that his offering to purchase the yearling from us was by way of recompense for not acceding to any request,' he explained. 'I think it may have been a sort of gesture on his part.'

In the 1985 Charlie and Traynor organised funds for Haughey's son Ciarán to establish a helicopter business in partnership with an American pilot John Barnicle, who put up just £60 each. Traynor organised things and Haughey approached people for money for Celtic Helicopters. They arranged to get money from Charlie's contacts. They included John O'Connell, the former Labour party deputy, former chairman of Bord Fáilte Joe Malone, and the beef magnate Séamus Purcell. There may have been nothing wrong with a father helping out his son, but Traynor appeared to cross the line of corporate ethics, by involving himself in the organisation of a rival firm while he was acting as a director of Aer Lingus, a semi-state body that had it own helicopter subsidiary, Irish Helicopters.

Of course, it seems ludicrous to highlight Traynor's lack of business ethics in this matter when one considers his other activities. He was already engaged in organising a massive tax evasion scheme for a number of business people and it can be demonstrated that he facilitated Charlie in diverting hundreds of thousands of pounds intended for the Fianna Fáil party.

Haughey used the party leader's fund to launder money. This was a fund initially established by Eamon de Valera's government in the 1930s to provide for a party secretariat and fund political research. From 1984 to 1992, the state contributed £1.05m to this fund, and Charlie topped it up to £1.5m with money donated to Fianna Fáil, or contributions towards a medical fund for Brian Lenihan to secure a liver transplant in the United States.

All cheques drawn on the account had to have two signatures of senior party members. The account, which was held at AIB branch in Baggot Street, was administered by Eileen Foy in Haughey's office, and she and Charlie were the only people who knew how much was in the account. The records of deposits in the account, from 1980 to 1983, were destroyed along with other bank records from the period, so what happened to the account during those years remains a mystery.

The cheques drawn on the account between 1984 and 1992 were all co-signed by Charlie and either Ray MacSharry, the party's finance spokesman, or by Bertie Ahern, the party's chief whip. Ahern signed most of the cheques in an accommodating and unquestioning manner. Despite his own accountancy background, he signed most of them blank. He would sign up to thirty at a time. One cheque dated 16 June 1989 was subsequently made out to cash for £25,000. This was deposited in Haughey's own account, as well as three other cheques made out in 1991. In February of that year, Ahern signed a whole book of blank cheques, which totally negated the control element of having two people sign the cheques.

Cheques co-signed by Ahern included two cheques for a total of £15,832 for Charlie's Charvet shirts. There were also cheques for a total of £15,000 for meals at Le Cog Hardi restaurant between April and December 1991, and there were three cheques made out simply to cash for a total of £22,500. Those three cheques were deposited in Charlie's own account. Of course, he was to claim that these were to cover legitimate expenses, such as entertaining in his own home, but then – as the call girl said in court during the infamous Profumo scandal in Britain – 'he would say that, wouldn't he?'

Only a fraction of the excess money has yet been explained. In 1986, some £134,00 extra was deposited in the leader's fund. The Irish Permanent Building Society contributed £100,000 of that to Fianna Fáil. The money was in the form of two £50,000 cheques made out to the party. Both were signed by Haughey and deposited in the leader's fund. Later £75,000 was withdrawn from the account in five cheques, which coincided with similar deposits into an account from which Des Traynor paid Haughey's domestic bills. A sixth cheque made out to cash for £25,000, which was signed by Charlie and Bertie Ahern, was also deposited in the account. In effect, the leader's fund was used to launder the £100,000 that was diverted, from Fianna Fáil.

Charlie was living so far beyond his means, that the £100,000 made little difference to his finances, which were again in a dreadful state. In 1986 Des Traynor left as managing director of Guinness & Mahon Bank to take up the position of chairman of Cement Roadstone Holdings (CRH), and the bank was taken over by the Japanese, who did not care whether Haughey was Taoiseach or not. They insisted that his loan and overdraft in the region of £900,000 be cleared up. Traynor moved Charlie's account to a subsidiary, Ansbacher Cayman. But the new owners still desired that Haughey's account should be straightened out. Traynor decided to raise the money by again tapping a number of business contacts. One of those he approach was the auditor of Dunne Stores, Noel Fox, who talked to Ben Dunne, the family member then controlling the business.

In January 1987 Dunne had handed over six cheques made out to 'bearer' for a total of £30,000 that somehow ended up in Charlie's account. Neither of them could remember the circumstances afterwards, but Dunne had apparently demonstrated that he was prepared to give money to Haughey, and he was more than amenable to the idea of helping when Fox told him about Traynor's approach. 'I think Haughey is making a huge mistake trying to get six or seven people together,' Dunne contended. 'Christ picked twelve apostles and one of them crucified him.' Consequently, Dunne offered to pay all the money himself.

He intended to source it outside the state, which was going to take some time. The first payment was a £285,000 sterling cheque drawn up in Northern Ireland on 20 May 1987. In December, there was a further cheque sourced in Northern Ireland for the sterling equivalent of £204,055, and the following summer Dunne provided a cheque worth

146

£471,000 from Switzerland. Thus from May 1987 to the summer of 1988, he gave Haughey over £960,055, and he also gave Ciarán Haughey £100,000 for services rendered, both in flying him and looking for a private helicopter for him. That same year Haughey bought a new yacht for £122,000, but the source of that money was never traced, though Dermot Desmond of the Brokerage firm, NCB, paid £75,546 to have the yacht refurbished. He said that this was really an interest free loan to be repaid only if the boat was re-sold.

In 1989 there were European, local, and general elections and the money came rolling in to Haughey's coffers. A total of £220,000 extra was deposited in the leader's fund. This included money collected to defray Brian Lenihan's medical expense for a liver transplant. That whole saga will be considered separately.

Mark Kavanagh gathered £100,000 for Fianna Fáil on behalf of the builders of the Financial Services Centre in June 1988. He was asked to put the money in the form of four cheques for £25,000 in 1989. He said that he handed the cheques to Charlie on election day. Haughey explained that Fianna Fáil would get half and £25,000 would go to Lenihan, while the remaining £25,000 would go to selected FF candidates. One of the cheques was lodged to his account and the other were exchanged for a draft for £50,000 and given to Fianna Fáil supposedly as a contribution from Michael Smurfit, who had contributed £60,000 through Des Traynor. Thus out of the £160,000 that was collected for Fianna Fáil and Lenihan, only £75,000 was handed over and the remaining £85,000 was retained by Haughey, who got another £150,000 from Ben Dunne in 1989.

This brought the total from Dunne to £1.1m. Ben stated that he never sought any favours from Haughey, other than asking him to arrange a meeting with Philip Curran, the chairman of the revenue commissioners. Nothing came of that meeting, but Dunne handed over a further £400,000 sterling for Charlie in 1990 and, without even being asked for money, he handed him £210,000 in cheques on one Friday in November 1991. He gave him three further cheques totalling £180,000 a year later after Charlie had retired from politics. In all he had given him over £1.93m, and he even offered him a further £1m to help him to cover his tax liability on the money, if he decided to declare it. Thus, it would seem that Dunne was not looking for political favours.

But the same cannot be said with any confidence about other people, because many of the people who made the contributions have never been identified. On 22 and 24 February 1988, there were two mystery bank transfers to Haughey's account of £195,000 and £49,700 respectively. Charlie said that he could not explain them, but for decades he had been suffering from convenient amnesia when it came to explaining embarrassing matters, especially about money. He was clearly evading taxes and would eventually be compelled to pay over six million euro in back taxes, penalties and interest.

Of course, tax evasion was rife in the country at the time. In 1988, Charlie's government introduced a tax amnesty allowing people to pay off tax previously evaded without penalties or interest. It was estimated that about £30 million in evaded taxes would be collected in this way, but over £500 million was actually collected in the amnesty that year. Tax evasion seemed to be a way of life in which even the Taoiseach was participating, but he did not avail of that tax amnesty himself.

Des O'Malley was first appointed to the cabinet as Minister for Justice in May 1970 during the arms crisis. In the ensuing months as arrangements were being made for the arms trial, the special branch reported seeing him with Charlie at the Rose of Tralee Festival. Peter Berry, the secretary of the Department of Justice, tried to give O'Malley a subtle warning, telling him that Brian Lenihan, the Minister for Transport and Power, had been seen with Charlie in Tralee. With the arms trial due to begin later in the month, Berry noted that it was inappropriate for any minister to be seen with Charlie before the trial, because the special branch, which had the former minister under surveillance, might get the wrong impression.

O'Malley promptly admitted that he had also met Charlie and added that they planned another meeting at Charlie's home the following week. Berry objected. If O'Malley was determined to meet Charlie, then the meeting should be in the minister's own office in Leinster House, where it could take place without the knowledge of special branch. O'Malley therefore met with Charlie in Leinster House for some thirty minutes on 9 September 1970. Afterwards he told Berry that the conversation had concentrated on Berry's statement in the *Book of Evidence* and the testimony he was likely to give at the trial.

'He said that Mr Haughey's principal worry was over my evidence and that he had asked if I could be "induced", "directed" or "intimidated" into not giving evidence or changing my evidence,' Berry recalled. When he asked if 'induced' meant bribed, O'Malley did not answer. 'The whole nature of the meeting,' Berry added, 'left me in no doubt that he (O'Malley) was pretending to Mr Haughey that he was a friend. It gave me a touch of nausea.'

O'Malley flatly rejected any suggestion of impropriety surrounding the meeting. 'I thought it quite appropriate at the time,' he later explained. 'I had told Mr Berry beforehand that I was meeting Mr Haughey and I told him afterwards what had transpired. But unfortunately the connotation is put on it that I made some kind of request to him which I certainly didn't. I factually reported what had happened because I thought it was appropriate that he should know.'

Thereafter relations between Charlie and O'Malley were strained. The latter was firmly in the Lynch wing of the party. He backed Colley for the leadership in 1979 and he led the abortive heave against

Charlie a little over two years later. O'Malley supported the McCreevy no-confidence motion later in the year, going so far as to resign from the cabinet before the meeting.

When the telephone-tapping scandal broke a few months later, O'Malley immediately dismissed Charlie's call for a judicial inquiry. 'The record of these enquiries is not very satisfactory,' he said. He was apparently in sympathy with those who wished to railroad Charlie. When Charlie survived again, Dessie was obviously in political trouble. At the Fianna Fáil Ard Fheis a few weeks later he was defeated when he ran for one of the five vice-presidential posts. This was the route Charlie had taken in his slow resurrection within the party following the arms crisis, but he was now firmly in control of the party and he was determined to block O'Malley.

Some of the dissidents were upset at the almost dictatorial way in which Charlie was allowed to commit the party to his own policy without any discussion within the parliamentary party. They were particularly critical of the way in which he reacted to the publication of the report of the New Ireland Forum in 1984.

His critics were being told that they should voice any concern within the parliamentary party, but as far as Charlie was concerned, any discussion had to give way to electoral considerations. The regular weekly meeting after the publication of the report was postponed for him to be in Cork for the photo call as the party's candidates submitted their nomination papers for the upcoming European elections. By the time the parliamentary party met, Charlie had firmly pronounced the party line and any backtracking would lead to speculation about his leadership – this time in the midst of the European election campaign. He therefore moved a motion congratulating the party's representatives 'on their splendid contribution to the purpose of the forum both in its work and the subsequent presentation of the report'. An amendment stipulating that the leader should only enunciate policy 'after discussion with the parliamentary party' was roundly rejected, and the motion was then carried unanimously.

Following the three hour meeting O'Malley was openly critical of the way in which debate on the report had effectively been stifled. With the campaign for the European elections already under way, his remarks were widely resented in party circles and Charlie seized on the opportunity of calling for the expulsion O'Malley from the parliamentary party. The haste in which a meeting was convened – with little more than twenty-four hours notice – was in stark contrast with the two weeks taken to convene the parliamentary party meeting to discuss the Forum report. Charlie personally proposed the removal of the party whip, and his motion was carried by a sizable majority.

Uno duce, una voce! P. J. Mara, the party press secretary, remarked facetiously to a journalist afterwards. 'We are having no more nibbling at my leader's bum'.

Early in the new year when the FitzGerald government was confronted with an internal crisis while trying to legalise the sale of condoms and other non-medical contraceptives without a doctor's prescription, there was a real chance the government would be defeated. Some members of the Roman Catholic hierarchy vociferously opposed the new bill and a number of Fine Gael and Labour deputies threatened to vote against the measure. Much to the annoyance of opportunists within Fianna Fáil, O'Malley spoke out strongly in support of the bill.

Although he had already been expelled from the parliamentary party, he was still a member of the Fianna Fáil organisation. In view of that membership, he did not take the logical step of actually voting for the bill after speaking for it. Instead, he just absented himself from the Dáil while the vote was being taken.

Charlie seized on this to secure O'Malley's expulsion from the organisation 'for conduct unbecoming a member'. Some people tried to intercede on O'Malley's behalf, but Charlie was adamant. 'It's him or me', he said.

O'Malley was permitted to address the meeting of the party's national executive called to discuss his expulsion. He requested that the vote should be taken by secret ballot, but Charlie called for a unanimous decision. 'I want it to be unanimous for the good of the party and the organisation,' he emphasised three different times. When it became apparent that this was out of the question, he demanded a roll call vote.

While the parliamentary party was free to establish its own procedure, the national executive was bound by the party's *Coru*, which stipulated that all votes should be secret. Yet none of the 82 members present dared to challenge Charlie on the issue. A roll call vote was taken and O'Malley was expelled by 73 votes to 9.

Interviewed on RTÉ radio the following morning, O'Malley said that his difficulties with Charlie went back to the time of the arms crisis. 'I came to know in some detail about those events and all the details surrounding them and I inevitably began to form certain opinions then and quite honestly those opinions have never left me,' he explained. But he refused to elaborate. When he adopted the same approach some months later on the *Late Late Show,* Gay Byrne challenged him to 'put up or shut up – stop saying these things, or else say what you mean'. But O'Malley still refused to clarify the matter.

In coming months he gave serious consideration to founding a new party. He still had not firmly made up his mind until Charlie became involved in controversy over the Anglo-Irish Agreement signed at Hillsborough Castle, near Belfast, on 15 November 1985. Charlie voiced strong objections against what he contended were the constitutional implications of the agreement. He vehemently denounced the very first article of the accord affirming 'that any change in the status of Northern Ireland would only come about with the consent of a majority of the people of Northern Ireland'. He said that this provision was 'in total conflict with the constitution and in particular, Article 2 of the constitution', which claimed sovereignty over the whole island.

'For the first time ever,' he emphasised, 'the legitimacy, which is contrary to unification, has been recognised by an Irish government in an international agreement ... From our point of view it gives everything away,' he said. 'It confirmed that status of Northern Ireland as an integral part of the United Kingdom and it confirmed that there would be no change in the status without the consent of the northern Unionists.'

Charlie's constitutional arguments ignored Article 2 (b) of the agreement which clearly stated that 'there is no derogation from the sovereignty of either the Irish government or the United Kingdom government'. While that clause may well have been inserted as a sop for northern Unionists, it also guaranteed the Republic's constitutional position because it meant there was no derogation of the Republic's *de jure* claim to sovereignty over the six counties. Admittedly the agreement contained a recognition of the fact that the area was under alien rule, but Article 3 of the constitution already recognised that fact.

FitzGerald had astutely anticipated Charlie's criticism and had carefully prepared a trap. The clause to which the Fianna Fáil leader took such extreme exception had actually been taken practically verbatim from the communique which Charlie and Margaret Thatcher had issued following their first summit meeting in May, 1980. Charlie suddenly found himself at pains to explain why the very words he had used five and half years earlier should now mean something different. If agreeing to those words constituted a sell-out, then it was he who had sold out in May 1980.

In an effort to depict the Hillsborough agreement in the best light possible, the government orchestrated a very successful public relations effort, which was undoubtedly enhanced from the Nationalist perspective by the hysterical reaction of Ian Paisley and the Unionists community in Northern Ireland. FitzGerald did not claim that partition was likely to be ended in the near future, as Charlie had intimated and Lenihan had indicated back in December 1980, but Paisley might just as well have said as much in his demagogic rantings. He described the agreement as the 'process of rolling Irish unification'.

There was dramatic drop in Fianna Fáil's public support and, for the first time in sixteen months, FitzGerald squeaked ahead of Charlie as the popular choice for Taoiseach. It was at this point that O'Malley launched the Progressive Democratic party along with Mary Harney, who was still a member of the Fianna Fáil organisation at the time.

The new party flourished initially, drawing considerable support from disillusioned Fianna Fáil voters and floating voters who had supported Fine Gael in November 1982. But there was little comfort for Charlie because satisfaction with his performance dropped to the lowest point since the black days of 1983. He actually trailed both FitzGerald and O'Malley as the people's choice for Taoiseach in a poll published on 18 January 1986.

There were two further defections from Fianna Fáil in the following weeks, as Pearse Wyse and Bobby Molloy joined the Progressive Democrats. Of the 22 deputies who had voted against Charlie's leadership in October 1982, only nine were still in the Fianna Fáil parliamentary party a little over three years later.

The most vocal of those critics were all outside the party with the exception of Charlie McCreevy, whose vulnerability was dramatically exposed in the run up to the local elections in 1985 when he was denied a party nomination to run for the Kildare County Council. There was no doubt whatever that Haughey had a firm grip on the party leadership at the time of the next general election in February 1987.

Eamon de Valera had failed to secure an overall majority in his first five general elections following the signing of the Anglo-Irish Treaty of 1921. Three of those general elections were as leader of Fianna Fáil. But this was generally overlooked by the media as they regularly decried Charlie as Fianna Fáil's greatest failure as a leader. In February 1987 he became the first leader of the party to fail to gain an overall majority in four consecutive general elections. Just three seats short of a majority, Fianna Fáil was very unlucky. With a total of less than 500 extra votes spread over eight specific constituencies, the party would have won 89 seats, which would have been very a comfortable majority.

Charlie was again blamed for the failure; this time with real justification. After all he was responsible for driving Des O'Malley out of Fianna Fáil, and he was thus indirectly responsible for the formation of the Progressive Democrats, who won fourteen seats. Four of those were former Fianna Fáil deputies and at least another half dozen were former members of the party. There could be little doubt that the advent of the Progressive Democrats had denied Fianna Fáil an overall majority. As Charlie sought to form a government, the media again concluded that he was fighting for political survival. If he failed to cobble together a government, it was generally believed that he would be toppled as party leader.

Realistically Fianna Fáil was the only party that could form a government. This time Charlie made it clear that he would not deal with anyone. He did offer to support the re-election of the speaker, Tom Fitzpatrick of Fine Gael. When the offer was described as stroke politics, he indignantly refused the suggestion.

'It would enhance the standing and the prestige of the office,' Charlie said. 'It was the tradition in previous years that the outgoing ceann comhairle was re-elected by the incoming Dáil.'

Fitzpatrick would have been willing to stay on, but he was instructed by Fine Gael to decline the offer. Fianna Fáil therefore approached Seán Tracy, an independent deputy, and he jumped at the offer.

Charlie felt he could depend on the support of Neil Blaney in the vote for Taoiseach, which meant that all eyes turned to Tony Gregory again. He was ready to make a deal, but Charlie insisted that there would be no deal this time. Gregory therefore told the press that he would not support the Fianna Fáil leader, which raised the unprecedented spectre of a hung Dáil.

John Kelly, the former Fine Gael minister, suggested a power-sharing arrangement between the two major parties, but Charlie ruled that out. 'Fianna Fáil is not interested now – nor will it be in the future – in arrangements of that kind,' he said. 'If need be,' he added, 'there will have to be another general election.'

On the eve of the Dáil meeting, the main story in the *Irish Times* was a report that Fine Gael sources were contending, if the Dáil failed to elect anyone, that Garret FitzGerald 'would not necessarily have to report to the president'. He could postpone his resignation for a couple of days in order to allow further consultations to find a candidate who would win a majority vote in the Dáil. John Murray, the attorney-general in Charlie's last government, argued however, that the Taoiseach would have to resign immediately under article 28.10 of the constitution.

At the time the whole thing looked like an invitation to flush out an alternative candidate from within Fianna Fáil. Back in 1948 Richard Mulcahy, the leader of Fine Gael, had been unacceptable to some of his party's potential allies in the Dáil. Fine Gael therefore put forward John A. Costello for Taoiseach and he was elected with the blessing of Mulcahy, who remained as party leader. Thus there was a precedent for having other than a party leader as Taoiseach.

Although four men – FitzGerald, Haughey, O'Malley and Spring – were nominated for Taoiseach, only Charlie had any chance of winning. The whole thing seemed to depend on Gregory, with the result that there was a distinct air of tension when he rose to speak in the Dáil.

He had waited in vain, he said, for the right wing parties to act responsibly in getting together to form a government. 'They are motivated by petty party self-interest and personality difference and have sought to divert attention from their irresponsibility by isolating me, as if the burden of responsibility rested with me alone,' he continued. Rather than precipitate another election, he said that he would abstain from voting. This was greeted with some applause and an audible sigh of relief from all sides of the house.

Charlie had successfully called Gregory's bluff. The voting ended in a tie – 82 for and against Charlie's nomination. He was then elected on the casting vote of the speaker. FitzGerald immediately rose to congratulate him and went on to say that Fine Gael would not attempt to bring down the government, if it sought to introduce the necessary corrective measures for the economy. Although FitzGerald resigned as leader of Fine Gael next day, his successor, Alan Dukes, pursued this policy as part of what became known as the Tallaght Strategy.

Brian Lenihan had been associated with Charlie in the public mind ever since the 1960s when John Healy dubbed him one of the three musketeers, along with Haughey and Donagh O'Malley. Lenihan was first elected to the Dáil in 1961, when he took the seat of the long time Minister for Justice Gerald Boland. During that Dáil term, he actually became Minister for Justice himself when he replaced Charles Haughey after his surprised appointment as Minister for Agriculture in October 1964. He liked to think of himself as keeping close to both of the main factions within Fianna Fáil. As Minister for Transport and Power in 1970 he tipped off the people behind the gun-running that the special branch were set to seize the weapons upon arrival, but he backed Jack Lynch in the ensuing arms crisis.

In the aftermath of the 1979 leadership contest between Colley and Haughey, there was confusion over Lenihan's role. Vincent Browne maintained Lenihan and Ray Burke were distraught on the night of the contest because that they had backed the loser. Lenihan had already told his family that he was faced with the choice of backing a fool or a knave. Years later he stated publicly that he had actually voted for Haughey in that contest.

Charlie retained Lenihan and most of Lynch's cabinet in his own government and appointed him to each of his subsequent governments. Lenihan became vocal in his support of Haughey during the various heaves against his leadership. In 1987, Lenihan was appointed to the prestigious post of Minister for Foreign Affairs and was retained even after he became ill with a serious liver complaint shortly afterwards. During the next couple of years, Lenihan deteriorated visibly. By April 1989 he was obviously dying. His family was told that his only chance of survival was for him to have liver transplant.

Charlie learned that Lenihan had only about a month to live from Catherine Butler, his personal assistant, who said that the Taoiseach broke down and wept at the news. Lenihan could not afford the cost of such an operation at the Mayo Clinic in the United States, so Haughey initiated a fundraising effort. 'There was nobody else,' he later testified, 'nobody else in the position, or able to, or prepared to take the initiative in that regard.'

Charlie asked Paul Kavanagh, the main Fianna Fáil fundraiser, to organise a collection. Kavanagh drew up a list of sixteen wealthy businessmen that he planned to approach. They were Fred Danza Agna, Oliver Barry, Michael Behan, Leo Cafollo, Ben Dunne, Edmund Farrell, Tadgh Gallagher, Larry Goodman, John Horgan, Gus Kearney, Dan McInerney, J. P. McManus, Oliver Murphy, S. F. Rafique and Séamus Tully. When Kavanagh showed this list to Charlie, he promptly crossed out the name of Ben Dunne.

'I never asked the reason,' Kavanagh later said. Having worked for Haughey for ten years, he knew the procedure. 'When he did something like that, that was it,' Kavanagh explained. 'You didn't ask why.'

The explanation would seem obvious enough in the light that Dunne had already agreed to contribute £1 million towards Haughey's personal expenses, but Charlie insisted that he knew nothing of that arrangement. Yet, his behaviour in relation to crossing off Dunne's name would seem to suggest otherwise.

The fundraising for Lenihan was complicated by political developments. On 26 April 1989 Charlie returned from a official visit to Japan to learn that Fianna Fáil had problems in the Dáil over a Labour party amendment calling on the government to increase an offer of a quarter of a million pounds to haemophiliacs infected with the AIDS virus. The amendment, which was passed over Fianna Fáil objections, allocated £400,000 for the victims.

For more than a year Fianna Fáil had been enjoying over 50% support in the public opinion polls, and Charlie saw the Dáil defeat – the sixth his government had suffered since taking office – as an excuse to call a snap election in the hope of securing the elusive 'working majority'. He immediately indicated that he was thinking of calling a general election which would seem to suggest that he had allowed his pique to get the better of his judgment.

As the general election would have to be held within thirty days of the dissolution of the Dáil, it would have meant that the election would have to be held before the end of May. As the European elections were already scheduled for 15 June, this would have meant two national elections within a month. If the haemophiliac question had been made an issue of confidence beforehand, he would have had no choice, but having failed to do this, he would now have difficulty justifying the unnecessary expense of two national elections so close together.

Thus he had to wait for almost three weeks before he could ask for an election. Having already shown his hand, however, it became all too obvious that he was waiting to hold a general election in conjunction with the European elections.

Albert Reynolds, the Minister for Finance, advised against a general election, and Fine Gael made desperate efforts to avoid one, going so far as to offer to negotiate a formal economic accord with the government to provide backing on agreed legislation.

During the legislative year beginning in October 1988, Fine Gael had voted with the government on 42 occasions and abstained 8 times, and only voted against 12 times. Such co-operation between the two major parties was unprecedented, with the result that there was a strong public perception that the general election was unnecessary. Nevertheless, on 25 May Charlie announced a general election to be held in conjunction with the European elections.

Meanwhile Charlie took the initiative in tapping a number of people for money for Lenihan. He summoned Tom Ryan of the Voluntary Health Insurance (VHI), which subsequently agreed at a board meeting on 18 May to make an *ex gratia* payment, and actually paid £57,247 in August following the transplant.

Haughey had already approached Edmund Farrell of the Irish Permanent Building Society for an election contribution for himself and Fianna Fáil. Farrell had persuaded his board to authorise £65,000 to the party and £10,000 to Charlie, who then asked Farrell on 7 June for a further contribution towards Lenihan's operation fund. 'Who should the cheque be made out to?' Farrell asked.

'Myself,' replied Charlie.

'On behalf of the members of the society, we are pleased to endorse a cheque for £20,000 to help meet the expense of Mr Lenihan's operation,' Farrell explained in a covering note. The cheque was made out to 'C. J. Haughey (B. Lenihan)'. Farrell also enclosed a cheque for £10,000 to help with Charlie's elections expenses. Those two cheques were endorsed by Haughey and deposited in the Bank of Ireland account of Celtic Helicopters at Dublin airport.

Various businessmen contributed on behalf of themselves or their companies. They included Larry Goodman, who gave £25,000; Edmund Farrell, John Magnier, Séamus Tully and Mark Kavanagh, who gave £20,000 each; Eamon de Valera and Nicholas Fitzpatrick gave £10,000 each on behalf of their companies, while Oliver Murphy gave £5,000. Those contributions came to a total of £130,000.

In the five week period around the time of Lenihan's operation over £180,000 extra was deposited in the party leader's account, in addition to money from the exchequer. It was not clear exactly how much of that was intended as a contribution towards the medical expenses and how much was for election expenses. But it can be established clearly that nothing like even £130,000 was contributed out of this money towards Lenihan's expenses. Hence, despite Charlie's assertions to the contrary, a considerable amount of money was obviously kept.

Haughey later explained that depositing the money in the account of Celtic Helicopters had been a mistake. On 13 June 1989 the £30,000 was withdrawn from the account in the form of a cheque made payable to cash. This cheque was delivered to the Taoiseach's office but it was subsequently exchanged for cash at AIB, Baggot Street, where the leader's account was held. It was not deposited in the leader's account, as the various deposits in the account at the time can be explained by other contributions. All trace of that the building society's contribution of £20,000 earmarked for Lenihan vanished at that point.

Money provided from the leader's account was used to pay various bills incurred by Lenihan in connection with the operation. For instance, £54,498.58 was paid to the Mayo Clinic from the account in 1989. In addition, a total of £10,007.12 was paid to the Department of Foreign Affairs in connection with expenses incurred by Lenihan. The following March another £5,727.23 was withdrawn to pay for three further international cheques to the Mayo Clinic, a nearby hotel, and a limousine service.

Eileen Foy testified that she thought that Charlie also provided the Lenihans with cash to cover their expenses, but she could not explain why she believed this. Anne Lenihan, Brian's wife, said that the only cash that she or her husband received was on the day that they left for the United States, when Haughey sent his driver over with £200 in an envelope. At the time, she thought it was a generous gesture. But on reflection, it hardly looked so, especially when there was a massive surplus in the account and the amount given would not even have paid for one of Haughey's shirts.

In early 1991, a bill for Lenihan's travel expenses to the United States was presented by the Department of Defence. The total cost of this came to £12,914.50. There should have been ample money in the leader's account to cover those expenses as there should still have been a surplus of at least £49,000, but Charlie called Paul Kavanagh to raise further money to cover Lenihan's expenses. He said that £50,000 extra was needed.

It was suggested to Paul Kavanagh that Philip Monahan, a property developer and neighbour of Lenihan, would possibly give that total himself, so Kavanagh approached him. Monahan duly wrote out a cheque for £25,000. This was deposited in the leader's fund, and the Department of Defence bill was paid that day.

The total amount contributed to the collection for Lenihan being conducted by Haughey was at least £155,000, just counting those confirmed contributions already noted. The amount paid out of the leader's account towards Lenihan's expenses came to just over £83,000, so there should have been a surplus of over £71,000 that Charlie was unable to explain.

When all of this was exposed little over a decade later, Haughey indignantly refuted suggestions that he had misappropriated the money. He said that what he did for Lenihan was 'the most compassionate thing I've ever done in my life.'

'I think it's absolutely preposterous that this whole genuine charitable effort on my part at the time should now, 20 years or so later, be sought to be turned against me in a most cruel fashion, that I would deliberately divert for my own purposes money which was subscribed by well-meaning people for the good and salvation of my friend, Brian Lenihan,' Charlie declared. 'I watched him fade away in 1988–1989. I watched over him. I protected him. I kept him in office when he was hardly able to perform the functions of his office.'

In effect, Haughey was virtually saying that he betrayed the trust of his own office to help his friend by keeping him in office too long. 'I kept his job open for him, did it myself in so far as it had to be done, and when he came out of hospital that time,' he said, 'I again looked after him in government, and personally.'

Charlie seemed to be protesting too much, as he was stung by the suggestion that he would misappropriate money in such circumstances. In fairness, it should be emphasised that his initiative probably did save Lenihan's life and afforded him a further six years. Lenihan's son Brian publicly declared during this controversy that it was to Haughey's credit that he did come forward to help his father at a critical time. 'Very much to his credit,' young Lenihan said, 'he came forward and said that he would help in every way possible.' The money was used to pay all of Lenihan's bills; it was the surplus that was misappropriated.

Of course, that does not in anyway excuse this behaviour. In all, when one includes his influence in persuading the VHI to contribute £57,247, Haughey was instrumental in raising over £200,000 for Lenihan's operation. He was proud of doing that for his friend, but he balked at the opposition's insistence on providing an extra £150,000 compensation for the more than one hundred haemophiliacs infected with the AIDS virus as a result of receiving tainted blood and blood products provided by state.

The whole blood saga was arguably one of the greatest scandals in the history of the state. Through a mixture of bungling, ignorance, incompetence and indifference, 104 Irish people were infected with the AIDS virus through tainted blood or blood products. A further 217 haemophiliacs were infected with hepatitis C. Nearly all of those were infected prior to Charlie's return to government in 1987, so the opposition's role calling for the £250,000 in compensation to be raised to £400,000 was understandable, but Haughey used the whole thing as a pretext for calling a general election in 1989.

ONE ELECTION TOO MANY

Fianna Fáil gave two reasons for calling the general election of 1989. One, there was a danger the government would be defeated on the health budget, which would necessitate a general election anyway. Two, it was argued that there was a need for political stability as Ireland was due to take over the presidency of the European Community at the start of the new year. Many people did not accept these arguments. They suspected it was an attempt by Charlie to shake off the opposition shackles that were forcing him to pursue responsible policies.

In the circumstances the Haughey Factor re-appeared. Although it never became as great an issue as in some of the earlier elections, it was always there and in tight races – where a comparatively small number of votes could mean the difference between victory and defeat – it became very important.

Ever since the *Taca* controversy Fianna Fáil had been particularly vulnerable to suspicion that it was prepared to do improper favours for businessmen in return for contributions to party funds. Whether this was unfair or not, it was nevertheless widely believed, with the result that the public tended to look with deep suspicion on any kind of cosy relationship between a Fianna Fáil government and the business community.

There had been some questionable incidents involving one of the businesses of beef baron, Larry Goodman. In 1986 the authorities discovered evidence of a scheme to defraud the EC. Documentation to secure EC export credit on an £80 million deal was falsified both by exaggerating the weight of the meat and including trimmings that were not eligible for export credit.

It was an obvious fraud in the eye of the authorities, but for some reason the fraud squad was not called in to investigate for almost two years, by which time there had been a change of governments. The company involved was penalised by the government withholding £1 million of EC money as a penalty.

When Barry Desmond of the Labour party raised the issue in the Dáil in March 1989, Charlie accused him of national sabotage. In light of what had happened, there were many questions that needed to be answered, but the government was not prepared to set up a judicial inquiry. When the Labour party and Progressive Democrats persisted with questions, Charlie sought to distance himself. He accused his opponent of trying 'to involve me in a matter about which I had no official knowledge and for which I had no official responsibility'.

Just what he meant by 'no official knowledge' was anybody's guess. He was personally informed of the fraud by the secretary of the Department of Agriculture in January 1988, but he apparently decided to go along with the low-key approach adopted under the previous government in order not to damage the image of the beef industry.

Although the policy had really been implemented before Charlie's return to power, he became particularly vulnerable when it was disclosed that Larry Goodman had been allowed the unprecedented privilege of keeping his private jet at the Army Air Corps base in Baldonnel. In addition, there were serious rumblings about export credit insurance given to his companies.

Iraq had been considered a bad credit risk because of the ongoing war with Iran, coupled with falling oil prices on the world market. As a result the coalition government suspended export credit insurance to companies trading with Iraq in 1986, but this was re-introduced in 1987 after Charlie returned to power. Although Iraq was given eighteen months credit, £53 million was already overdue and there was a further £119 million outstanding at the time of the election. The Irish tax payer was going to have to foot that bill, if Iraq defaulted.

The uneasiness over this, coupled with the perception that the election was unnecessary, tended to have a corrosive effect on the Fianna Fáil campaign. As a result the party's support declined steadily in the three weeks before polling day. In the first poll published after the election was called, for instance, Fianna Fáil's support dropped to 47%, to 45% the following week, and to 41.1% a week later in the actual vote on election day.

Party workers found a lot of resentment on the doorsteps. Having campaigned strongly against health cuts in 1987, they found themselves having to explain why Fianna Fáil had instituted even more severe cuts, curtailing programmes that Haughey had introduced while Minister for Health in Jack Lynch's last government.

'It gives me not the slightest bit of pleasure to have to cut back the very programmes I put in myself,' Charlie explained during the campaign. He made a particularly damaging admission on the health situation during a phone-in programme on RTÉ radio, when he said that he 'wasn't aware of the full extent of the problems and difficulties and hardship it was causing'.

This was an extraordinary admission, tantamount to acknowledging that he did not know what his government was doing. Some people saw it as an indication that his political judgment was slipping, and that impression was compounded by the election results, which were little short of disastrous from his standpoint.

In the outgoing Dáil, Fianna Fáil had 81 seats, but it returned with only 77, seven short of an overall majority. The only bigger losers were the Progressive Democrats, who lost eight of their 14 seats.

The party's dramatic reversal had the impact of making what had once been unthinkable now look attractive. As Seán Tracy could be re-appointed speaker, the six seats won by the Progressive Democrats just happened to be the number that Charlie needed to form a government. On his past record he had been ready to pay dearly for the necessary support and Mary Harney realised there was an opportunity for her and her colleagues – all of whom were former members of Fianna Fáil – to salvage something from the election disaster.

'However we may dislike certain people or parties,' she said, 'we have to play our part in giving this country a government for the foreseeable future.' She was clearly signalling the possibility of an arrangement, but Pearse Wyse seemed to throw a wet blanket over the idea of any co-operation while Charlie remained as leader. 'I believed that no man, including Mr Haughey, has the right to stand in the way of stable government,' he said. 'In no circumstances could I bring myself to vote for him as Taoiseach.'

The Progressive Democrats were pledged to vote for the Fine Gael leader, and they decided to keep their commitment when the Dáil met to select a Taoiseach on 28 June. But in the interim Des O'Malley and Pat Cox, who had just been elected to the European parliament, held exploratory talks with Charlie. They insisted that the price of Progressive Democratic support would be a coalition. When Charlie said he could 'never sell' that to Fianna Fáil, O'Malley smiled. He said that Charlie should not 'make a mistake in under-estimating his ability to sell anything to his party'.

As expected Charlie's nomination was defeated by 86 votes to 78, but so also were the nominations of Alan Dukes and Dick Spring. Under the constitution, Charlie would remain as Taoiseach until a successor was elected, but there was some confusion as to the correct constitutional procedure, as this had never before happened. Charlie proposed that the Dáil adjourn until 3 July to give him a chance to form a government. He said he would not be advising the president to dissolve the Dáil at this stage, as it would not be in 'the best interests of the country to precipitate another general election' so soon, if this could be avoided. He and his cabinet colleagues would continue in office and the 'day to day business of the government will be carried on uninterrupted', he said.

Alan Dukes raised no objection. Prior to the first meeting of the last Dáil in 1987, it will be remembered that Fine Gael sources had been claiming that the Taoiseach could have up to forty-eight hours. But Dick Spring insisted that Charlie was constitutionally obliged to go to the president to resign his office formally.

Charlie said he had advice from the attorney-general that 'time was not of the essence' and that he had 'up to a week' before having to resign. It was ironic the same person had said the opposite in relation to the possibility of Garret FitzGerald delaying for a couple of days two years earlier.

Article 28.10 of the constitution stipulates: 'The Taoiseach shall resign from office upon his ceasing to retain the support of a majority in Dáil Éireann unless on his advice the president dissolves Dáil Éireann and on the reassembly of Dáil Éireann after the dissolution the Taoiseach secures the support of a majority in Dáil Éireann'. The Taoiseach was obviously obliged to resign unless he called for another general election.

Much of the argument was really academic anyway, because the following paragraph of the constitution stipulates that 'the Taoiseach and the other members of the government shall continue to carry on their duties until their successors shall have been appointed'. It was just a question of procedure, but in such matters procedure is extremely important.

Charlie was leaving himself open to the charge of refusing to resign in defiance of the constitution. He and Neil Blaney had been the first ministers in the history of the state to refuse to resign when called upon to do so by the Taoiseach during the arms crisis. Now Charlie would be setting a constitutional precedent.

During a two-hour recess he was convinced by colleagues that, regardless of the advice from the attorney-general, it was politically imperative that he should resign as soon as possible.

Immediately after the recess he announced his intention of tendering his resignation to the president. He added that he would not ask for a dissolution but would continue to try to form a government. The Dáil then adjourned for four days, until the following Monday, 3 July 1989.

The Progressive Democrats made it clear that they were not interested in propping up a minority Fianna Fáil government, no matter what inducements were offered to them. They were only interested in a coalition, but Fianna Fáil had a longstanding policy of not going into coalition with anybody.

The Fianna Fáil national executive voted unanimously against coalition and Charlie went on RTÉ's *This Week* programme on 2 July to say that he was totally opposed to the idea.

This, of course, raised the spectre of another election, but this would now be strictly a matter for the president, because he now had the authority to refuse to dissolve the Dáil as the Taoiseach had ceased to retain majority support. Charlie contended, however, that the 'accepted wisdom' had always been that the president would never exercise this power.

When the Dáil reconvened next day, Charlie asked for a further adjournment until the afternoon of 6 July. Dukes agreed but not before making a hard-hitting speech in which he criticised Charlie's attempt 'to prejudge the response that the president might make to advise on a dissolution of the Dáil'. It was ironic that Charlie, of all people, should adopt such an attitude.

His approach now was in sharp contrast 'with his actions in January 1982,' when he tried to get the president to reject Garret FitzGerald's request for a dissolution of the Dáil, O'Malley observed.

When the cabinet met next day, it was evenly split on the issue of coalition with senior members like Albert Reynolds, Pádraig Flynn, John Wilson and Michael O'Kennedy firmly opposed. Brian Lenihan, on the other hand, felt they had no choice. He argued that, under the circumstances, they would be able to sell the idea of coalition to the party.

Flynn stunned his colleagues with a vicious attack on Charlie, whose lust for power had put them in the invidious position, he said. Later that afternoon he went on RTÉ's *Today at Five* to say that a coalition was out of the question. 'All the members of the cabinet are unanimous for no coalition,' he said. 'The national executive, the parliamentary party and the grassroots have indicated this is a core value which we must preserve.'

When Charlie met the Progressive Democrats shortly afterwards, he formally agreed to form a coalition, subject to an agreement on a joint programme for government. On being asked about remarks concerning opposition within the party, he was dismissive.

'I haven't told them yet,' Charlie replied.

Next day, Thursday, 6 July, the Dáil reconvened and Charlie asked for a further adjournment until 12 July. Dukes again agreed, but warned that this was the last time. 'One thing is perfectly clear,' he said. 'The issue before us must be resolved before this House meets next Wednesday.'

Some deputies were becoming uneasy about the delay. Roger Garland of the Green party noted that the Dáil was dithering 'while the world goes down the tube'. He complained about the destruction of the world's rain forests and the ozone layer. As a result of the greenhouse effect, the polar ice caps were melting and he forecast the inundation of a large part of Bangladesh, as well as low-lying areas of Dublin, Cork and Limerick.

'He's only looking for the floating vote,' one Fianna Fáil backbencher interjected.

If Garland thought the Dáil could have had the slightest impact on any of those matters within a week, he was the only one.

Details on policy matters relating to the programme for government were negotiated by Albert Reynolds and Bertie Ahern for Fianna Fáil, and Bobby Molloy and Pat Cox for the Progressive Democrats. Things on which they were unable to agree and matters relating to the actual makeup of the government were then left to the two leaders.

Fianna Fáil was insistent that Progressive Democrats were proportionally entitled to only one seat in the cabinet, but O'Malley insisted on two. He realised that Charlie was under strong pressure from within the cabinet and he actually expressed sympathy for the Taoiseach at one point.

The parliamentary party allowed Charlie freedom to negotiate a coalition, but not before Máire Geoghegan-Quinn made some bitter comments. 'Don't ask me to accept that what is being done is in the national interest,' she said. It was simply being done to satisfy the leader's desire for power.

Most of the backbenchers, however, were so anxious to avoid a further election that they favoured coalition. 'They're more enlightened than some of my cabinet,' Charlie remarked caustically. 'They are only a crowd of gobshites.'

By the eve of the Dáil meeting the only outstanding issue was the question of whether the Progressive Democrats would be offered one or two seats in cabinet. Albert Reynolds told RTÉ that the party had authorised Charlie to give only one seat, but Charlie gave in to O'Malley's demands and agreed to appoint him and Molloy to the cabinet and Mary Harney as a minister of state. In addition, the Progressive Democrats were promised three seats in the Senate out of the eleven to be appointed by the Taoiseach.

'Never in the history of Irish politics has so much been given by so many to so few,' grumbled one Fianna Fáiler.

'Nobody but myself could have done it,' Charlie proudly declared.

With a presidential election due in November 1990, there was speculation that Charlie might run for the seven-year term. He was expected by many to step down as Taoiseach at the end of Ireland's presidency of the European Community in July 1990, and it seemed natural enough that he would move on to Áras an Uachtaráin for a seven year term at this stage of his political career, especially when there were questions about his health.

In December 1989 Charlie discouraged these rumours by effectively touting the candidacy of Brian Lenihan at an annual Fianna Fáil dinner. 'He will still be one of us whatever high office he is called to during the next decade,' the Taoiseach said to tremendous applause.

Lenihan had been quietly campaigning for the office for months, and had done absolutely nothing to discourage speculation about his own ambitions for the office. 'I would be honoured, as any Irishman would be honoured, to run for the presidency,' he declared.

Despite his open benediction, however, Charlie had real misgivings, because Lenihan's election would undermine his majority in the Dáil. The government would have to win the ensuing by-election in Lenihan's Dublin West constituency and, of course, Charlie had some unhappy memories of the by-election there eight years earlier. In the circumstances some of the government became uneasy, and Charlie did nothing to allay their disquiet. In fact, he quietly encouraged an alternative to Lenihan, going so far as to send out feelers to Fine Gael about the possibility of running an agreed candidate like the distinguished civil servant, T. K. Whittaker.

Lenihan betrayed his own suspicions in April when he told the press that Charlie was 'a tremendously loyal person to his friends, generous in spirit and a very kind and considerate person in all his personal relationships and dealings.' He was trying to put pressure on the Taoiseach, as there were indications that John Wilson, the Minister for the Marine, was also interested in running for the presidency. If he won, Fianna Fáil would have little difficulty winning a by-election in his Cavan-Monaghan constituency.

'The more suspicious of my supporters felt that Mr Haughey was behind the Wilson gambit,' Lenihan wrote. But Leinhan's campaign had already gained an unstoppable momentum, and he brushed aside the Wilson challenge to win the Fianna Fáil nomination by 54 votes to 19.

From the outset Lenihan was an odds-on favourite to win the presidential election. Over the years he had enjoyed a high profile, especially in recent months after his successful liver transplant. He was well liked by politicians on all sides of the Dáil and also by the press. He was the kind of man who facilitated journalists and, unlike Charlie, he never took offence at their criticism.

Prior to the start of the campaign proper, therefore, Lenihan enjoyed a considerable lead in the polls. He had more than double the support of his nearest rival, Mary Robinson. During the campaign she began to eat into his lead as expected, but her left wing views on matter like divorce and contraception, were seen as a distinct liability among conservative voters. The various public opinion surveys were indicating that if Brian did not win on the first count, he would win easily on transfers from the Fine Gael candidate, Austin Currie, who did not get into the campaign until too late. He and his party was floundering in their efforts to boost his candidacy by trying to depict Lenihan as unsuitable for the office on the grounds that he was too close to Charlie and could not therefore be trusted to act independently. 'It is difficult to see how the habits of loyalty to Mr Haughey for half a lifetime will be abandoned by Mr Lenihan if elected president,' Currie said at the launching of his campaign.

On RTÉ's *Questions and Answers* on 22 October 1990 Garret FitzGerald noted that Lenihan had facilitated Charlie in trying to interfere with the discretionary power of the president by trying to get Hillery to refuse a dissolution of the Dáil after the coalition government was defeated on John Bruton's budget eight years earlier. Lenihan dismissed this, because no president had ever used the option.

'Why the phone calls to try to force him to exercise it?' Garret asked, alluding to what happened in 1982.

'That's fictional, Garret,' Lenihan replied.

'It is not fictional, excuse me, I was in Aras an Uachtaráin when those phone calls came through and I know how many there were.'

A member of the audience asked Brian directly if he had made any phone calls to the Aras that night.

'No, I didn't at all,' he insisted. 'That never happened. I want to assure you that never happened.'

Lenihan had forgotten that he had told a student in May that he had called President Hillery that night and had actually spoken to him.

'I got through to him,' he said. In hindsight, he explained that the whole thing was a mistake because the president was not the type of man who would break new ground. 'But, of course,' Brian added, 'Charlie was gung-ho.'

In an article in the *Irish Times* on 27 September the student, Jim Duffy, wrote that Charlie, Lenihan and Sylvester Barrett had made phone calls to the president on the night of the budget fiasco. Dick Walsh, the political editor of the newspaper, was anxious to run a follow up story, but Duffy was reluctant. He allowed Walsh to hear the taped interview and agreed to the *Irish Times* running a low-key story on 24 October to the effect that it had corroborative evidence.

The whole thing was by now gathering a momentum of its own. Gay Byrne challenged the *Irish Times* to publish the evidence, if it had any. And Lenihan reaffirmed his denial on RTÉ radio's *News at One*, as well as *Today at Five*, on which his campaign manager, Bertie Ahern, mentioned Jim Duffy and suggested that his tape had been stolen.

With the political temperature rising Duffy decided to release the pertinent segment of the controversial tape after Bertie Ahern had named him on RTÉ. The *Irish Times* then called an extraordinary press conference. Rather than running the story as an exclusive on its own pages, it gave the story to the world, setting off a political firestorm.

Lenihan was caught completely by surprise. He rushed over to appear on RTÉ's evening news programme to explain his side of the story without even hearing the tape. He only heard it for the first time on the programme. Rather than candidly admit that he had no recollection of the interview, he tried to bluff his way out by looking straight into the camera.

'My mature recollection at this stage is that I did not ring President Hillery. I want to put my reputation on the line in that respect,' he said.

The interviewer, Seán Duignan, realised that Lenihan could not have it both ways. Either he wasn't telling the truth now, or else he did not tell the truth to the student.

'I must have been mistaken in what I said to Duffy on that occasion,' Lenihan replied. 'It was a casual discussion with a research student and I was obviously mistaken in what I said.'

But it could not have been just a casual slip; it wasn't just one mistake. Duignan quoted from the transcript of the conversation.

'But you made a phone call?' Duffy asked.

'Oh, I did,' Lenihan replied.

'Sylvester Barrett made one?'

'That is right.'

'And Mr Haughey?'

'That is right.'

'Well,' Lenihan interrupted Duignan, 'in fact, that is wrong, and I want to emphasise it here. From my mature recollection and discussion with other people, at no stage did I ring President Hillery on that occasion or any other time.'

'They are all going to come after you demanding that you pull out of the race,' Duignan suggested. 'Do you not think that in all the circumstances you should?'

'I will not pull out of the race. I am not going to do so on the basis of a remark made to a university student, to whom I was doing a very great service in providing background for the material he was making on the presidency.'

It was a pathetic performance, made all the worse by Lenihan's ridiculous efforts to project sincerity by looking straight into the camera and using the phrase 'mature recollection' four different times. Either he was lying now, or else he had spun a cock and bull story to the student. If the latter was true, it was certainly ludicrous to describe the interview as 'a very great service'.

What he said to Duffy 'was a casual oversight', he explained minutes later during an interview on radio news. 'I am telling you the honest truth. And I like to be honest. I have been honest all my life in politics.'

'What state of mind could you have been in to be so very wrong over such a very wide area?' Olivia O'Leary asked him some hours later on *Today Tonight*. 'One knows that you've been sick recently. But were you on some drugs or something?'

'Not at all,' Brian replied breaking into a broad smile. 'That's an outrageous suggestion.'

Much later in his book, *For the Record*, Lenihan provided a plausible explanation for his behaviour when he admitted that at the time of the Duffy interview he was on strong drugs to ward off rejection of his new liver. A common side effect of those drugs is a partial loss of memory, but he only admitted this long after the campaign had ended.

During the actual campaign, his behaviour seemed inexplicable. He had obviously been lying to somebody and by protesting his honesty, he seemed to be lying to everybody and insulting the intelligence of the electorate.

173

There was uproar in the Dáil next day when the opposition tried to raise the issue of the Lenihan tape and the telephone calls to the Aras. 'Brian Lenihan should be hauled in here and hung, drawn and quartered,' Jim Mitchell of Fine Gael declared.

Charlie was incensed. 'The leader of the opposition is hurling false accusations around the House,' he said, 'before he makes any more accusations about telling lies or untruths, he should look behind him at Deputy Garret FitzGerald, who had been completely exposed as telling lies.' He had to withdraw the accusation of telling 'lies' or 'untruths,' but of course the damage was done by then.

In football parlance, Charlie had gone over the top. He was accusing FitzGerald of lying because he had said on the controversial *Questions & Answers* programme that if the various Fianna Fáil people had not called the Aras on the night in question, somebody had done a good job of imitating them. This was taken by some people to suggest that he had actually overheard the calls, but Garret had already made it clear that he was making no such claim. He was simply told at the Aras that the various people had telephoned.

That night the Progressive Democrats decided to demand Lenihan's resignation from the government. On Monday, Charlie had Ahern explain the situation to Lenihan, but the latter said that he would not resign as it would destroy his campaign.

Charlie called an impromptu session of the Fianna Fáil members of his cabinet at his home to discuss the situation. Neither Brian, nor his sister, Mary O'Rourke, were invited. The Progressive Democrats were insisting on Lenihan's resignation, Charlie explained. Many of those present thought it was the only way out of the impasse and there was little doubt that the Taoiseach favoured this course.

On Tuesday morning, Brian broke off campaigning in the south to fly to Dublin to meet Charlie at his home. They had a twenty-minute meeting at which Charlie explained that the government would collapse if Brian did not resign. 'The Taoiseach advocated that the best option open to me was my resignation,' Lenihan recalled. 'He said my resignation would help rather than damage my campaign for the president. He said most people would respect me for standing down in the national interest in order to avoid a general election. Pressing the point further Mr Haughey said that if I resigned, Dessie O'Malley would issue a statement congratulating me on my decision.'

'I listened to all this patiently,' he continued. 'I then countered that my resignation would be tantamount to an admission that I had done something wrong as Tánaiste and Minister for Defence which rendered me unfit to serve as a member of the cabinet.'

Lenihan protested his honesty. 'I put it to the Taoiseach that he and Mr O'Malley knew that I was telling the truth because both of them were on the Fianna Fáil front bench on the night the phone calls were made.' But that was only part of the problem.

O'Malley had succinctly summarised the situation on an RTÉ radio interview on Sunday. 'Mr Lenihan has given two diametrically opposed accounts of what happened and they can't both be true,' he said. For some reason Lenihan seemed curiously unable to see that protesting his honesty in the circumstances seemed to be compounding the lie. Charlie explained that the Progressive Democrats were insistent 'and the only acceptable solution' was his resignation.

The meeting had to be cut short as Charlie was due to meet Queen Beatrix of the Netherlands who was arriving at Dublin airport on a state visit. Ahern told Lenihan that the Progressive Democrats were going to pull out of the government, if he had not resigned by five o'clock that afternoon.

At Dublin airport Charlie was asked by waiting reporters about resignation rumours.

'Brian Lenihan did not offer his resignation nor did I seek it,' he replied. 'Anything like that would be a matter for my old friend, Brian Lenihan personally. I would not exert pressure on him in that regard, nor would my colleagues.'

He clearly thought that Lenihan was going to resign voluntarily. They met again after lunch. 'This time Mr Haughey was pushing resignation harder than before,' Lenihan noted. 'He handed me a three page prepared resignation statement.'

Brian promised to give Charlie his answer before five o'clock. When he did it was a refusal. 'If I resigned, my credibility and reputation would be destroyed,' Lenihan felt.

That evening Ahern and Pádraig Flynn were sent to persuade him, but he refused to meet them. At that point, Haughey had apparently resigned himself to the idea that the government would fall, because he did not believe that he could weather the storm within the party if he sacked Lenihan, but then came word of a poll to be published in the *Irish Independent* next day.

The survey found that Lenihan was trailing very badly, with just 31% support against 51% for Mary Robinson. Faced with such figures, it was obvious that fighting a general election so that Lenihan could retain his job would be extremely risky, and there is nothing more likely to concentrate the minds of politicians than the possibility of losing their seats. When the Fianna Fáil parliamentary party met next morning Charlie found that it would be safe to dump Lenihan. The meeting expressed confidence in the Taoiseach to do as he thought fit. Word was passed to the Progressive Democrats that Lenihan would be given the choice of resigning or being dismissed.

The drama was being played out behind the scenes as the Dáil debate on the no confidence motion began. Charlie took the offensive. 'I would rather, any day, have Brian Lenihan who would, for whatever reason, give an impulsive inaccurate version of something that happened eight years ago, than a group of Fine Gael conspirators who, with a cold ruthless determination, planned to trap and destroy a decent man,' he said. 'There is not the slightest doubt that Brian Lenihan did not speak to President Hillery on the telephone on that night of January 27, 1982. In fact, President Hillery did not speak on the telephone to anyone in Fianna Fáil that night. The Tánaiste was carefully set up by Fine Gael, with the willing collaboration of a Fine Gael activist, in a way that breached the ethics of research.'

Charlie was personally stung by the recent accusations that he had actually threatened the army officer at the Aras over the telephone that night. This was something that only came out during the latest controversy. The opposition was charging that this was a criminal offence and should be investigated. 'My father was an army officer,' Charlie declared, his voice vibrating with emotion. 'I myself have been an officer in the defence forces. I was brought up to believe in the integrity of our defence forces and have the highest respect for them. I would never, and never have, insulted an army officer in any way, and I never will. I reject that allegation with contempt and I ask why is it being brought up now after eight years. Why is it being raised now and being cast at me in this way?

'The people opposite, who are making this allegation, have been in government themselves,' Charlie continued. 'They had all the records at their disposal. They knew all about the gossip and chat going on since 1982. Why did they not investigate it? They did not because they knew it was a tissue of lies and a fabrication and that is what I brand it here in this House.'

Dick Spring made a virulent speech, which many people found offensive. 'This debate is not about Brian Lenihan when it is all boiled down,' he said. 'This debate, essentially, is about the evil spirit that controls one political party in the Republic. And it is about the way in which that spirit has begun to corrupt the entire political system in our country. This is a debate about greed for office, about disregard for truth, and about contempt for political standards. It is a debate about the way in which a once great party has been brought to its knees by the grasping acquisitiveness of its leader. It is ultimately a debate about the cancer that is eating away at our body politic – and the virus which has caused that cancer, An Taoiseach Charles J. Haughey.'

Shortly after six o'clock Lenihan telephoned Charlie. It was a short call lasting little over a minute. At the outset Charlie asked if he intended to resign.

'No,' Lenihan replied.

'It would have helped your campaign you know.'

'We'll agree to differ on that.'

'Brian Lenihan has been a friend, a loyal and trusted colleague with whom I have served in the Dáil for well over a quarter of a century,' Charlie told the Dáil minutes later. 'Most people in this House will understand that what I have to do I do with great sadness and great sorrow.' Lenihan had failed to comply with the request for his resignation. 'Accordingly,' Charlie added, 'I propose to exercise my constitutional prerogative and advise the president to terminate his appointment as a member of the government.'

'Charlie won't be able to live with this,' Chris Glennon of the *Irish Independent* was told by a seasoned backbencher, who predicted that the Boss would 'probably stand down in a few months'.

Charlie was castigated for abandoning his old friend, but in this instance he really had little choice. He made mistakes in the affair, but his biggest mistakes were not that he did not give Brian enough support, but that he overstepped the bounds of propriety in the way in which he supported him – by his attacks on Garret FitzGerald and Duffy, as well as his statement to the press at Dublin airport.

Lenihan had put his own personal considerations before the government, and the party. It was he who got into the mess. He really had only himself to blame, but he tried to blame a whole range of people from Charlie, to FitzGerald, to Duffy and the *Irish Times*. His subsequent explanation about being on strong drugs and not remembering the Duffy interview was both plausible and believable, but his real problem was in denying that calls had been made to the Aras in the first place. There would have been no controversy had he told the truth on *Questions and Answers*.

There was nothing wrong about informing the president that Fianna Fáil was ready to form a government. If Fine Gael were contending that Paddy Hillery was incapable of making an independent decision after talking to anyone, that would have been even more insulting than trying to contact him.

Lenihan's dismissal provoked a strong reaction from the grassroots of the party and a great wave of support for him. He began to regain lost ground by leaps and bounds and might even have turned about the election had it not been for some unfortunate remarks by Pádraig Flynn during a radio programme on which he seemed to question Mary Robinson's suitability as a wife and a mother. That put paid to whatever chance Lenihan had. He did head the poll with 44.1% of the vote, against Mary Robinson's 38.9% but she got 76.7% of Austin Currie's transfers to win by over 86,500 votes. For the first time in the history of the state, Fianna Fáil had failed to get its man into the presidency.

Tension ran high within the party afterwards, but the expected challenge to Charlie's leadership never materialised. It was not until a year later in the midst of a series of business scandals that an attempt was made to topple him and then Brian Lenihan was among the first to come out openly in support of the man who had fired him.

In May 1991 when the *World in Action* programme highlighted alleged abuses of the beef intervention system by Larry Goodman's companies, the Progressive Democrats demanded a judicial inquiry. A similar demand the previous year had been denied by the Fianna Fáil government, but now the party was in coalition and Charlie had no choice. He conceded.

At the time he was riding high in the polls, enjoying a 56% favourable rating. Although his popularity was running well ahead of his party, he was nevertheless blamed by many people when Fianna Fáil fared comparatively badly in both the local and European elections the following month. And things went further wrong in the early autumn with the eruption of a whole series of financial controversies, beginning with the Greencore scandal.

In 1987 the Irish Sugar Company – or Greencore as it would become known following privatisation in 1991 – gave an interest-free loan of £1 million to four of its executives in order to purchase a shareholding in Sugar Distributors. Eleven months later Irish Sugar bought their shareholding for over £8 million – a profit of over £7 million in just eleven months for a mere personal outlay of £10,000 each.

When the whole transaction came to light at the beginning of September 1991, Chris Comerford, the company's chief executive, was persuaded to retire from Greencore, but not before negotiating a golden handshake worth about £1.5 for himself. News of this exacerbated the public outrage, and gradually a whole series of different business scandals came to the fore.

Questions were quickly raised about transactions regarding the acquisition of a new headquarters site for Telecom Éireann as well as the purchase of the old teachers' training college at Carysfort as a graduate business school for University College, Dublin. There were also controversies over a sewer pipe laid through Charlie's estate in Kinsealy, the spending of over £166,000 by the Electricity Supply Board on wind experiments on his island off the south-west coast, and the leaking of information to a company partly owned by one of Charlie's sons.

The Telecom controversy arose following reports that Michael Smurfit, the chairman of the board of Telecom Éireann, had a financial stake in United Property Holdings (UPH), which once owned the building purchased for a new headquarters for Telecom Éireann. He had a 10% share in UPH, a property development company mainly owned by Dermot Desmond, the founder and chief executive of National City Brokers (NCB), which had handled the privatisation of Greencore and had recently been retained to advise on the privatisation of Telecom Éireann. UPH had purchased the controversial site for £4.4 million and then sold shortly afterwards for £6.4 million. Dermot Desmond helped Hoddle Investments to acquire the building, which was then sold to Telecom for £9.4 million. It had more than doubled in price at a time when property values were actually dropping.

Examining the various business controversies is beyond the scope of this study, except in as much as Charlie was dragged into the story. He was known to have been friendly with people like Goodman, Desmond, Smurfit and Bernie Cahill, who was not only the chairman of the board of Greencore but also of Aer Lingus and Feltrim, a mining company largely owned by Charlie's son, Conor. These people were part of what was being called the Golden Circle – a group of top businessmen for whom the government seemed particularly facilitory.

As top businessmen with proven track records in having vitalised their companies, they were probably the country's best Irish hope of providing extra employment. Hence it was natural that the Taoiseach should have extensive contacts with them. Nevertheless he appeared to try to distance himself from them in his latest radio interview.

Desmond was just a 'business friend' as opposed to a 'personal friend', Charlie contended. He proceeded to call on him, Smurfit, and Seamus Páircéir, the chief executive of UPH and chairman of the Custom House Docks Authority, 'to stand aside' while the various controversies were being investigated. In each instance he was careful to stress that he was not implying that any one of them had done anything wrong. 'I say all that without any implication, the slightest scintilla or suggestion that there is anything wrong,' he emphasised.

Nine years earlier he had been roundly denounced for not asking the attorney-general to step aside when the MacArthur affair broke. Now that he was asking these people to stand aside, he was castigated because he did not forewarn them of his intention. No matter what he did, his opponents were going to criticise him for doing the wrong thing.

Next day he was drawn further into the growing list of controversies when Nora Owen of Fine Gael raised questions about a sewer pipe that had recently been laid through his Kinsealy estate by Dublin

County Council, reportedly to service some nearby cottages. The work, which cost £78,000, had been deemed unnecessary by the council in 1985; so there were therefore some legitimate questions that needed to be answered. But Owen proceeded to hype up the affair in the Dáil by charging that this was not the first time that Charlie had been involved in this kind of controversy.

'After all, hasn't he experienced this before on his landholding on the outskirts of Dublin in the Donaghmede area in the late 1960s?' she said. 'In that instance, rumours and stories abound of undue pressure put on corporation engineers to extend pipes on to his land. Whether or not these rumours or allegations are true, the facts speak for themselves. The Taoiseach's former land was rezoned, thereby greatly inflating the value of the land, and many hundreds of houses are now built on that land. One can be forgiven for sensing a touch of *déjà vu!*'

The controversy over Charlie's land, which had been an election issue in 1969, had initially been prompted by charges that he had supposedly benefited from recent tax legislation introduced by himself, but that charge was convincingly discredited at the time. There were also intimations that there was something immoral about the way the value of the property had appreciated from £50,000 to a little over £200,000 in just ten years, but while that kind of jump in value seemed extreme in relation to previous decades, it was actually quite modest when compared to either of the next two decades.

The controversy surrounding the land had nothing to do with extending pipes in 1969. It seemed that rumours were growing with time. Yet nobody in the media challenged Owen's extravagant claims, which were reproduced *verbatim* in the *Sunday Tribune*, even though she did not cite one shred of evidence to support them.

A further controversy followed after the disclosure that NCB had fouled up after being commissioned in 1986 to do some work for Irish Helicopters, a subsidiary of Aer Lingus. A report containing confidential information supplied to NCB by the Aer Lingus subsidiary was mailed to a rival firm, Celtic Helicopters. Due to a postal error, however, the material was delivered to Irish Helicopters. That had been resolved quietly between the various companies some time ago, but suddenly it became the subject of public controversy, no doubt because Celtic Helicopters was partly owned by Charlie's son, Ciarán.

'The Taoiseach must say if he had any hand in inducing Mr Desmond of NCB to attempt to pass on this information to his son's company,' John Bruton demanded under the protection of Dáil privilege.

As a result the media were able to highlight the affair in a way that suggested that the whole thing may have been the result of Desmond's friendship with the Haugheys. It was ironic that NCB had actually been hired while the FitzGerald government was in power. There was no evidence that Desmond was personally involved, but this did not deter Bruton or the media. Some of them asked whimsically if Charlie – having redefined his friendship with Desmond – was about to re-define his relationship with his son, Ciarán.

When controversy erupted over the purchase of Carysfort, Charlie insisted that the place had been bought at the instigation of the UCD authorities. 'UCD proposed to us that they acquire Carysfort,' he emphasised during his radio interview on 22 September. 'UCD carried out an examination of Carysfort through their own mechanism and decided that the asking price for it was great value.'

'Was the UCD approach perhaps made at the prompting of the government?' he was asked.

'No,' Charlie replied. 'Certainly not.'

The government was criticised for not buying Carysfort when it was offered for sale in August 1989. The asking price then was £8.5 million. The chance was passed up then, but the government provided the money for UCD to buy the college twelve months later for £8 million. In the process £500,000 was saved on the asking price. In other walks of life, those responsible might be complimented, but not in politics. Even when the government gets something right, the opposition will inevitably complain on some pretext or other. In this instance the government was accused of not acting fast enough.

Carysfort was sold for £6.25 million to an individual business-man, Pino Harris. Critics insinuated that the government could have bought it for that price. But would the owners have sold it to the government for the same price? After all the price dropped because the government was not interested. In such dealings people frequently wonder if they might have done better with other tactics, and this case was little different, except that the opposition introduced what might be called the sleaze factor.

On previous occasions some elements of the media would have come to Charlie's defence by pointing out the inconsistencies in the arguments of his opponents. Even during the GUBU period of 1982 when even some of his harshest critics – people like Geraldine Kennedy and Vincent Browne – accepted that the media had been unfair to him, there were a number of editors from whom Charlie could at least expect a sympathetic hearing – people like Douglas Gageby of the *Irish Times*, Tim Pat Coogan of the *Irish Press* and Michael Hand of the *Sunday Independent*.

Gageby had insisted on balancing his newspaper's political comments by employing John Healy as a regular columnist. But when Gageby retired, Healy left the *Irish Times* following the appointment of a new editor, Conor Brady, who had been in charge of *The Sunday Tribune* during the GUBU period. Since then there had also been a major shake up in the Irish Press group, now headed by Vincent Jennings, who had caused a sensation in 1982 with his signed editorial in the *Sunday Press* castigating Charlie following the Dublin West by-election defeat. There was no longer any national editor sympathetic to Charlie, with the result that critical stories found a more ready access to the news columns. This naturally complicated an already difficult political situation for him.

When four Fianna Fáil backbenchers issued a joint statement criticising Charlie on 27 September, they received extensive national publicity. Had 24 backbenchers come out in a similar way in support of him, their actions would probably not have received nearly as much coverage as the four who were critical of him. Indeed, only the previous weekend *The Sunday Tribune* had a banner front page headline: 'Fianna Fáil backbenchers want Haughey to resign as leader'. This was the lead for a story about a survey of 51 backbench deputies by the newspaper on the leadership question. Twenty-four indicated Haughey should stay, and 13 indicated he should go, while the remainder refused to comment. Had only two deputies called for Charlie's resignation, the headline would have been technically correct, but there could be little doubt that it was misleading.

Distortions could be found not only in misleading headlines and the way in which undue prominence was given to critical reports, but also in the biased analyses of political commentators, as well as the uncritical reporting of unsupported – and sometimes unsustainable – accusations made by opponents.

The publication of Garret FitzGerald's autobiography in the midst of the scandals also hurt Charlie. As the first autobiography published by any former Taoiseach, it attracted enormous media attention and comparisons were inevitably made in which Charlie was depicted in a less than flattering light.

When Garret appeared on the *Late Late Show*, for instance, there were a number of pointed references by people in the audience alluding to Charlie's 'lust for power', and the mysterious way that he had 'acquired enormous wealth'. Although his name was never actually mentioned, there was no doubt that those people were referring to him, and their snide insinuations on the most popular Irish television programme had an insidious impact by subtly projecting an air of unspeakable sleaziness.

In response to a question from Gay Byrne, Garret explained that his 'flawed pedigree' remark in 1979 had been taken out of context. He was merely observing that questions had been raised about Charlie that had never been raised about any of his six predecessors.

In his life time de Valera had been blamed for starting the civil war and for deliberately prolonging it. In addition, he was accused of being directly involved in the killing of Michael Collins. Yet by implication, Charlie was now being accused of worse. In a veiled allusion to the Carysfort controversy, Garret complained that the government's decision had been taken without any cabinet memorandum on the subject. This, he depicted, as a complete departure from normal procedure, even though his own government had actually acquired the old School of Engineering from UCD without presenting a memorandum to the cabinet. It was FitzGerald's government which had initiated the move to acquire a new office for the Taoiseach. But Charlie had been pilloried ever since he moved in earlier in the year, because the whole thing had cost so much at a time when hospital wards were being closed throughout the country due to financial constraints.

An official from the Department of Finance produced a report suggesting that changing the plans should cut costs. Among the changes proposed was the scrapping of plans for a fountain in front of the building. Haughey would not hear of the suggestions. 'Shred them,' he told one of his aides. 'And the official who made the suggestions.'

The aide did not understand what he meant of about the official who drew up the report.

'You can fucking shred him, too!' Haughey explained.

A very impressive job was done on the office building, which was variously dubbed the 'Taj Mahaughey' and the 'Chas Mahal'. Charlie was disappointed to find, however, that toilet for his office was not en suite. He had to go out in the hall to gain access, and, worse, the toilet was not heated. When he complained, an official of the Office of Public Works told him that the radiators in the hall would heat the toilet. 'There you are,' Charlie said, flipping the key on the desk in front of him. 'Try it on the way out, and I hope it freezes the balls off you.'

Many of the accusations being made against Charlie could just as easily have been directed against Fine Gael. At the centre of most was the implication that his friends had ripped off the state and that they would never have had the opportunity, if it were not for his friendship with them. This involved all kinds of unwarranted assumptions. No evidence had been produced that Bernie Cahill or Michael Smurfit had personally done anything wrong. Moreover, it should be noted that both had been appointed to their public positions by FitzGerald's government. In addition, the fraudulent claims made by the Goodman company for export credit subsidies had been made while Fitz-Gerald was in power. His Minister for Agriculture, Austin Deasy, had actually helped to set up the Egyptian deal involved in the initial fraud, though of course there is no evidence nor would we suggest Deasy was aware that the Goodman company was going to engage in any fraud. It should also be noted that Dermot Desmond's company was first hired as a consultant by Aer Lingus, while Jim Mitchell of Fine Gael was the relevant minister. Of course, it would be grossly unfair to ac-cuse any of the Fine Gael ministers of wrong doing in these matters, and it was just as unfair to make such accusations against Charlie.

In Irish society people are entitled to a presumption of innocence, but now virtually all of the media were presuming Charlie's guilt and ignoring all other possibilities. If Fine Gael people were guilty, they would have had a vested interest in setting Charlie up as a scapegoat. Likewise, if businessmen in the so-called 'golden circle' had been rip-ping off the country, they would have had good reason to get him out so they could have his successor play down the scandals on the pretext that the man responsible had been ousted and further publicity would be damaging to the country.

The media people should have stuck to the facts and not allowed themselves to be stampeded into a highly personalised campaign. In-stead of presenting an unbiased account of events, they went whoring after false demons. 'The scandals that broke in the summer of 1991 were ones unconnected with him, but once the publicity dam burst, much mud hitherto retained behind the barrier of libel laws and media discretion burst out, and engulfed him,' Garret FitzGerald admitted within hours of Charlie's decision to retire in January 1992. It seemed that even he believed the Taoiseach was an innocent victim of the business scandals.

Charlie was essentially tried and convicted by the media without a shred of firm evidence against him. In a review of the year, Gerald

Barry, the political correspondent of *The Sunday Tribune*, noted that 'no single piece of directly incriminatory evidence has been produced against the Taoiseach'. But the media treated the absence of hard evidence as if it were an irrelevant technicality.

In the Carysfort controversy Charlie and the government were initially condemned for not acting fast enough – for not purchasing the college when it was first put up for sale. Later, when they did act, they were accused of moving too fast and not going through the normal bureaucratic procedures. In short, they were too slow and too hasty. In other walks of life the critics would be told they must pick one or the other, but the media was quite prepared to allow Charlie's opponents to have it both ways.

He opened the confidence debate in the Dáil with a strong defence of his government on 16 October. 'Irish political life is going through a traumatic period with many disturbing features,' he said. The 'disclosure of reprehensible behaviour of a small number' of businessmen had been 'added to, hyped up and exaggerated by a massive campaign of vilification and character assassination of unprecedented intensity without regard to evidence, proof or justification.

'We have had a campaign of personalised attack by way of unfounded allegation, innuendo, accusations of guilt by association and all the other traditional despicable weapons of such campaign,' he continued. 'The object of the campaign was nothing less than to undermine and destabilise this government and to damage the credibility of individual members, particularly myself.'

The purchase of Carysfort was 'an entirely praiseworthy and progressive step,' he maintained. 'The transaction was carried out in a perfectly straightforward manner and I was not involved in it. I gave it my full support.'

'I think you gave it more than support,' Ruairí Quinn said.

'I defy the deputy to prove anything of that kind,' Charlie snapped back.

Before the debate was even over, however, Mary O'Rourke, the Minister for Education, admitted that she had made the initial approach in the matter to the president of UCD on her own initiative. But Charlie had played a more active role than even she realised. He actually had a couple of private meetings with the head of the UCD School of Business to discuss the acquisition.

Some opponents charged that there was no need for the state to subvent UCD in the whole matter, because arrangements had already been made with business interests to have a graduate business school built at no cost to the taxpayer. Ultimately, of course, the taxpayer would probably have ended up paying an awful lot more, if only by way of taking up the shortfall as a result of tax concessions given to the businessmen. Building a new graduate school from scratch would undoubtedly have cost considerably more than the £9.7 millions that it cost the state to purchase and renovate Carysfort. Moreover it would have been a disgraceful waste of resources, both financial and physical.

On the basis of the evidence produced, Charlie's biggest mistake in the whole Carysfort controversy was his denial that the government had taken the initiative. He should have admitted it. Indeed, he could have been proud of the fact that he had sliced through the bureaucratic red tape.

When Fianna Fáil and the Progressive Democrats went into coalition, it was decided that their programme for government would be renegotiated after two years, and the Progressive Democrats were now threatening to withdraw their support if agreement was not reached before a vote of confidence was taken.

There had been intermittent negotiations throughout the summer and an agreement had appeared imminent when Albert Reynolds walked out of the talks and balked at some final concessions. Charlie had apparently been prepared to concede those, with the result that Reynolds was credited with forcing the Progressive Democrats to back down when they gave in on some of the Fianna Fáil demands at the eleventh hour.

Although the government then survived the confidence motion, there were rumours in Leinster House that Reynolds would lead a heave against Charlie for the leadership of Fianna Fáil within a week. The plan was for Reynolds, Ahern and Flynn go to him and ask for his retirement. If he refused, as expected, they would show him a motion of no-confidence that they would table for the next parliamentary party meeting.

Charlie was worried enough to hold extensive consultations. 'Why are they trying to humiliate me?' he asked.

Ahern advised him on 22 October to indicate that he had a retirement date in mind. Charlie heeded the advice.

Next day he appealed at the weekly meeting of the parliamentary party to be allowed to quit the leadership with dignity at a time of his own choosing. He talked about a 'time frame' for his departure. He gave deputies to believe that he wished to complete a scheduled meeting with Prime Minister John Major of Britain in December and attend the EC summit at Maastricht later in the month, as well as oversee the introduction of the budget in January.

'I will know when it is time to step down,' he said.

It was all reminiscent of his appeal to a similar meeting on 27 January 1983. As then, his remarks were interpreted as an indication that he intended to go in the near future, and as on the previous occasion, Ray Burke openly said that he believed that Charlie was about to step down. Ahern assured deputies that the Taoiseach would go after completing his political agenda, but the Reynolds camp saw the appeal as a sign of weakness. Charlie was mortally wounded and supporters of Reynolds were moving in for the political kill, just as Charlie would do himself in similar circumstances.

They argued that it would be best if he were forced out before there were any more damaging disclosures, but Reynolds was being out-manoeuvred by Charlie. Deputies were moved by his private entreaties to be allowed to go with dignity and not to be kicked out ignominiously after thirty-five years of service to the party.

There was similarities with events leading up to the abortive heave by O'Malley in February 1982. Deputies who had privately expressed a desire for change began to waver, and Ahern now seemed to be playing the role that Martin O'Donoghue had played in calling on O'Malley not to go through with the challenge almost ten years earlier. Ahern told Reynolds that he would not back a heave at this time.

'He brought us right up to the brink,' one Reynolds supporter complained, 'and then he opted out'.

Friday, 25 October, was to be the day for the challenge. When Charlie went to open a new shopping centre in his constituency that morning, he looked like a very worried man. His voice quivered with emotion as he began to address the gathering.

'It's always good to be among your own when the going gets tough,' he said. Everyone knew what he meant when he said that this was likely to be one of the more pleasant duties he would have to perform that day. If Reynolds challenged him, he was obviously going to have to call for his resignation, but Reynolds lost his nerve. He announced that the challenge was being shelved to give Charlie an 'honourable time frame' to complete his political agenda.

'I am not interested in any way in bitter divisions opening up within Fianna Fáil,' Reynolds said. 'I have long experience and sharp memories of that situation and I want no part of it ever again'. It was like an echo of what Des O'Malley had said when he talked to the press after calling off his challenge on 25 February 1982.

After the O'Malley heave collapsed in February 1982, Charlie was given a breathing space of some seven months before the McCreevy challenge, but this time he was not even given two weeks. By the following Wednesday he was back in the middle of a political storm.

The previous week he had indignantly refuted an intimation by Dick Spring that Bernie Cahill had not been asked to step aside from Greencore because he had too much on Charlie. Dick contended that it was Charlie who suggested to Cahill that NCB and his friend Pat O'Connor should be appointed as advisers to Greencore on its privatisation.

'I reject that with contempt,' Charlie replied. 'That is totally untrue and it does the deputy no credit to make those sort of unfounded allegations. I suggest to him on that score that he too await the outcome of the present investigation when he will find –'

'The Taoiseach had no meeting?' Dick interjected.

'I had no meetings. I suggest to him on that score that he too await the outcome of the present investigations when he will find that he will owe me an apology.' At the end of a further exchange, Charlie reaffirmed that 'no such meeting took place'.

It quickly became apparent, however, that he had met Cahill and there was evidence to prove that on 26 May 1990 Cahill had flown by helicopter from his home in West Cork to Kinsealy. What was more the Irish Sugar Company had paid for the trip. Cahill admitted this at an extraordinary general meeting of Greencore shareholders on Wednesday, 30 October. At this meeting, he said, he showed Charlie the list of companies from which a stockbroker would be chosen to advise on Greencore's privatisation, but denied 'any undue pressure' had been put on him to support the appointment of NCB. It was already on the list. Although pressed a number of times, he persistently side-stepped questions about whether Charlie had actually recommended NCB.

Many people thought that Cahill's confirmation was proof that the Taoiseach had lied to the Dáil, but Charlie denied this. 'I did not say, as is now being suggested, that I had no meetings with Mr Bernard Cahill,' he explained. 'What I said was that no meeting of the kind suggested by Deputy Spring took place.'

In the context of his initial remarks, however, what Charlie had initially denied was the suggestion that he had recommended the appointment of NCB to Cahill. If he had, so what? Charlie was Taoiseach and there was nothing wrong with recommending the best people for any position. Politicians of all parties regularly make representations on behalf of people or companies. So long as no undue pressure was applied, there was absolutely nothing wrong with making recommendations, and Cahill had confirmed there was no undue pressure in this instance. But Haughey's behaviour reeked of gross impropriety against the backdrop of essentially accepting a so-called interest free loan worth £75,546 from Dermot Desmond of NCB to refurbish his yacht. Charlie was seriously compromised by his acceptance of this loan.

As with the Carysfort controversy, Charlie had walked into trouble by denying involvement with Cahill. Whether he had actually lied may be open to question, but there was no doubt that he had deliberately tried to mislead the Dáil.

In the past this kind of dispute in the Dáil would have been quickly forgotten, but now there were television cameras in the chamber. The earlier part of his initial remarks, where he denied meeting Cahill, had been shown that night on television and were now repeated. Taken by themselves, these seemed conclusive that Charlie was saying that he had not met Cahill, but he did indeed subsequently qualify his initial denial by stipulating that there had been 'no such meeting'.

Deputies know that the use of a word like 'such' is pregnant with significance. But he should have remembered that he was going into homes all over the country through the medium of television. His subtle nuance had not been included in the edited highlights. Whether or not deputies had actually been fooled, there is no doubt that the viewing public was deceived, especially by the edited highlights. As a result there was further speculation about a heave within Fianna Fáil. It was ironic that such a fuss should have been kicked up over this affair. Charlie had been misleading the whole country between 1983 and 1987 with his criticism of health cuts, the Hillsborough Agreement and the Single European Act, and most of the party had gladly gone along with him.

Now, however, Charlie McCreevy challenged Haughey to ask for a vote of confidence in his leadership at the next parliamentary party meeting, but the challenge was brushed aside as the Taoiseach took the offensive by suggesting that Spring was deliberately deflecting attention from the Greencore scandal by his attacks on the government.

P. J. Mara then pulled a little stunt on Charlie's behalf. He set the press up by suggesting that Spring had been associated with the property developer Pat Doherty, who claimed to be the principal owner of Hoddle Investments, the company which ultimately sold the controversial building to Telecom Éireann. 'If we are going into guilt by association,' P. J. told reporters, 'one of the things that will emerge in the Dáil will be the association between Mr Pat Doherty and Mr Dick Spring.' He was very careful with what he had to say. In order that there would be no confusion, he actually read the single sentence from a piece of paper.

The press swallowed the bait, hook, line and sinker. The whole thing made front page headlines suggesting that Charlie believed he had the dirt on Dick, who was worried enough to go scurrying through his diaries.

The ruse worked. The press turned the spotlight on Spring, though there was nothing to the whole thing. Doherty announced that Dick had once been introduced to him at a function in the Irish embassy in London, but he doubted that the Kerryman even remembered the introduction.

Charlie was making no apologies. He asked how many questions the opposition would have tabled, if somebody had told the press that the Taoiseach had once met Pat Doherty. Nobody needed to answer that!

The media were outraged. They had been made to look stupid. Charlie was accused of misleading the people and Mara was denounced for 'acting as a professional character assassin'.

Next day, Seán Power – one of the 'gang of four' backbench dissidents who had criticised Charlie back in September – proposed a formal motion calling for Charlie's removal as leader at the next meeting of the Fianna Fáil parliamentary party. Reynolds announced his support of the motion next day The sense of drama was heightened as Reynolds was about to be interviewed on RTÉ television's evening news. Gerard Collins seemed near to tears during an interview in the Dáil studio. He accused Albert of 'frightful political immaturity' and made an emotional appeal to him not to go through with the challenge. 'You will wreck our party right down the centre and burst up the government,' Collins said.

This had been the first real political crisis since the introduction of television cameras in the Dáil. The highlights in recent days had been depicting a most unruly setting with politicians trying to score cheap points off each other. On top of all this came the tear-jerking appeal by Collins. The whole thing was beginning to look like a bad political play in which ham actors were turning a tragedy into a farce.

'For some time now there has been considerable political instability, which has led to an erosion of confidence in our democratic institutions,' Reynolds declared. 'This uncertainty must not be allowed to continue.' He added that the country needed 'strong and decisive leadership', with the result that he would be supporting the motion.

As Article 28 of the country's constitution enshrines the concept of collective cabinet responsibility, Albert should have resigned from the government. When he did not, Charlie was obliged to ask for his resignation, but Reynolds refused. The Taoiseach therefore asked the president to remove him.

Albert was apparently hoping his dismissal would provoke the kind of sympathy that Lenihan received a year earlier. Pádraig Flynn followed the same path in forcing Charlie to have the president dismiss him after coming out in support of Power's motion, but eleven other ministers came out strongly for Charlie, as did Brian Lenihan.

On Friday, the eve of the parliamentary party meeting, Charlie gave an extended lunchtime interview on RTÉ radio. He denounced the whole thing as a 'power grab'.

'When Albert talks about political stability and wishing to avoid political instability that seems to be very much like a bookie complaining about gambling,' he said. 'This is just a new type of campaign directed, I believe, quite simply, not so much at getting rid of me, as a campaign to install Albert Reynolds as Taoiseach.'

It was ironic that Charlie's opponents should be turning to Albert. After all he was one of 'the gang of five' who claimed credit for pushing Jack Lynch and organising Charlie's rise to power in 1979. Indeed it would seem that he was more than just one of the gang, seeing that he was only one of the five who was immediately appointed to the cabinet.

Reynolds appeared to be moving with a precipitate haste by being unwilling to await the results of the various investigations. His supporters argued that it was necessary to get Charlie out before there were any more embarrassing disclosures. Everyone expected political sparks from the Beef tribunal, but Reynolds was liable to be dragged into that himself in a way that would raise questions about his much vaunted fiscal prowess. This may well have had something to do with his impatience. It was a case of now or never.

Financial mistakes had undoubtedly been made by the Haughey government, but the biggest mistake of all was probably the re-introduction of export insurance on beef exports to Iraq after these had been suspended by the FitzGerald government. This monumental blunder could cost the state well over £100 million and Albert was the individual minister responsible for its re-introduction. When the money involved in all the other scandals was added together, it amounted to only a fraction of the state's potential exposure under the Export Credit scheme.

The media seemed to be touting Reynolds on his own terms without even questioning his overall record, which was distinguished more for its style than its substance. He had avoided taking a stand on a whole range of issues – on contraception, education, divorce, women's affairs, or even Northern Ireland. He had nothing to say in the debates on some of the most momentous issues of the past decade – the Pro-Life Amendment, the Anglo-Irish Agreement, the Divorce Referendum, and the Single European Act. Most of his political contributions had been confined to economic and financial matters.

By the eve of the parliamentary party meeting on 9 November Charlie was confident enough to have his own people put forward an amendment calling for a vote of confidence in his leadership, which was something he had pointedly refused to do when challenged by McCreevy earlier in the week. The media, which had been predicting his demise suddenly began to hedge. Having got it wrong so often in the past, the political pundits did not actually write off him this time. They said he might survive in an open vote, but he would be defeated in an secret ballot.

The first part of the parliamentary party meeting was taken up with a procedural debate on whether the vote on the motion should be secret or open. Haughey's opponents contended that it should be secret, as he had been elected by secret ballot. He had also had his position confirmed by secret vote during the last heave in February 1983.

Charlie argued that he was in opposition the last time. When he had been in government at the time of the McCreevy motion, it had been by open vote, which Reynolds and Flynn had supported.

The public was bombarded with cliches about democracy and the secret ballot. But surely it was not in the interest of democracy to facilitate gutless politicians who lacked the integrity to stand up for their own beliefs. A secret vote on the leadership issue would have been patently undemocratic in this instance. While it is vital that people should have a secret vote in choosing their representatives, it is equally important that the representatives should then vote openly so the people can assess how they are being represented. This is why all votes in the Dáil are taken openly.

After more than three hours of debate, the party voted openly by 44 to 33 for a roll call vote on the actual motion. Thereafter the eventual outcome was a virtual foregone conclusion.

When the meeting reconvened after a short break Reynolds was among the first to speak. He complained that 'disinformation' had been circulated about him. There was an unfounded story, for instance, that Larry Goodman had loaned him £150,000 to keep one of his business interests afloat. In addition, he said that 'a very prominent businessman' from Dublin had been investigating his business dealings going back to the late 1950s. His home in Longford had been under surveillance by people in a white Hiace van, and somebody had been acting suspiciously near his Dublin apartment.

Jim Tunney, the chairman of the parliamentary party, proposed a committee be set up to investigate the charges. This was agreed. Reynolds, John Wilson and Tunney being selected.

The atmosphere was electric as Albert went on to accuse Charlie of instigating the campaign of disinformation through the government information service, because of the rumours that Reynolds was preparing to challenge for the leadership. He denied that he was making a grab for power. Indeed, having lost the procedural vote, he clearly recognised that he was now involved in a lost cause. He said that he was throwing away power because of his principles. There was a deathly silence as he wound up. 'It is enough for evil to prosper that good men do nothing,' he concluded.

The discussion on the actual motion dragged on for a further ten hours, well into the early Sunday morning. Much of the initial tension dissipated as critics were allowed the opportunity to let off steam.

Several people were critical of Haughey's arrogance. Senator Don Lydon complained that he had been summoned to the leader's office and bawled out for making a public speech on Northern Ireland without permission. Lydon said he was then contemptuously dismissed from the Taoiseach's office, but in his stunned state he could not find the door in the midst of all the new wood panelling.

After a while Haughey looked up at the bemused senator still in his office.

'What are you doing here?' he asked.

'I can't find the door, Taoiseach,' Lydon replied.

'Then why don't you jump out the fucking window?' Haughey rejoined.

If Lydon had expected the meeting to be outraged at the Taoiseach's conduct, he must have been sorely disappointed, because the meeting erupted with laughter.

Pádraig Flynn waited until after midnight to speak. He reminded the gathering that it was now a quarter of a century to the day since Charlie's father-in-law, Seán Lemass, stepped down as Taoiseach. He had been party leader for seven years. Charlie had been for almost twelve years, but he still had no intention of accepting the invitation to quit.

Before the actual vote Charlie called on his supporters to ensure that there would be no triumphalism. He clearly did not want a repetition of the disgraceful scenes outside the Dáil in the aftermath of the McCreevy motion in October 1982.

As expected the vote on the amendment expressing confidence in Charlie's leadership was easily carried by 55 votes to 22. There was no triumphalism on the part of Charlie's supporters, but there was a disingenuous display by his ousted opponents congratulating themselves for supposedly standing on principle. 'I made the ultimate sacrifice to be able to be free to go into the parliamentary party and say what I wanted to say and to vote no confidence in Mr Haughey,' Reynolds declared on returning to his constituency. 'Everybody can take their own message out of that.'

If principle had been the motivating factor, however, surely he would have gone ahead with his challenge a fortnight earlier. His timing and tactics suggested that his move had more to do with ambition and poor political judgment. There was not even that modicum of self-sacrifice which should have required him to resign from the cabinet rather than force the Taoiseach to dismiss him in order to preserve the principle of 'collective responsibility' required by the constitution.

Charlie used the occasion of the dismissal of the two cabinet ministers to make his most extensive cabinet reshuffle of the four different governments which he had set up. Among the eight changes he announced the introduction of two new ministers – Noel Davern as Minister for Education and James McDaid as Minister for Defence. The latter's nomination provoked a storm and landed Charlie in an unprecedented controversy. Some 20 months earlier McDaid had been photographed coming out of the Four Courts with James Pius Clarke, a convicted member of the Provisional IRA. The supreme court had just ruled against a request for Clarke's extradition to Northern Ireland.

McDaid had taken a personal interest in the case because he knew that Clarke had not been involved in an attempted murder for which he had been convicted in Northern Ireland. They had both been members of the same Gaelic football club and on the night of the crime, Clarke and McDaid had both been at a stag party in Letterkenny. Under the circumstances he felt he had a moral duty to defend Clarke, but he obviously got caught up in the euphoria of the moment after the supreme court found in Clarke's favour. One of the photographs taken outside the Four Courts showed McDaid smiling broadly with his hand on Clarke's shoulder.

Neither John Bruton nor Dick Spring made any reference to the press photographs in their addresses. It was Proinsias de Rossa, the leader of the Workers' Party, who first raised the issue of McDaid's presence outside the court. This was like throwing a bone to Fine Gael wolves. Jim O'Keeffe and Michael Noonan launched into bitter attacks. The latter produced newspaper clippings of the Clarke case with a photograph of McDaid in the background. Looking directly at Des O'Malley he intimated that O'Malley should have followed George Colley's example by insisting on a veto over the appointments of Ministers for Justice and Defence before agreeing to serve in Charlie's government.

O'Malley, who had raised no objection to McDaid's appointment in advance, had not been aware of the incident outside the Four Courts. He withdrew from the chamber to read up on the Clarke case.

As the storm began to gather momentum McDaid went to Charlie's office at about 6.45 that evening. 'He said that he had expected the attack but didn't expect anything as abusive as this,' McDaid said afterwards.

The *Irish Times* took this as an admission that Charlie had been aware of the photograph before he made the nomination. But what he had actually been expecting was the normal critical reaction from the opposition. No matter whom he selected he was likely to be criticised in the charged personalised atmosphere prevailing in Leinster House, even if he had selected a member of Fine Gael.

McDaid naturally felt aggrieved. 'I explained my involvement in the James Pius Clarke case and suggested that any other TD in the same circumstances would have done the same for a constituent, especially for somebody he believed to be totally innocent,' he explained.

Charlie arranged for McDaid to meet O'Malley and Molloy. He told them what had happened and emphasised that he had no sympathy whatever for the Provisional IRA.

'I sincerely believe he is in no way supportive of the Provisional IRA or any other violent organisation,' O'Malley explained afterwards. 'But I had to say to him that he had compromised himself, unfortunately.'

Molloy, who was a former Minister for Defence, explained that somebody wishing to join the army as a mere private would not be accepted, if he had been photographed with members of the IRA.

'You didn't have to be a psychiatrist to realise that they were having a major problem with the situation,' McDaid admitted. 'They made it clear that in any other portfolio, except Justice, there would have been no problem at all.

'Making a long story short,' McDaid continued, 'when I was going out the door I was under no illusion but that they could not see to my appointment.'

He went back and reported what had happened to Charlie, who said that he would talk to the Progressive Democrats again himself. McDaid then withdrew to his own office to prepare a statement for the Dáil to explain his involvement in the Clarke case.

'It was at that point I made my mind up there was never going to be any peace for me in the role of Minister for Defence and took the decision to go into the chamber and announce my withdrawal,' he explained. 'I went back to the Taoiseach and told him. He agreed my decision was the correct one and I went into the chamber.'

Before McDaid could make his statement, however, he had to endure a vitriolic attack from the Fine Gael spokesperson on defence, Madeline Taylor-Quinn. 'I wonder now, given the proposed appointment,' she asked at one point, 'will the terrorist organisations of this country be privy to very secret matters?'

There was utter indignation in the Dáil. The word was already out that McDaid was withdrawing, but Taylor-Quinn had not yet heard it. Her attack added considerable insult to the injury already felt on the Fianna Fáil side.

McDaid made a dignified statement: 'In view of the attacks made on me and to avoid the slightest suspicion, however unwarranted, attaching to the Minister for Defence, and in the broader national interest, I have requested the Taoiseach to withdraw my nomination as a member of the government.'

There was outrage on the Fianna Fáil benches. People had never before seen such indignation in the chamber. Many deputies demanded a meeting of the parliamentary party the following morning. Charlie was willing, but Jim Tunney realised that time was needed to allow tempers to cool, as such a meeting would be much too divisive in the circumstances.

Charlie undoubtedly made a mistake in selecting McDaid for his Minister for Defence. He essentially admitted as much himself the following day when he said that it would not have been 'appropriate, in the circumstances, to proceed with the appointment.'

There is no room in that sensitive ministry for even the slightest suspicion of any kind of ambiguity towards the Provisional IRA. McDaid had compromised himself outside the Four Courts, though not to the extent of justifying the deluge of invective, some of which was a flagrant abuse of parliamentary privilege. He had been a victim of clear character assassination.

Only a week earlier John Bruton had caused uproar in the Dáil with his accusations that P. J. Mara was a character assassin, because of his little ruse over Dick Spring's supposed association with Pat Doherty. Yet what P. J. did in that instance was very mild in comparison to the conduct of Fine Gael representatives in McDaid's case. Of course, Fine Gael was not really going after McDaid at all. The whole thing was part of the on-going effort to gut Charlie and, like the IRA, they did not give a damn whom they hurt in the process.

What was Charlie's mistake this time? That he didn't see or remember a face in the background of a photograph on the front pages more than a year earlier, neither did O'Malley, Bruton, or Spring. Charlie knew McDaid was not an IRA sympathiser, and his failure to remember the incident was therefore as understandable as it was unfortunate.

Nevertheless the whole thing did him incalculable harm. In recent months his authority was being undermined by a handful of brash, young, backbench dissidents who were shouting their mouths off in public from within his own party. They were affording critics fodder with which to berate him. The size of his vote of confidence would normally have allowed him to enforce a more rigid discipline, had he not been undermined by his blunder in the McDaid affair.

Charlie was castigated not only from the opposition benches, but also in the lobbies by members of his own party, especially Reynolds supporters who accused him of 'gross misjudgment' because of his failure to stand up to the Progressive Democrats. For them it was another case of the tail wagging the dog. Lyndon B. Johnson, the former American president, was fond of a particularly crude saying: 'When you got 'em by the balls, their hearts and minds will follow'.

The Progressive Democrats had Charlie, and when they put on the squeeze, he submitted and the Reynolds gang screamed.

DOHERTY'S DAGGER

A number of political fuses were lit at the Beef tribunal in December 1991 and the new year began with predictions that one of those would lead straight to the Taoiseach's office. Documentary evidence had been presented to the inquiry that Donal Creedon, the secretary of the Department of Agriculture, had 'advised' Charlie on 25 January 1988 of a serious fraud involving one of the Goodman companies claiming EC export subsidies. When asked in the Dáil about this fraud in the spring of 1989, Charlie declared that he had 'no official knowledge' of the matter, and he proceeded to accuse Barry Desmond, the deputy leader of the Labour party, of national sabotage for raising the question.

The fraud really had nothing to do with Fianna Fáil. It occurred before Charlie's return to power. It was an abuse by a Goodman company exaggerating weights on documents claiming EC subsidies from the Department of Agriculture. This had been detected while the Fine Gael–Labour coalition was still in government.

On 15 January 1992 Donal Creedon, told the Beef Inquiry about his conversation with the Taoiseach four years earlier. He had gone to talk to Charlie about other matters and just mentioned the fraud 'in passing' as he was being ushered out of the office, he said. The Taoiseach 'didn't register any reply, good, bad, or indifferent,' according to Creedon. 'My view is that he wanted to get rid of me as quickly as possible.'

The big news on television on that night was not Creedon's testimony, however, but a report that RTÉ's *Nighthawks* programme would be carrying an interview in which Seán Doherty, the speaker of the Seanad and former Minister for Justice, would be suggesting that other members of the cabinet had known about the tapping of journalists' telephones in 1982. Even before the programme was aired, his remarks were being hyped on news bulletins.

It was news orchestration in the most blatant form. People were being given news of forthcoming news, and then what they got was not really news at all, but a rehash of an old story in which Doherty was complaining about having been left to carry the can for the telephone-tappings of 1982. He had said much the same thing before in a 1984 interview with *Magill* magazine, though this time he went a little further with his insinuation that Charlie may have been in some way involved. 'I felt let down by the fact that people knew what I was doing,' he said.

The media assumed he was insinuating that Charlie actually authorised the taps on the telephones of Geraldine Kennedy and Bruce Arnold in 1982. Reporters naturally pressed him to be more specific in the following days, but he refused to comment on the matter. It may have been more than a coincidence that Albert Reynolds and his supporters suddenly raised the tempo of his campaign for the Fianna Fáil leadership. On Friday afternoon, Marian Finucane's *Liveline* programme was devoted to him, and Pádraig Flynn was the main guest interviewed on RTÉ's *This Week* programme a couple of days later. He suggested that Charlie had no intention of stepping down when his limited agenda was completed, and he said Doherty should be more specific. The same day *The Sunday Tribune* was hyping the Doherty story with a picture of the controversial senator on the colour wrap-around with a large bold caption: 'GUBU or GAGA?' Inside there was an extended profile of Pádraig Flynn.

Was it just a coincidence that these events were being orchestrated by some of the same people who had been active in the push to oust Jack Lynch in 1979? Reynolds and Doherty had been members of the gang of five who led the earlier campaign. Indeed, they were the only two of the five whom Charlie rewarded with cabinet posts. Flynn had been prominent in that campaign, and Vincent Browne was the first journalist to whom they entrusted the story. The whole thing was an ominous reminder of the push against Lynch.

Having fended off reporters for almost a week, Doherty gave a press conference on 21 January at which he announced that he had been lying when he said that Charlie did not know about wire taps before the story broke in December 1982.

'I am confirming tonight that the Taoiseach, Mr Haughey, was fully aware, in 1982, that two journalists' phones were being tapped, and that he at no stage expressed a reservation about this action,' Doherty emphasised. 'As soon as the transcripts from the taps became available, I took them personally to Mr Haughey in his office and left them in his possession.

'When I indicated on RTÉ's *Nighthawks* programme, that I felt let down by lack of support from people who had known what I was doing I was referring exclusively to Mr Haughey,' Doherty added. He was speaking out after nine years, he said, because Charlie had succumbed to pressure from the Progressive Democrats to introduce phone-tapping legislation 'at a time when it could only do maximum embarrassment to me as Cathaoirleach of the Seanad.'

His announcement undoubtedly had a lot more to do with the leadership struggle within Fianna Fáil. He had the power to deliver a fatal political blow by telling what he knew about the events of 1982. He declared that he had not only lied for Charlie but surrendered his Front Bench position and had even given up the party whip voluntarily.

'Why should we believe Seán Doherty now?' Doherty asked rhetorically.

'Because,' he explained, 'I am resigning my post. You only do that for the truth.' His concern for the truth was rather touching, but he had just said that he gave up his position in 1983 to foster a lie. There were contradictions and serious flaws in his statement, but these were initially ignored by the media.

The whole thing had been carefully organised. Doherty's press conference was timed to secure maximum media impact. It began late in the evening so that journalists had barely enough time to file their stories before deadline. Printed copies of the text of Doherty's statement were handed to the journalists, so there was really no need for him to read it before the television cameras, especially when he was refusing to answer questions. The whole thing was being done for effect.

Faced with pressing deadlines, there was little opportunity for journalists to reflect. They had to write by virtual instinct, and the natural instinct of most of the media was critical of Charlie, with the result that their stories afforded Doherty's statement more credibility than if there had been time to examine it carefully. Of course, whether they would have examined it carefully, if they had the time, was in itself doubtful.

As well as being an attack on Charlie, Doherty's statement had been a defence of his own actions in connection with the tappings. He said that these originated after he had gone to Deputy Garda Commissioner Joe Ainsworth to complain about cabinet leaks and it was Ainsworth who had proposed the tap on Bruce Arnold's telephone.

Nine years earlier, however, Ainsworth stated that it was Doherty who requested the taps, and there was actually no reference to cabinet leaks then. Arnold had been writing primarily about the infighting within Fianna Fáil and foreign policy in relation to the Falkland's war, not about cabinet matters. Nobody ever identified any item in his articles that might conceivably have been considered a cabinet secret. At the time the justification for the tap was that Arnold was considered 'anti-national', whatever that meant.

Yet in the rush following Doherty's latest press conference, his self-serving statement was taken at face value by the press, which then set off a political storm. RTÉ journalists had just gone on strike, with the result that radio and television news was drastically curtailed and there were no current affairs programmes that might have balanced the instant analysis of the printed media.

Charlie denounced Doherty's allegations as 'absolutely false' at a press conference the following afternoon. 'I wish to state categorically that I was not aware at the time of the tapping of these telephones and that I was not given and did not see any transcripts of the conversations. I also wish to say that I have always abhorred the principle of phone-tapping except where absolutely necessary to prevent serious crime or subversion by paramilitary organisations.'

It was not, he said, until January 1983 that 'Mr Doherty came to see me in the company of another colleague and revealed to me his involvement in these events'. Reading from a carefully prepared text, Charlie referred to a number of discrepancies in Doherty's latest statement.

Doherty said, for instance, that he forwarded the transcripts to him over a period of several months, but this was impossible, according to Charlie, because Doherty had only been given transcripts on one occasion. Charlie proceeded to quote from several of Doherty's earlier contradictory statements. 'Mr Haughey did not know that I was tapping these journalists' phones', Doherty had told Gerald Barry in an RTÉ interview on 24 January 1983.

Why did he not tell him? Barry asked.

'Because he would have stopped it,' replied Doherty.

Unlike his accuser, Charlie fielded questions from assembled reporters. It was one of his more impressive and confident performances, but his opportunity to shine was greatly undermined by the RTÉ strike. The radio and television audiences missed much of what went on because the dreadful sound quality failed to pick up most of the questions.

In response to questions Charlie said that Ray MacSharry had been the colleague who accompanied Doherty to his office. He was sure he could confirm what went on.

But MacSharry was unable to do so. He said he had gone to the office on another matter that day and had not heard what Doherty actually said. Hence Charlie's best chance of totally discrediting Doherty was gone. People were going to have to decide for themselves between his and Doherty's version of events.

Charlie had tried to blame Doherty for the mess, but in the last analysis it was the Taoiseach's responsibility because he was the one who appointed Doherty as Minister for Justice in the first place. It was a blunder, but Charlie made no effort to remove him, even though he now said that he had already made some preparations to set up a judicial inquiry into Doherty's conduct before leaving office in 1982. Yet he made no effort to prevent Doherty being elected speaker of the Senate in 1989.

'Why did you support his elevation to the position of Cathaoirleach of the Seanad?' one of the journalists asked.

'I didn't support, I left that to the Senate group,' Charlie replied. 'In fact, for the first time, I did not nominate anybody to the Senate group. I let them take their own decision.' If he had opposed him, it was most unlikely that Doherty would have been elected. At any rate Charlie would now have been able to maintain that he had acted consistently with his supposed disapproval of Doherty's earlier behaviour.

Over the years many of Charlie's problems stemmed not so much from his actions, or alleged actions, as from his denials. At the arms trial, for instance, he contradicted the sworn testimony of four different people – Peter Berry, Jim Gibbons, Capt. Kelly and Anthony Fagan.

Was Charlie right and were all the others wrong?

In the circumstances of the time, Charlie could have justified authorising the use of money both for arms and for propaganda as a means of relieving the distress for which the money was allocated by the Dáil. But he testified that using the money for such purposes was 'absolutely' out of order.

'Public funds were misappropriated,' he insisted. 'That is a criminal offence.' But it was his office which had supplied the money for the arms and for *The Voice of the North*.

Capt. Kelly testified that he 'certainly' told Charlie's personal secretary, Anthony Fagan, what was happening to the money. Fagan, in turn, testified that he believed Charlie knew and he thought it 'inconceivable' that he did not tell him, but he was not able to refer to any specific occasion on which he told him.

In the context of Charlie's whole career it seemed that he was conveniently ignorant about too many things – whether it was in relation to the arms crisis, the telephone-tapping or his own financial affairs.

When Donal Creedon started to tell him in 1988 about the beef fraud, he obviously did not want to know. Possibly he felt more comfortable in a position where he could deny any knowledge.

When things went wrong, Charlie would disclaim responsibility and repudiate somebody else. He would maintain that he acted with total propriety himself, but even giving him the full benefits of any doubts, it was difficult to avoid the conclusion that he could be very economical with the truth.

His credibility, damaged by the earlier controversies, was further undermined after his return to power in 1987 when he made policy u-turns on the Anglo-Irish Agreement, the Single European Act, health spending, extradition, birth control legislation and coalition. He was further hurt by evidence that when he was publicly saying that he had no intention of asking Brian Lenihan to resign, he had already asked him and was actually pressurising him to do so. On top of these were his denials of involvement in the Carysfort deal, and the controversy over his meeting with Bernie Cahill.

If it had not been for all the other contradictions over the years, people might not have been as ready to believe Doherty. For the Progressive Democrats, however, it no longer mattered whether Charlie or Doherty was telling the truth. The persistent controversies were undermining the work of the government and it was obvious that these were not going to stop as long as Charlie was Taoiseach. They therefore issued a thinly veiled ultimatum warning that they would withdraw their support if he did not step down.

Charlie had sacrificed too many of his political supporters in the past. He had dropped McDaid and sacked Lenihan at the behest of the Progressive Democrats. Now it was his own turn and colleagues were no longer ready to risk their political careers to save him. His past had caught up with him.

In November he said he would go in his own time after he had completed his agenda, which included a meeting with the British prime minister, the EC summit at Maastricht and the introduction of the next budget on 29 January 1992. With the Progressive Democrats unwilling to back down, he announced on 30 January that he would be retiring as leader of Fianna Fáil on 7 February 1992.

Many people had thought he might try to hold out and pull off just one more escape, but John O'Connell advised him at a private meeting to resign because he could not guarantee that the £50,000 that he received from Mahmud Fustok would not come out. Haughey decided to go with grace and dignity. He informed O'Connell of his decision in writing. Suddenly opponents were saying things about him that had not been said for decades.

'He could not have inspired so much loyalty in his own party for so long,' Garret FitzGerald wrote, 'if he did not possess some remarkable qualities which are inherently difficult to pin down – a magnetism and capacity to relate with people which made it difficult even for his bitterest political enemies to dislike him personally and an instinct for generosity which made him something of a "soft touch".'

Even John Bruton paid a glowing tribute. 'Over more than the twenty years I have known him, I could never fault him for his courtesy and commitment to working in the Dáil,' Bruton said. 'Charles Haughey would probably not thank me for fulsome tributes; neither would his supporters or mine. But I must say I would be sorry to see him leave the Dáil. We would miss his style and shafts of wit.'

Yet there could be no doubt that Charlie's political style had got him into endless trouble. Some of his principal opponents had great style. They were good, decent men who got on great with the media, but there was little substance to their political achievements. Charlie, on the other hand, had a brilliant legislative record, but he was the man the media loved to hate.

'He did more than his critics ever did,' former Taoiseach Liam Cosgrave remarked.

People liked Charlie 'for lending some colour to a particularly drab period,' Conor Cruise O'Brien once wrote. But, of course, there was much more to it than that. He put the bureaucrats in their place and told the media where to go. He wanted to be loved by people and so he tried to give them what they wanted in the short term, which all too often was not what they needed in the long term.

'It is going to be a damned boring scene without Charlie to kick around,' his longtime critic Charlie McCreevy acknowledged. The gutting of Charlie Haughey had been one of Ireland's greatest spectator sports for more than a quarter of a century.

'MY GLORY WAS I HAD SUCH FRIENDS'

Although Haughey remained as a member of the Dáil for the next ten months following his resignation as Taoiseach, he essentially bowed out of active politics. He was indirectly in the news in August 1992 when it was reported that his son Conor had been given a loan to pay for refurbishing of the yacht, *Celtic Mist*, which was in his name. The loan had been authorised by Dermot Desmond, who had power of attorney over the account of the Isle of Man company, Freezone, which had been involved in selling the controversial building to Bord Telecom.

That story was a portent of things to come, but it did not set any alarm bells ringing at the time. Haughey was gracefully slipping into retirement. Even Bruce Arnold had some nice words to write about him.

'Charlie Haughey achieved a great deal. And it is grossly unfair to him that there should now be a sense of relief at his not being there,' Arnold wrote in the *Irish Independent* on 22 August 1992. The former Taoiseach had vast experience going back to the time of the First Programme for Economic Development in 1958. 'He was brilliant on that, and on the economy generally over the years since then, and the legacy lingers on, marred by other things,' Arnold wrote. Nobody could doubt that Haughey had left a flawed legacy, but some of his critics seemed unwilling to give him any credit for anything he had ever done.

The Fianna Fáil National Executive hosted a dinner in Haughey's honour on 1 October 1992. He was presented with oak carvings of Leinster House, Government Buildings and Dublin Castle, to mark his years as a Dáil deputy, as Taoiseach, and as president of the European Council of Ministers in 1990. In his address, he paid tribute to his friends by quoting from Yeats:

> *Think where man's glory begins and ends*
> *And say my glory was I had such friends.*

His failure to mention his successor Albert Reynolds even once during the speech was rather pointed. Reynolds did refer to Haughey in his speech, but there was no danger that he was going to be accused of being effusive. 'The greatest tribute we can pay to the achievements of Charles Haughey is to be able to say in a few years' time that his government laid the basis for a long period of Fianna Fáil rule, even if there had to be a few years of Fianna Fáil-led coalition in the middle.'

Reynolds was obviously still smarting over Fianna Fáil's coalition with the Progressive Democrats, which he had dismissed as a 'temporary little arrangement'. Just how temporary would become apparent little over four weeks later in the drama of the Beef tribunal.

Haughey began four days of testimony at the tribunal on 13 October 1992. For the first time in 133 days of testimony, the hearing room was full at Dublin Castle. The proceedings turned into virtual theatre, as the former Taoiseach was tough and combative, much to the amusement of the spectators. He seemed to relish being at the centre of attention again. The proceedings were compared to a testy Dáil question time.

'This is not Dáil Éireann,' the chairman Liam Hamilton remarked at one point.

'Although some may be forgiven for thinking that now,' Haughey replied, evoking laughter from the public gallery. 'May I say, sir, that you would have made a big contribution to Dáil Éireann,' he said to Hamilton, who had actually been an unsuccessful candidate for the Labour party many years earlier.

'If that was the case you might not have been Taoiseach,' Hamilton replied.

'And if I had chosen the courts, I might have ended up as president of the high court,' said Haughey.

The two main issues that Haughey had to deal with were his involvement in both the abortive Goodman Plan and the re-introduction of the Export Credit Insurance Scheme. His involvement in both was only peripheral, according to himself.

He reaffirmed his complaint that the former deputy leader of the Labour party, Barry Desmond, had tried to sabotage the Irish beef industry. He said that the allegations made against himself by Desmond and Tomás Mac Giolla of the Workers' Party 'were absolutely absurd and recklessly made.' He was equally caustic about the Progressive Democrats, who, he said, were accurately anticipated in the poem, 'Leaders of the Crowd,' by W. B. Yeats:

> They must keep their certainty accuse
> All who are different of base intent,
> Pull down established humour; hawk for news:
> Whatever their lose fantasy invent.

When someone pointed out that it was Haughey himself who appointed Des O'Malley as Minister for Industry and Commerce, the former Taoiseach conceded with mock humility, 'Nobody's perfect'.

Adrian Hardiman, then a well-known member of the Progressive Democrats and now a supreme court judge, and Diarmuid McGuinness were representing Des O'Malley at the tribunal. As McGuinness was cross-examining, Haughey asked him, 'Are you a PD?'

'Unlike Mr Hardiman, who underwent a voluntary conversion, and my client who underwent a forcible conversion,' McGuinness replied, 'I am not a PD'.

Although Haughey was often entertaining in the witness box, he was only minimally revealing. He was intent on denouncing the allegations made against him. 'At the end of the day,' he argued, 'they don't amount to a row of beans.' And the allegations against the Irish beef industry did not amount to much more, in his view. 'If there had been breaches of regulations in the Irish beef trade, they are only trotting after what has been perpetrated in other countries,' he said. 'I don't know what we're all doing here.'

He was especially critical of the 'yellow press type of television programme', which suggested that he and Goodman were long-standing friends, whereas, in fact, he had never even met the man before 1987. In all the two of them had fourteen meetings between then and 1990.

'We met exclusively to deal with official matters,' Haughey explained. But he took no notes at any of those meetings, and he was particularly vague about what they discussed.

On the other hand, he said there were documents to suggest that there was 'a very substantial correspondence' showing that Goodman had been much closer to FitzGerald. But the tribunal was told at that point that FitzGerald wished it to be known that – notwithstanding a report on the files by one of his staff that he had met with Goodman 'on a regular basis' – he had, in fact, only met him 'at most' on three occasions.

The main thrust of Haughey's evidence was that Goodman came up with a plan that had great economic potential for the beef industry in Ireland. 'It was not a question of the government wanting to advance Mr Goodman's companies, rather than it wanted to advance the interest of the economy and the Goodman Company would be the vehicle for that,' the former Taoiseach explained. 'Here was a proposal based on an indigenous industry, based on the beef industry and on a company with a proven record of success. It would have been lunacy not to decide yes,' he emphasised.

He gave a contradictory explanation for his involvement in compelling the IDA to drop a performance clause that would have required the Goodman companies to produce a certain number of jobs before receiving any grant. He admitted that he was 'almost certain' that he discussed the performance clause with Goodman four days before it was modified by the government, but he denied instructing the secretary of the Taoiseach's Department, Pádraig Ó hUigínn, to intervene.

Ó hUigínn had already testified that he had, indeed, talked to the IDA on his own initiative. It was just a pure coincidence that he had made the call shortly after Goodman's meeting with Haughey.

James Nugent, counsel for John Bruton, was sceptical about this testimony of Haughey and Ó hUigínn. 'I have to put it to you that his evidence and your evidence are not credible,' he said.

'I don't think defending your client justifies your right to make such an allegation,' Haughey snapped. 'I won't take it from you.'

'Don't try to bully me,' said Nugent.

'And, don't you try to bully me,' Haughey shot back. 'Don't think you can question my credibility. I won't take it.'

They clashed a number of times during the former Taoiseach's testimony. Nugent seemed to be playing the media. At one point in his cross-examination of Haughey, he appeared to be addressing the reporters.

'I don't like talking to the back of your head,' the former Taoiseach complained.

'I am here to ask the questions,' Nugent snapped at another point. 'You are here to answer them!'

'You are trying to make mysteries out of straight-forward facts,' Haughey protested. 'If you are intent to lecture me on my role, I may presume to lecture you.'

He was particularly dismissive when asked what he thought of Bruton's accusation that he had hassled the IDA into giving Goodman the deal of a lifetime. 'I would be inclined to be apoplectic, if I were not a sane person,' Haughey replied, and he went on to characterise the Fine Gael leader as 'the Admiral Stockdale of Irish politics'. When he was complimented afterwards on using this comparison, Haughey reportedly asked, 'Just who is this Stockdale character?'

Admiral James Stockdale was Ross Perot's running mate in the on-going American presidential election campaign. Stockdale had recently showed up as a kind of bumbling individual, almost totally out of his depth in a television debate with the other two vice-presidential candidates, Dan Quale and Al Gore.

During his testimony Haughey seemed to admit that he may actually have gone too far in putting pressure on the IDA, but if that was the case, he thought the civil servants should have rectified it. 'The government from time to time takes decisions and afterwards departments point out, 'look, you can't do that,' he explained. 'So formulae are found which make them workable – that's the job of good officials.' It was his way of cutting through bureaucratic red tape and getting things done.

'We took our decision at government and that was the end of the matter as far as we were concerned,' he said. 'But, in all these circumstances, it is the duty of the officials, secretaries of the government departments to clear up any of these sort of legal difficulties, which government decisions may give rise to.' He was contending, true to form, that if he had made a mistake, it was somebody else's fault!

By law, the IDA had the right to determine the extent to which it would facilitate the Goodman plan and undue government pressure was not only improper but also illegal. Although cross-examined by seven barristers, none of them was able to make more than a coincidental link between the timing of Haughey's meetings with Goodman, and the subsequent pressure put on the IDA to adjust its terms for supporting of the company's plan. Yet the weight of those coincidences became overwhelming, in the last analysis

'It was obvious that "the Authority" would not have deleted the clause were it nor for the intervention of the government', Liam Hamilton concluded in his report. The government had exceeded its authority in directing the IDA to remove the performance clause, and 'this direction was made either at the instigation of the then Taoiseach or the secretary of his department.'

Even though the government did bend over backwards in trying to facilitate the Goodman Plan, this was somewhat academic, as it was never implemented because Goodman did not get it all his own way. The whole thing did 'not cost the Exchequer a penny,' Haughey argued. In a sense, he was right, but it cost the country a small fortune on legal fees inquiring into the whole thing in order to placate his critics.

On the re-introduction of the Export Credit Insurance Scheme on the beef for Iraq, which was a costly *faux pas*, Haughey sought to dump all the responsibility on the head of Albert Reynolds, whom he accused of re-introducing the scheme without his knowledge or approval. 'All I can say to you is that Mr Reynolds was an experienced businessman aware of the complexities of international markets and trading and aware of all the pitfalls,' Haughey said. 'It was just another on-going departmental scheme administered by the minister in the department without reference to me.'

'Goodman states that he would have discussed all matters that were of importance to him whenever he got the opportunity but had no clear recollection of discussing Export Credit Insurance with the Taoiseach on any specific occasion but emphasised that he would have discussed it whenever he got the opportunity', Hamilton noted in his report. Haughey could not remember discussing it, but he appointed Reynolds as Minister for Industry and Commerce, with the result that he bore ultimate responsibility for the mistakes made by him, whether he discussed the scheme with him or not.

At the end of his testimony, Haughey announced that he was leaving to return to his 'books and bucolic pursuits'. He slipped gracefully into official retirement on 5 November 1992 when the government came crashing down after Reynolds was accused of being 'dishonest' in his testimony at the Beef tribunal. On formally retiring Haughey indicated that he would not write his memoirs and would not be making any further public statements.

Haughey did do some charity work and he seemed to be enjoying his retirement. While at Kinsealy he went riding regularly on Portmarnock strand on his hunter, *Gatsby*, and he took a keen interest in his racehorses, especially *Flashing Steel*, which won the Irish Grand National on Easter Monday 1995, when the Taoiseach John Bruton was presenting the trophy.

Haughey continued to perform the official opening of the Dingle Regatta. There was an extraordinary story in the *Irish Independent* on 27 August 1997. In covering the opening of Dingle Regatta the previous day, Miriam Lord reported that Haughey had 'fallen off the *Celtic Mist*' in Dingle Harbour and had to be plucked out of the sea by a marine rescue helicopter. 'That's what happens, when you are enjoying your retirement and have no responsibilities,' she wrote. 'You fall into the sea.'

It was Miriam Lord who had gone overboard, because there was no truth to the report. She was apparently joking, but the story obviously was garbled. If Haughey had actually fallen into the sea and been rescued in that way, it would have been front-page news, not just buried in the middle of the newspaper.

Miriam telephoned Haughey to apologise next morning. He undoubtedly had grounds for a legal action, but he graciously accepted her apology. When she asked how he would like her to apologise in print, he told her to do it whatever way she wished, or not to bother at all. He was content with her telephone call and he told her she could forget it.

'Sorry. Sorry. Sorry. I'm as sick as pig', she began an open letter to Haughey next day. 'I have done you a dreadful disservice.' She admitted that he had never fallen off the *Celtic Mist* and had not been rescued by air corps. Haughey rescued Miriam on that occasion.

He was only out of the Taoiseach's office for little over a week when an incident occurred in Miami, Florida, that was to have profound long-term repercussions. The police arrested Ben Dunne as he threatened to jump from a high-rise hotel building. He was high on cocaine and apparently thought he could fly. The saga of his involvement with Haughey would gradually unravel as an indirect consequence of his erratic behaviour that night.

In the aftermath of the Miami incident, his sister, Margaret Heffernan, ousted him as chief executive of the family business. A bitter family feud followed as he sought to break up the family trust. She was horrified to learn from a company accountant in July 1993 that her brother had given Haughey over £1 million of company money. It was bad enough giving it to a politician, but giving it to Haughey was the last straw, because her father had detested him ever since an incident between them at a trade exhibition in New York in the 1960s. Ben was unwilling to provide his sister with details of the cheques he had given to Haughey.

'If you don't tell me,' she warned, 'I'm going to keep digging.'

'You can look all you like,' he replied. 'You'll never trace them.'

She confronted Haughey personally. 'I said it had come to my knowledge that my brother had given him £1.1 million,' she explained. He had actually given him at least £1.93 million.

'I can't be responsible for what your brother says,' Haughey replied. He went on to say that Ben 'was unstable'. When she tried to press him about the money, he avoided the issue. 'He kept going back to the stability of my brother,' she said.

'I was as non-committal as I could be to Mrs Heffernan, because that's the first time I heard this rumour about this million pounds,' Haughey later contended. He said he only referred to Dunne as being unstable in the light of her remarks. 'I may have said "From what you describe, Margaret, it would seem that your brother is acting in an unstable way",' he explained.

In March 1994 Noel Smyth, Ben Dunne's lawyer, told Haughey that the story of the Dunne money might be made public. Haughey response was to lie, to say that he had never received any money from Dunne. In fact, throughout his numerous meetings and some forty different telephone conversations with Smyth during the next couple of years, Haughey never actually admitted that he had received money from Dunne, but Smyth did not need an admission.

'If Mr Haughey wanted to make some other case I was leaving that really to him,' Smyth explained. 'I knew I had sufficient documentary evidence.'

The Dunne family feud was resolved in November 1994. Dunne was bought out for some £100 million, but solicitors for Dunnes Stores still tried to recover the money from Haughey. On 13 November, they wrote to him with details of the payments that they contended were 'improperly diverted' to him.

'As no such monies had ever been paid to me by Mr Ben Dunne

or any of the companies mentioned, no question of repayment arises,' Haughey replied next day. 'I take grave exception to the use of the words "improperly diverted" and the implication that I was aware of such conduct by or on behalf of Mr Ben Dunne.'

Haughey's stalling tactics began to unravel in December 1996 when the Dáil requested Judge Gerard Buchanan to investigate payments made by Dunne to Michael Lowry, after he was forced to resign as a minister in the Rainbow coalition. Haughey's name became linked with the disclosure that £20,000 had been paid to his wife for his election expenses in 1989. It was also disclosed that Haughey's son Ciarán had been paid £10,000 for helicopter services and his brother, Fr Eoghan Haughey, had been paid £2,000 for masses. But then *Phoenix* magazine broke the story that Haughey had been given over £1 million. Because of the Buchanan report, the government established a tribunal under Mr Justice Brian McCracken to investigate Dunne's payments to politicians. The tribunal had already been set up when Noel Smyth showed Haughey three bank drafts that Dunne had given him at Abbeville in November 1991. Viewing the drafts as 'lethal', Haughey admitted to Smyth that they 'could be a cause of some embarrassment.'

'I think he said "is there any way we can get rid of these?"' Smyth later testified. It was reminiscent of Haughey's question to Des O'Malley about Peter Berry's forthcoming testimony shortly before the arms trial.

Haughey had told Smyth in 1993 that he had not availed of the tax amnesty, with the result that Smyth concluded that he was likely to have trouble with the revenue commissioners. Dunne had therefore authorised him to offer Haughey 'up to £1 million' more towards the cost of settling his tax affairs. Smyth urged Haughey to make a full disclosure about the money.

Although he acknowledged the 'very gracious offer', Haughey said it was 'impossible' for him to accept it, even though Smyth warned that the tribunal, with its very extensive powers, was likely 'to get all the information sooner rather than later.' He again advised Haughey to do himself a 'huge favour' by making a clean breast of things. But Haughey tried to brazen it out.

Throughout most of the time that the McCracken tribunal sat, he denied that he had received any money. On 7 July 1997, he submitted an eight-page statement denying that any meetings took place between Ben Dunne and himself at Kinsealy, or that he had received three cheques totalling £210,000 from him in person, but this time he had gone too far. He stated that he first heard of the Dunne money when Margaret Heffernan confronted him in July 1993. He added that he then telephoned Des Traynor, who said that he would be meeting her himself to 'hear what she had to say but that I need not be concerned about these rumours as they were without foundation.'

That was unbelievable. The tribunal had enough evidence to convinced Haughey's own lawyer that his client's position was untenable. The tribunal sitting was suspended for the day and the next morning Haughey submitted a revised statement accepting that he had indeed received the money and he had misled the tribunal.

'As a result of reviewing the excellent work of the tribunal and considering the very helpful documentation recently received from Mr Ben Dunne's solicitor, I now accept that I received the £1.3 million from Mr Ben Dunne and that I became aware that he was the donor to the late Mr Traynor in 1993, and furthermore, I now accept Mr Dunne's evidence that he handed me £210,000 in Abbeville in November 1991,' Haughey declared. 'In making this statement, I wish to make it clear that until yesterday, I had mistakenly instructed my legal team.'

Haughey testified before the tribunal in Dublin Castle on 15 July 1997. Members of the public had been gathering in the early hours of the morning to gain access to the tribunal chamber. Haughey arrived before 7.30 a.m., eluding reports and photographers. He was no longer the same combative witness who had appeared before the Beef tribunal less than five years earlier. At the outset, he read a prepared statement in which he expressed regret for his behaviour in not co-operating with the tribunal 'in the manner which might have been expected of me.'

He insisted that he did not know where any of the money had come from until July 1993, but he admitted that his statement 'was incorrect' that Traynor had dismissed the story as a rumour when he first talked to him about it. 'I can only suggest that I was reluctant to face the inevitable consequences of disclosure,' he explained.

He clearly tried to dump the responsibility for the handling of his finances on Traynor, who had died in 1994. 'I never had to concern myself about my personal finances,' Haughey said. 'He took over control of my financial affairs from about 1960 onwards. He sought, as his personal responsibility, to ensure that I would be free to devote my time and ability to public life and that I would not be distracted from my political work by financial concerns.'

'Traynor had complete discretion to act on my behalf without reference back to me,' Haughey continued. 'In hindsight, it is clear that I should have involved myself to a greater degree in this regard.'

'My private finances were perhaps peripheral to my life,' he contended. 'I left them to Mr Traynor to look after.' Of course this was not the case with the three cheques worth £210,000 that Ben Dunne had handed to Haughey, who said that he could not remember that incident. But he accepted Noel Smyth's documentary evidence and Dunne's word that it did happen.

It was pointed out that a sizable loan taken out by Celtic Helicopters was paid off from an off-shore account that had been set up for him by Traynor in the Ansbacher Bank. Haughey said that he was unaware of this transaction but that Traynor would have known it was acceptable to him to use such funds for family-related business. Although Haughey had been spending much more than his official salary, he denied that he lived extravagantly.

'I didn't have a lavish lifestyle,' he told the tribunal. 'My work was my lifestyle and when I was in office I worked every day, all day. There was no room for any sort of an extravagant lifestyle.'

He had to concede, however, that as recently as 7 July 1997, he had been 'persisting in accounts of events which were short of the truth.' Yet, while he was on the stand, neither he nor any of the lawyers referred to his deception as lying.

'It wasn't a full explanation,' he insisted.

'It was pretty economical?' counsel asked.

'I hate to use that phrase,' Haughey relied.

'It was not true, Mr Haughey, isn't that right?

'It was not a full explanation.'

When he emerged from the tribunal, a crowd of up to 1,000 people had gathered outside Dublin Castle. There was a smattering of applause, but his loyalists were quickly drowned out by booing.

On 25 August 1997 the tribunal report was published in which McCracken concluded that it as 'quite unacceptable that a member of Dáil Éireann, and in particular a cabinet minister and Taoiseach, should be supported in his personal lifestyle by gifts made to him personally.'

The report was a devastating indictment in which the judge made little or no effort to hide his annoyance at the way that Haughey had prevaricated and lied. He had wasted the time of the tribunal by repeatedly ignoring requests for information. Then, when he did provide answers, he lied in three separate written submissions. The judge also concluded that the former Taoiseach had not been honest in his actual testimony either.

'The tribunal considers Mr Charles Haughey's evidence to be unacceptable and untrue,' he wrote, citing eleven different instances in which he described the former Taoiseach's evidence as 'not believable', 'quite unbelievable', 'most unlikely', 'beyond all credibility', or 'incomprehensible'.

Since Haughey admitted that he knew about a £105,000 loan from the Agricultural Credit Corporation during the late 1980s, McCracken found it strange that he 'did not admit to being aware of any other loans.' He did not believe the story about not remembering the three cheques given to him by Ben Dunne in November 1991.

'It is not believable that a person could not remember an event such as this, which was quite bizarre,' McCracken contended. 'It is also most unlikely that if Haughey gave those bank drafts to Des Traynor, Traynor did not reveal that other moneys had been received from Dunne at an earlier date.'

The judge refused to believe several aspects of the former Taoiseach's story involving his relationship with Des Traynor. For instance, McCracken found it 'unbelievable' that Traynor managed all of Haughey's financial affairs since the 1960s without reference to him. Moreover, it was 'quite unbelievable that Traynor would not have told in some detail of the difficulties and it is equally unbelievable that Haughey would not have asked.' It was incredible that he would not have discussed the tax implication with Traynor. McCracken argued that it was 'far more likely' and 'far more consistent with his subsequent actions' that the tax implications were discussed and 'that it was decided that the money should be kept off-shore and that its receipt should never be acknowledged.' Since Traynor had apparently been 'a meticulously careful person', it was unlikely, according to the tribunal report, that he would 'have used any money in the Ansbacher deposits, which were held for the benefit of Haughey, to support Celtic Helicopters unless he had the authority of Haughey to do so.' After Traynor's death in 1994, it was 'beyond all credibility' that the former Taoiseach 'would not have become very concerned as to his affairs, and particularly concerned to ensure his assets were secured.'

At one point during Haughey's testimony, McCracken noted that the former Taoiseach admitted that he had received financial statements from Traynor. 'The clear impression is that despite his earlier denials, Haughey had in fact received statements dealing with his accounts which he read and noted, and therefore he did not ask about his affairs, because he was already aware of them.' The judge went on to state that 'the tribunal thinks it probable that he was at all times aware that money was being held for his benefit in Ansbacher Cayman Limited.'

'While he may not have known the exact sums of money which he was spending,' McCracken argued, 'he must have known that large sums of money were being spent on his behalf, despite his denial of having a lavish lifestyle.'

The judge stopped short of actually accusing Haughey of perjury as that would be a judgment for a court of law. The clear implications of the report were that Haughey had obstructed the work of the tribunal and perjured himself. 'It is not for the tribunal to determine whether Mr Charles Haughey should be prosecuted,' McCracken wrote. 'This is a matter for the director of public prosecutions,' but he added rather pointedly 'that the circumstances warrant the papers in the matter being sent to the director of public prosecutions for his consideration as to whether there ought to be a prosecution, and the tribunal intends to do so.'

In the aftermath of the McCracken report, two more judicial tribunals were set up under high court judges to investigate allegations of political corruption. One tribunal under Michael Moriarty was to investigate the Ansbacher and related payments to politicians, while the second tribunal under Fergus Flood, was to investigate corruption in relation to the planning process, which included allegations of payments to politicians.

The other tribunals exposed further payments not only to Haughey but also to some of his cabinet appointees. This form of sleaze reached its nadir in June 1989 when, after being introduced to members of the cabinet, the builder Tom Gilmartin was asked by a Fianna Fáil functionary to deposit £5 million in an offshore account for the party.

'You people make the effing Mafia look like monks!' Gilmartin exclaimed.

'You could end up in the Liffey for that statement,' the functionary replied.

Haughey was billed for £2 millions by the revenue commissioners for his failure to pay income tax on the money provided for him by Ben Dunne, but he appealed the assessment. The case was heard in camera in October 1998 before Ronan Kelly, an appeals commissioner. His task was to sit independently of the revenue commissioners to evaluate the assessment and decide whether it should stand, be reduced, or dismissed.

The revenue commissioners insisted that the McCracken report identified Ben Dunne as the donor of £1.3m given to Haughey. Offshore companies paid the money – Equifex Trust Corporation, registered in Zug, Switzerland, which forwarded £621,000 sterling, and Tutbury, a company in the Isle of Man, which provided £410,000 sterling. A further £182,650 sterling was provided by Dunnes Stores in Bangor, Northern Ireland. Haughey's legal team contended that, in law, the actual donors were the off-shore companies from which Dunnes Stores withdrew the money for the benefit of the former Taoiseach. The shareholders of the companies would be the actual donors, but, as these were not identified, the appeals commissioner Ronan Kelly had no real option but to conclude that the money came from outside the state and was not therefore liable to income tax under existing laws.

When the decision was announced on 15 December 1998, it was greeted with a storm of protests. The revenue commissioners indicated that they would be appealing the finding to the circuit court, where the proceedings would be open to the public.

The revenue commissioners lodged an appeal to the circuit court against the verdict of the appeals commissioner in essentially dismissing the £2 million tax assessment against Haughey. Moreover, he had been returned for trial in March 2000 on charges of obstructing the McCracken tribunal. If convicted, he could have been fined £10,000 and sentenced to two years in jail, but a series of events conspired to postpone and eventually prevent the trial.

No Fury Like a Woman Scorned

For more than 30 years Gay Byrne's *Late Late Show* had been the most popular television programme on RTÉ, before his decision to retire in 1999. The second last programme on 14 May 1999 featured Terry Keane, who raised many eyebrows by talking openly about her 27-year affair with Haughey. By then, even the 'dogs in the street' knew about that affair, according to Byrne.

She had been making snide references to the affair in her column in the *Sunday Independent* over the years, and it had been parodied week after week on *Scrap Saturday*, a popular comedy radio programme. She said she was telling her story because Kevin O'Connor was bringing out a book, *Sweetie*, which she said would distort the affair. She said she was motivated by a desire to ensure that the relationship was accurately depicted as 'a genuine love affair.'

'I hear from people who had seen the script that it was a very loveless relationship, punctuated only by expensive dinners or trips on yachts,' she explained. 'It wasn't like that. I wanted to show that it really was love.'

Although he was 'a consummate politician, he was not consumed by politics,' according to Terry Keane, a journalist who began a torrid affair with him. 'I viewed Charlie as a bit of a wide boy with a terrible reputation as a womaniser,' she wrote. 'There was a whole series of Charlie stories, some true, some false and some frankly lurid.' She began her affair with him on 17 January 1972 at Club Elizabeth, a nightclub in Leeson Street that was frequented by politicians. At the time, she was in her early thirties, the fashion editor of the *Sunday Press* and temporarily separated from her lawyer husband.

She was in company with Haughey, whom she teased and treated rather contemptuously. 'I don't have to put up with this,' he finally snapped in exasperation. 'I'm going home.'

'Don't go,' Terry responded. 'I'll dance with you instead.'

'There was some sort of empathy,' she later explained. 'I felt that I would also be like that if I wasn't the centre of attention. I suddenly thought: "He's attractive". He oozed sex appeal and had the most beautiful mouth of anybody I'd ever seen.'

After that night, he invited her to London, where they stayed in an apartment owned by his friend John Byrne, the property developer. That was the first of a number of foreign trips. During one of their early trips to London, he introduced her to 'Cristal' champagne. As the waiter was returning with a bottle of the expensive wine, a customer checked the vintage, much to the indignation of Haughey.

'Who's that fucker and what is he doing with my champagne?' he snapped.

'I couldn't stop laughing: the facade of sophistication demolished at a stroke,' she noted. 'But that's Charlie'. That was the side of him that the people with old money sneered at and denigrated him as *nouveau riche*.

At the time Haughey was at low point in his political career, being shunned by politicians he had previously considered friends. He was venomous about the arms crisis, feeling that he had been victimised, and much of that venom was reserved for Lynch. There was no doubt he was implicated but the Taoiseach had obviously turned a blind eye and then made him the scapegoat, dismissing him from the cabinet while he was still in hospital after his riding accident. 'He didn't even have the decency to wait until I was back on my feet', Haughey would often complain.

The short fellow still had a firm conviction that he would be Taoiseach one day, and he talked to Terry for hours about how he was going to make his way back, this time to the very top. She found him exciting and great fun to be with.

'We were waltzing off to London and Paris all the time for trysts,' she wrote. France was Haughey's favourite. Napoleon, the little emperor who up-ended all of Europe, was 'his hero and inspiration,' according to her. Haughey loved French things, wines, restaurants, clothes, architecture and history. In the coming years, they would stay in various places in France and Germany without worry, but Haughey was leery of London, because of the danger of being outed by the tabloid press. He and Terry were not discreet about their affair, especially in Dublin, where it was an open secret among journalists. The two of them were married to other people. She got back together with her husband for some time, but throughout it all she and Haughey frequently met at different Dublin hotels, such as the Russell, Hibernian and Sachs, where they often dined or drank openly. There were numerous stories of tiffs between them; most were probably apocryphal. If she threw as many glasses of champagne in his face as rumoured, she would have drenched half of Dublin, not to mention all the dinners she supposedly dumped in his lap. She wrote about one night when she ordered him out of her car in Merrion Street after he had too much to drink.

He telephoned her next day.

'So you got home,' she said.

'Of course,' he replied. 'I met some citizens who carried me on their shoulders and were thrilled for the opportunity.' This was Charlie's natural arrogance. Within a month of the start of the affair, he was already on the road to political recovery.

He was actually amused when *Private Eye* mentioned the affair. He called Frank Dunlop to get a copy of the magazine. And he doubled up with laughter when he began reading it. 'Jasus, Frank, she'll go fuckin' bananas when she reads this'. He pointed to a reference to 'the aging Terry Keane'.

Although she wafted on about Haughey's achievements, the audience at the *Late Late Show* did not seem inclined to believe that he ever did anything worthwhile. 'They have forgotten all the good things he has done,' she said. 'When Ireland was a begging bowl, Charlie went out and eyeballed people in Europe and the world.'

She felt he was being treated unfairly and resented it when somebody in the audience suggested that Haughey had done as much damage to politics as the paedophile priest, Fr Brendan Smyth, had done to the Catholic Church in Ireland. 'Brendan Smyth buggered little boys,' Keane said. 'Charlie has never done that. Charlie took money from people who were very willing to give it to him so that he would go out and not have to worry about his own finances, that he could go and run the country, which he did brilliantly and brought us the Celtic Tiger and the prosperity we have today,' she argued. She was crediting him with too much, but then others were not giving him any credit at all.

Over the years, so many rumours about Haughey turned out to be untrue that there were still some who doubted Terry Keane's story. For instance, there was the totally unfounded story that Haughey had an affair with Emer O'Kelly of RTÉ. She first heard the story in 1980, but it was not until the wake of the Keane exposé that she found an opportunity to deny the story. There was also another false story that did the rounds for decades about how Eamonn Andrews had supposedly given Haughey a right hammering one night in the 1960s. One version of the story was that he had made a pass at Eamonn's wife, Gráinne. This supposedly happened at different places – at Haughey's home, at the Gresham Hotel, or at Jury's Hotel, depending on who was telling the story.

Andrews and his wife did attend a party at Haughey's home before he moved to Kinsealy. 'Charlie received us personally and graciously, as was his wont,' Andrews recalled. 'And he did make an innocent pass at Gráinne, who was looking particularly fetching. Both she and I would have been somewhat peeved had he not. But it was hardly the sort of pass to warrant a punch on the nose.'

The story persisted until Andrews finally became exasperated when it was repeated in the *News of the World*. He sued for libel and secured 'a few thousand pounds and an apology in open court'. On returning to Dublin, Andrews invited Haughey to his house for a champagne celebration.

'I'll come,' Haughey said, 'provided it's Dom Perignon!'

It was, and Haughey came. Andrews had purchased some sixty copies of the offending newspaper and he made a carpet of those all the way in from the doorway. The rumour persisted, but at least it had financed a good party.

Unfounded rumours about Haughey's famous fall from the horse in 1970 also persisted. Over a quarter of a century later twisted versions of that story were still being told. It was actually reported that Haughey was beaten close to death by the father and brother of a young woman after they supposedly caught him in bed with her, upstairs in the Grasshopper Inn in Clonee, Co. Meath. But there was no truth to the story.

Haughey's behaviour tended to encourage some of the rumours. In 1991 when he officiated at the start of the Dingle Regatta, he was still Taoiseach. He arrived in Dingle on the *Celtic Mist*, clearly in a happy mood. It had just been raining and there was a crew of young women in one race. The Taoiseach called out to them, 'Are ye'r knickers wet?'

He then gave an interview to a young woman reporter. 'I suppose,' he said at the end of the interview, 'a ride would be out of the question!'

There was a young male photographer with her at the time, so this was obviously not a proposition. It was Haughey's way of saying to the young people that he was still 'with it'. Some people would say, no doubt, that his behaviour was confirmation of the old Irish adage, 'the older the goat, the giddier!'

'He is not an oil painting – never was,' Joanne McElgunn wrote in the *Sunday Independent*. 'Women were metal and he was a powerful magnet.' He tended to flirt shamelessly, and they loved it.

'Once C. J. patted my bottom,' McElgunn continued. 'The company and the consumption of two gins and tonic, might just have saved him from the sharp edge of my tongue. In retrospect, I was strangely flattered. I know many women with whom he had only shaken hands.'

Terry Keane was certainly proud of her love affair with Haughey – the 27 years of which she went on to detail in a series of articles in the *Sunday Times*. Those included a photograph of them kissing while she was stretched out on the floor. That photograph dispelled any lingering doubts about the truth of the affair. But she was taken aback by the intensity of the public reaction to her articles.

'I certainly was surprised by the fallout after the first extract from them,' she said. 'Perhaps naively I didn't expect such a shock wave of reaction.'

For a while, she tried to defend him, especially in relation to money. All Ben Dunne got for the million pounds plus that he gave to Charlie Haughey was an invitation to a few parties at Abbeville and some family weddings, she told Marian Finucane in an RTÉ interview. 'If anybody is foolish enough to give a million pounds to be included in someone's social circle, that's up to them.'

Anybody who thinks that they could buy favours from Haughey does not know the man. 'They don't understand Charlie's character,' she said. 'Charlie would think the million pounds was his by right'. As was mentioned earlier, she added that 'it would be like the three wise men putting gold, frankincense and myrrh in front of the Saviour and that he would have no obligation because of a gift.' Ben Dunne continued to assert that he never got nor sought any favours. The Moriarty tribunal uncovered further cheques totalling £180,000 that Dunne gave to Haughey in November 1992. This was after Haughey had lost his political clout. In fact, he had actually quit politics, so those cheques would tend to support Dunne's contention that he was not looking for political favours. Ben even offered later still to provide the further million that Haughey would need to cover his tax liabilities if he came clean about the money Dunne had given him.

Between 1987 and 1997, when the story of the Dunne money first broke, Haughey spent a lot more money than he earned. Just where he got all the money is still not clear. The Ansbacher accounts controlled by Des Traynor, which the McCracken tribunal suspected might contain up to £40 million, were actually much more extensive. In all, there were about a hundred different Irish residents involved in those accounts and the total money ran into the hundreds of millions of pounds. Despite reckless remarks by some politicians suggesting that all those people involved were criminal tax evaders, a number of those accounts were perfectly legal and being used for legitimate business reasons.

In the midst of the further Ansbacher disclosures in September 1999, Terry Keane was back in the news when she auctioned off some paintings of Haughey and other memorabilia of their affair. News of the items to be auctioned first broke as the lead story on the front page of *The Examiner* on what was – unknown to the editorial staff – the eve of the Haughey's forty-eighth wedding anniversary. The unseemly timing of the hurtful gesture seemed like a confirmation of the lines of William Congreve:

> *Heav'n has no rage, like love to hatred turn'd*
> *Nor Hell a fury, like a woman scorn'd.*

The Moriarty tribunal uncovered other cheques that Ben Dunne diverted to Haughey, bringing the total of his contributions to £1.9m, but there was still no suggestion that Dunne had obtained any improper favour from Haughey, or the government.

A whole plethora of issues about his financial affairs were raised by the Moriarty tribunal, particularly in relation to Charlie's handling of money contributed to Fianna Fáil and his use of the party leader's fund, especially in relation to the money contributed towards Brian Lenihan lifesaving operation. Questions were also raised about propriety of using the leader's fund to pay for either Charlie's household bills, or his Charvet shirts, or using £26,000 to help Deputy John Ellis stave off bankruptcy, because if he was declared bankrupt, he would have to vacate his Dáil seat and the government would lose its majority. The National Irish Bank was even persuaded to write off a debt of £263,540 owed by Ellis about the same time.

There can be no real doubt that Haughey misappropriated the £100,000 given to Fianna Fáil by Irish Permanent Building Society in 1986, or that there was a vast surplus in the money contributed for Lenihan's liver transplant, or that a substantial amount of the £160,000 handed over by Mark Kavanagh and Michael Smurfit for Fianna Fáil in 1989 was allegedly misappropriated.

Rather than answered the various questions, however, Haughey appeared to prevaricate and even tried to frustrate the investigation. He challenged the right of Moriarty tribunal to investigate his bank accounts and those of wife, daughter, and two sisters on constitutional grounds. In April 1998 the high court held that the failure to give members of his family advance notice of the discovery orders executed on their accounts was unfair, but not sufficient to void the proceedings of the tribunal. On the other hand, the court ruled that Haughey's own complaints against the tribunal itself were 'bordering on the absurd'. The judge, Hugh Geoghegan concluded that 'some invasion of Mr Haughey's constitutional rights, such as his right of privacy et cetera, is justified having regard to the legitimate public concern,' because of valid questions were raised by his acceptance of gifts.

'Ethical behaviour in public office surely incorporates more than simply refusing to take bribes,' the judge contended. An office-holder was obliged to behave in a way that did not give rise to a public apprehension or inference of impropriety. In Geoghegan's judgment, there was already evidence that Charlie's conduct had given rise to such apprehension by accepting the money from Ben Dunne. The judge concurred with the conclusion of his colleague Brian McCracken that 'Haughey's whole life style' would appear to have been 'dependent upon such gifts.'

Geoghegan ruled that Haughey had to pay half the cost of the high court hearing. The former Taoiseach appealed this to the supreme court but lost in 1999. As a result, he was saddled not only with half the high court costs, but also the whole cost of the supreme court hearing. It was estimated that those costs could run as high as £500,000. This was only part of his growing financial problems. The revenue commissioners had lodged an appeal in the circuit court against the verdict of the appeals commissioner in dismissing the £2 million tax assessment against Haughey, but this was eventually settled out of court in April 2000 when Charlie agreed to pay £1,009,435 in tax arrears and interest on the money given by Dunne. Of course, this was only an interim settlement as the Moriarty tribunal had uncovered other monies given or appropriated by Haughey. He had little trouble paying the money, because of the explosion in property prices around Dublin. He was offered £5m for just 10 acres of Kinsealy. In August 2003 he sold the remainder of the property to Manor Park home builders, controlled by Joe Moran for around a reported 45 million euro. He had, in fact, become a fabulously wealthy man, but now in his twilight years, he was being hounded by his past.

The director of public prosecutions directed that Charlie should be charged with obstructing the McCracken tribunal. If convicted, he could have been fined £10,000 and sentenced to two years in jail. When he was due to make his first appearance in court on 14 October 1999, members of the Socialist Worker's party staged a virtual circus outside the courthouse, parading around with different placards reading:

Jail the Corrupt Politicians
Make Haughey Pay his Tax
Jail the Ansbacher Crooks

Although there were rarely more than a couple of dozen protesters, they made an enormous amount of noise with their rhythmic chants backed up with a loud hailer:

Charvet Charlie what's the score?
One law for the rich, one law for the poor!

Charlie Haughey what's the crack?
We want the shirt off your back.

Your island, your yacht, your shirt, you're caught!

Haughey had given the media the slip at the McCracken tribunal by going into Dublin Castle a couple of hours before the proceedings were due to begin. This time the media were not about to be deceived – they had television cameras covering all the entrances to the Four Courts from 7 a.m., even though the proceedings were not due to begin until 9.30. At about 9.10 Conor Haughey, Charlie's eldest son arrived, and told the photographers that his father was inside already.

'How did he get in?' one asked.

'He just got up before you.'

As the photographers followed him into the yard of the Four Courts a blue Mercedes drove up quickly behind them, a garda opened the door of court, and Haughey dashed in before the photographers could get any shots. They were disgusted as they were now going to be the butt of complaints from colleagues covering the other entrances.

'This could not happen in England,' a disappointed TV3 cameraman complained. 'They would never open the court early to suit somebody charged with a criminal offence.'

It was widely rumoured that Charlie would plead guilty as the evidence against him was overwhelming, but that was never his way. His trial was set from March 2000, but a series of events conspired to postpone it. When Jack Lynch died in October 1999, Haughey attended the funeral in Cork. It was the last great Irish political funeral of the twentieth century. In symbolic terms it differs enormously from the first great political funeral of the century, that of Jeremiah O'Donovan Rossa on 1 August 1915. That turned into a clarion call to arms when Patrick Pearse delivered the funeral oration. 'The fools, the fools, the fools,' he said, 'they have left us our Fenian dead, and while Ireland holds these graves, Ireland unfree shall never be at peace.' Pearse used that occasion as an opportunity to establish himself as a spokesman for militant Irish Nationalism, and he then used that platform to lead the Easter Rebellion less than a year later. Lynch, on the other hand, was celebrated as the man who blocked another call to arms in Northern Ireland in 1970. 'For that alone Jack Lynch deserves his place in history', Des O'Malley declared in his funeral oration.

Listening to people in Cork one sensed that Jack Lynch was already on the road to canonisation. Indeed, some seemed ready to suggest that he performed his first miracle by getting Charlie Haughey, Des O'Malley and Albert Reynolds to sit together in the church during the funeral mass. The text of O'Malley's graveside oration was already being circulated. 'The safe existence of this democratic state in which we live today is very much Jack Lynch's political legacy,' he would say. 'We could have caved in to sinister elements and put our country at mortal risk.' Reporters reading those comments in advance were certainly convinced that this was an attack on Haughey, who attracted more attention than the Taoiseach outside the church. For years, Haughey has enjoyed the kind of celebrity status that tends to upstage a bride at a wedding or a corpse at a funeral. Now that celebrity was tarnished by a notoriety that became apparent in a sense of ridicule. People were openly joking about his shirt. Some cheered Haughey, while others jeered, but it was neither the time nor the place for such demonstrations. Most people remained respectfully silent.

Haughey had the guts to pay his respects in hostile circumstances. It was, in a way, reminiscent of that day in December 1979 when he sat alone on the government benches and taunted his tormentors by listening to their invective in silence. He did not go to the graveside, but one sensed that he still had a pervasive presence, because of Des O'Malley's graveside oration.

There had already been considerable publicity surrounding the proceedings at the Moriarty tribunal, where it had been disclosed that Haughey had received or appropriated over £8.5m in contributions over a 17-year period.

Charlie's lawyers again argued that he could not receive a fair trial in the climate, and in June 2000 Judge Kevin Haugh agreed. He cited the publicity at the Moriarty tribunal, the campaign being waged by member of the Socialist Worker's party, and what he considered a prejudicial comment by the Tánaiste, Mary Harney. In an interview with the *Irish Independent,* she was asked if she thought that Charlie should be jailed as a result of the allegations made at the Moriarty tribunal.

'I do, yes,' she replied. 'He should be convicted.'

Her comments were certainly not contempt of court, because she was not talking about Charlie's conduct before the McCracken tribunal. She was referring to different matters but it all contributed to a poisonous climate in which a fair trial would be impossible, in the opinion of Judge Haugh. The director of public prosecutions appealed this decision to the high court, but it upheld the lower court's decision and suggested that the charges could be re-entered at a more suitable time.

In the next nine months, Charlie was called to testify before the Moriarty tribunal during three different periods. The first time was on 21 July 2000 when he spent two hours a day for five days on the witness stand. These shortened periods were in deference to his age and the disclosure that he had been suffering from prostate cancer for some years. He was back on the witness stand again on 21 September for eight further days, and the third period of examination began on 18 February 2001. It was confined to one hour a day for twenty days.

He was afforded the opportunity to refute all the allegations about the misappropriation of the money. He again tried to lay the responsibility for his financial affairs on Des Traynor. He argued that he had received 'considerably less' than the £8.5m being cited by the Moriarty tribunal, but he declined to speculate on how much less. 'I cannot say that because,' he contended, 'these figures are so complex and extend over such a long period of time that in pursuance of my duty to the tribunal, I engaged the services of a very expert forensic accountant to help the tribunal in unravelling these figures and he, too, is of the opinion that the figure was exaggerated.'

He sought to justify the use of the money in the leader's fund to pay his own household bills because he used Kinsealy for entertainment purposes, and the money given to Fianna Fáil was given to use as he decided. 'For me as a political person, these were Fianna Fáil's to be used as I saw fit, but given to me as a political leader and because of my work as a political leader,' he argued. He scrapped plans for an official residence for the Taoiseach, thereby saving the state a considerable amount of money.

'Abbeville would be staffed, manned by people from the Taoiseach's office at weekends because we would be meeting people, receiving deputations, entertaining people, and a whole variety of activities undertaken on behalf of Ireland, the government or the party,' he argued. 'We would be very active receiving deputations, visitors, individuals from Northern Ireland. Abbeville was ideal from that point of view, because a lot of these people wouldn't like to be coming, facing the glare of publicity in Government Buildings or in Leinster House, and Abbeville had privacy and confidentiality.'

He reacted indignantly to the suggestion that he had misused the money contributed for Lenihan operation. Without even waiting to appear the tribunal he issued a press release refuting any suggestion of misconduct. 'It was Charles Haughey the leader of Fianna Fáil who initiated and spearheaded the humanitarian project of raising funds that would enable Brian Lenihan's wife and family to take him to the Mayo Clinic in the United States for the life-saving liver transplant operation,' the press release emphasised: 'The funds raised were properly applied.'

Before the tribunal, he said that the £20,000 given for Lenihan by the IPBS had been mistakenly deposited in the Celtic Helicopters Account, but that this mistake had been quickly rectified. Certainly, the money was taken out of that Celtic Helicopter account the following week, but it was cashed and there was no corresponding deposit in the leader's fund. He had no convincing explanation for how the vast sums of money contributed by IPBS ended up in his account after he had endorsed the two £50,000 cheques made out to Fianna Fáil in 1986. Haughey endorsed all of the cheques and the whole £120,000 was apparently diverted into Haughey's coffers. So, was £85,000 of the £160,000 handed over by Mark Kavanagh and Michael Smurfit in June of 1989.

He could only argued that it was doubtful that he had ever approached Smurfit, but if Traynor was involved, it would have had nothing to do with Fianna Fáil, because he never collected money for the party. But there is ample evidence that he helped Charlie to misappropriate money intended for Fianna Fáil. Over the years, Haughey had demonstrated that he was a prolific liar, even under oath, so little credence could be placed in any of his testimony unless there was evidence to back it up. There was ample evidence over the decades that he could be very generous, and Brian Lenihan certainly did not suffer as a result of any of the misappropriations, because ultimately all of Lenihan's expenses were paid, thanks in no small measure to the efforts of Haughey, even if he did help himself handsomely in the process.

'Why are you saying these things?' Charlie pleaded at the tribunal. 'Are you trying to humiliate me?'

The tribunal had already identified the donors of at least £155,000 given to Haughey for Lenihan, but only £83,000 of that was used for him. 'You are wrong, you are wrong, and I think you are trying to make a false accusation, and I reject it,' Charlie told his interrogator at the Moriarty tribunal. He took particular exception to the way in which the media depicted his gift of £200 'as a sort of contemptible miserliness on my part ... The fact is that I, to save my friend's life, took an initiative, instituted the raising of funds, all of which funds were spent in his best interests and I did not, and couldn't and wouldn't take one penny of those fund for any other purpose,' Haughey told the tribunal in February 2001.

'I am certain and I think I will be able to persuade you that all the monies in that fund, all the monies that were raised were dispensed for him, medically or otherwise,' he added. 'I totally reject, totally reject, here in this tribunal or anywhere else, that for one moment in all those circumstances, a man who was in fact closer to me than one of my brothers, that I would for one moment deliberately have diverted money raised to save his life, to any purpose and certainly not to my own purpose.'

On this occasion, he no longer had the powers of persuasion. A poll conducted by the *Sunday Independent* found that 87% of the people did not believe that Haughey had 'never touched' the Lenihan money.

In April 2002 Charlie came to a final settlement with the revenue commissioners to pay £5m in back taxes and penalties, in addition to the £1m that he had paid a couple of years earlier. This was an admission that he had indeed received money for his own personal use, but everybody knew that by then. His past had caught up with him.

Charles Haughey was first appointed to a government position in 1960 when he was appointed parliamentary secretary to the Minister for Justice by the government of his father-in-law, Seán Lemass, but there was no question of nepotism. The appointment was widely welcomed, and he assumed the task of guiding through a whole raft of legislation. As the Dáil was about to break up in August 1961 James Dillon, the Fine Gael leader, complimented Charlie 'on the skill with which he has had the recourse to his brief. He has read out to the House learned discourses on various aspects of this legislation which, I have no doubt, will be quoted from the official reports hereafter as evidence of his exceptional and outstanding ability.' Referring to Haughey's 'carefully-prepared briefs' as a testimony of 'his extraordinary erudition', Dillon hoped to be as well briefed himself when his own party came to power. 'Indeed,' he continued, 'I hope I shall make half as good use of the brief'. This was a significant tribute from the leader of another party just before an election – and even more extraordinary when compared to later remarks by Fine Gael leaders, including Dillon himself.

Having only made it to the Dáil on his fourth attempt in 1957, Charlie headed the poll in 1961 was promoted to Minister for Justice. Again, his promotion was welcomed on all side of the Dáil, and there were no suggestions of nepotism. His promotion was seen as earned.

'Haughey was a dynamic minister,' Berry recalled years later. 'He was a joy to work with and the longer he stayed the better he got.' He was quick to master the bureaucratic mystique of the department and the method in which policies were formulated and implemented. Berry, who had served in the Department of Justice under fourteen different ministers beginning with Kevin O'Higgins back in the 1920s, noted that 'Haughey learned fast and was in complete control of his department from the outset.' In fact, he rated him 'the ablest' of all those ministers. 'He did not interfere in minor details,' Berry explained, 'but where political kudos or political disadvantage might arise he was sharp as a razor.'

He handled the calling off of the IRA's campaign with finesse and was responsible for passing a huge volume of legislation, modernising the country's antiquated legal system. He introduced the succession bill, which ensured that a man had to provide for his wife and children in his will and could not leave everything to the church. In 1964, he was appointed Minister for Agriculture following the resignation of Paddy Smith. During the next two years he worked to build up the national cattle herd, and James Dillon, who prided himself on his Agricultural expertise, rated Charlie as 'an excellent Minister for Agriculture'.

After Jack Lynch took over as Taoiseach, Charlie was appointed Minister for Finance, and again distinguished himself. The country was enjoying unprecedented prosperity and he had the vision to introduce a number of imaginative yet comparatively cheap giveaways, such as free travel for the elderly. The country was subsiding public transport at the time and this was simply a means of getting something in return for the subsidisation.

In 1970, Haughey was dismissed from the cabinet when he became implicated in the arms crisis. As Minister for Finance, he provided the money to purchase the weapons at the heart of the controversy and he used his statutory powers to instruct to the customs to admit the consignment without inspection. He was subsequently charged with conspiring to import arms illegally and beat the charges in court, because in the view of the jury the Minister for Defence, who had the authority to authorise the importation, was aware and had essentially authorised the importation. But in the course of the trial, Charlie did enormous political damage to himself by taking the stand and contradicting the evidence not only of state witnesses but also his co-defendants. He obviously lied and had to stick to those lies throughout the remainder of his political career.

Charlie made it back into government in 1977 when he was given the poison chalice of the Ministry for Health, but he did an excellent job, securing money to build hospitals and introduced a free hospitalisation for people earning under a £5,000 a year. He also introduced the first law legalising the sale of contraceptives in the country. It was a weak law, but it was a beginning and made it much easier for his successors to introduce amending legislation. Charlie also had the vision to introduce legislation to ban the advertising of tobacco more than twenty years before his British or American counterparts. By the end of his term as Minister for Health and Social Welfare, he was elected Taoiseach, despite the hostility of most of his government colleagues.

Haughey distinguished himself at the Department of Health, which proved a virtual political graveyard for many of his contemporaries. In April 1978 Senior Counsels Thomas McCann and Ronan

Keane warned the Eastern Health Board that the practice introduced by the previous government of withholding part of the pensions of medical card holders in nursing home was unconstitutional. The advice was passed on to the Department of Health, but nothing was done. Almost nine years later, on 27 March 1987, Haughey's government authorised a draft bill to regularise the illegal charges, but for some inexplicable reason this was not carried further. In 2005 the Supreme Court ruled that the charges were unconstitutional. This left the state facing a bill of as much as €2 billion. If Haughey is to be blamed so could his predecessor and his ten successors at the Department of Health.

Interviewed for the RTÉ television series, *Seven Ages*, Garret Fitz-Gerald stated that Haughey was 'an excellent minister in many posts – in fact, I think, every position he was in, he was a good minister.' Of course, that did not stop Garret from making his flawed pedigree speech.

Haughey unquestionably achieved more as a minister before his election to Taoiseach than any of his predecessors, or successors for that matter. But his first two terms as Taoiseach were little short of disastrous. He recognised that the country was living way beyond its means, but he only made the situation worse. In 1982, he presided over a short-live government that became synonymous with GUBU, as a result of a whole series of grotesque, unbelievable, bizarre and unprecedented events. In opposition, he led Fianna Fáil during a particularly destructive period, in which he put his own political welfare above the welfare of the country, going as far as trying to wreck the Anglo-Irish Agreement of 1985. He also sought to purge the party of his opponents, which probably cost him an overall majority in 1987.

As Taoiseach, he was sometimes woefully misdirected, but he nevertheless led a government that is generally credited with achieving a virtual economic miracle in turning a near bankrupt economy around in the late 1980s. He laid the foundations of the Celtic Tiger economy and was the politician most associated with the introduction of the Financial Service Centre, which proved a phenomenal success.

Even Charlie McCreevy, the man who was so critical of the auction politics and Haughey's economic performance during his first two terms as Taoiseach, later credited him with reforming the economy after returning to power in 1987.

'To Mr Haughey's eternal credit,' McCreevy stated in July 2003, 'he will always be remembered as the man who turned the country around. Because we were bankrupt. We were the next case for the International Monetary Fund. There may be lots of things that Mr Haughey did that people could not approve of but he turned this country around.'

He also played a considerable part in the early stages of the peace initiative in Northern Ireland. 'As Taoiseach, he played a major role in the peace process,' John Hume explained. 'When I began my dialogue with Gerry Adams I privately and confidentially informed him and I kept him regularly informed and he was very supportive. Our object was to get a joint declaration from the British and Irish governments. He worked closely with me to prepare what that declaration should be and he also worked very closely with John Major. That Joint Declaration, which was finally announced by John Major and Albert Reynolds led directly to the ceasefire.'

All too often people who seek to assess Haughey's legacy do so without examining his achievements. They just say that his personal avarice destroyed everything he accomplished. That might be a fair assessment, but only if they first consider his achievements.

While in power Charlie undoubtedly achieved much more than Garret FitzGerald. During little over four years in power, for instance, Haughey's government turned the economy around, while it got worse during FitzGerald's comparatively similar period in power. Garret promised a constitutional crusade to change the constitution and laws in order to convince northern Protestants that they had nothing to fear from the south, as it had become a modern pluralist society. He envisaged constitutional changes to drop the proscription on divorce and deal with what the Unionists considered the offensive implications of Articles 2 and 3.

Haughey denounced the suggestion of currying favour with the Unionists. He told a Fianna Fáil meeting on 17 October 1981 that any changes in the constitution 'should be undertaken on their merit, not with a view to impressing northern Unionists, the British, or anybody else.' Complaining that FitzGerald's constitutional crusade was 'unnecessary, divisive and unhelpful,' Charlie added that it was 'the first time in history that a crusade was started by the infidels.'

His use of the word 'infidels' could be taken as a rather snide way of questioning FitzGerald's religious convictions, as he was an admitted agnostic. Haughey stampeded Garret into endorsing the wording for the Pro-Life Amendment in 1982. The Fine Gael leader then felt compelled to go through with the proposal, even though he publicly warned that the wording was so flawed that it could actually lead to the legalisation of abortion in certain circumstances. FitzGerald tried to change the wording but some of his party was so insistent that he had to let the issue be put to the people without amendment, and the proposal carried. This was seen as a victory for Haughey, but Garret was subsequently proved right in 1992, when the supreme court ruled that a teenage rape victim in what was called 'the X-case' was entitled to an abortion in line with the wording of the Pro-Life Amendment. It was ironic that the only constitutional change that FitzGerald's government was able to implement was one that he did not want.

His greatest accomplishment was undoubtedly the Anglo-Irish Agreement, which he forced through despite Charlie's cynical opposition. Notwithstanding the success of the Anglo-Irish Agreement, however, FitzGerald was decisively defeated when he introduced a referendum to remove the constitutional proscription on divorce in 1986. He had set out to prove that the Catholic bishops did not rule the twenty-six counties, but it seemed that he merely demonstrated that they still enjoyed a virtual veto in Irish political affairs. By then the economy was in a shambles. Garret had tried to pursue the necessary economic policies but he was attacked at every turn by Fianna Fáil. Under Charlie's leadership the party famously proclaimed that 'health cuts hurt the poor, the sick, and the handicapped', but then he implemented even more drastic health cuts on coming to power.

Faced with Fianna Fáil's dishonest and opportunistic opposition, FitzGerald was a virtual political prisoner of the Labour party in government. He felt unable to make the economic cuts that he realised were necessary to revive the economy. The country was therefore virtually bankrupt in 1987 when Haughey got back into power on the casting vote of the ceann comhairle.

'It is important that the narrowness of the margin by which Deputy Haughey was elected should give rise to no doubts as to the possibility of the new government in this Dáil as at present constituted taking the steps that have become necessary in the national interest,' Garret told the Dáil following Haughey's election as Taoiseach. 'None of us is or need to be in doubt about the gravity of the problems facing us or about the fact that they can only be overcome by an effort of political will involving a commitment and a degree of united effort on the part of all of us in politics which is outside the normal framework of what has in the past been secured or what has seemed possible to secure given the adversarial character of our parliamentary system,' Garret assured the Dáil.

'It will not be easy for an opposition to support some of the measures the government will have to take,' he said. 'Yet we will do so. It will not be easy for the government to take these steps but they must do so.' This was a piece of supreme statesmanship in which he placed the national interest ahead of his party and his own political position. He outlined the necessary policy and then stepped down as Fine Gael leader, leaving it to Alan Dukes to implement what became known as the Tallaght Strategy.

Within little over a decade just about all of the reforms that Fitz-Gerald had advocated in the 1970s were implemented – the pluralist society, the deletion of the constitutional ban on divorce, eliminating the offensive implications of Articles 2 and 3, and ending the political interference of the Catholic Church were all achieved. Some of his former lieutenants especially Dick Spring and John Bruton, were in the political forefront in securing those changes. For instance, Bruton played a pivotal role in pushing through the divorce referendum, even though he had strong personal reservations, but he realised that it was an important step in demonstrating that the country had become a tolerant society. Various people got the political plaudits, but Garret was the person who had articulated the need for those changes and generated the enthusiasm and idealism to fire the cause.

In the last quarter of the twentieth century the Republic of Ireland underwent a virtual revolution that was much greater than the social or economic changes of the first half of the century. With the hindsight of history it is obvious that FitzGerald ultimately achieved what he set out to do. In his reserved, unostentatious way he was the political colossus of the latter half of twentieth century Ireland.

At the time, however, Charlie was widely considered the more accomplished politician. He played his part in the changes. He was the first one to get legislation enacted legalising the sale of artificial contraceptives. He was a brilliant operator who essentially took Fitz-Gerald's political clothes when they suited him, with the result that he appeared to be the winner – the shrewd political operator not only outplayed and defeated FitzGerald but also had earlier replaced, if not ousted, Jack Lynch, the most popular Irish politician since Daniel O'Connell. Haughey was also the virtual personification of ostentation in Irish politics. He went to Paris to witness, if not share in, Stephen Roche's victory in the Tour de France in 1987. He also went to Rome to see Ireland play Italy in the quarter final of the soccer World Cup in 1990, when he invited opposition leaders to join him, thereby muting the kind of criticism that had surrounded his earlier trip to Paris. He enjoyed the trappings of power.

His aide P. J. Mara would go ahead to announce that 'An Taoiseach is coming.' He would tell the people not to refer to him as 'Mr Haughey', but as 'Taoiseach'. He could be very conscious about the dignity of his office, but there were others times when he showed scant respect for the office.

An American couple wandered into a Dingle bar where Charlie was clearly enjoying himself one evening. A local Fianna Fáiler brought them over to introduce them to the Taoiseach. Haughey promptly complimented the woman, grabbing her bottom and squeezing. The locals watched in amusement as the Yanks fled in a mixture of horror and indignation.

Charlie once rounded on Dick Walsh of the *Irish Times* for persisting in calling him Mr Haughey, rather than Taoiseach. 'Have you no respect for the office?' he asked.

Walsh replied that it was precisely because he had so much respect for the office that he persisted in calling him 'Mr Haughey'. Yet, Charlie did try to build bridges to his critics and enemies. He visited Walsh in hospital on one occasion and brought him a copy of Andrew Boyle's bestseller, *The Climate of Treason*. Of course, it was a joke, but not to be outdone, Walsh asked Charlie to autograph it. Haughey declined – his sense of humour was not as good when he was on the receiving end.

In the early days, Haughey helped to build an aura of success around himself by exhibiting the trappings of wealth. He lived regally in a magnificent mansion set in palatial grounds. He engaged in horseracing, the renowned sport of kings, as both an owner and a breeder. He owned his own yacht as well as his own island off the coast of Kerry, and he helped set up his son in the helicopter business.

Charlie affected the studied gestures of Napoleon and frequently behaved in an imperious manner towards those around him. He courted publicity by a variety of means, as he clearly loved the limelight. He entertained lavishly. He had a reputation for generosity to the point of profligacy. He was known as a soft-touch for hard luck cases. He was one of the people caught in the 'Dear Mary' scam by the *Sunday Independent*, which sent out begging letters to prominent people, supposedly from a single mother, looking for the price of bringing her young son into Dublin to see Santa Clause. Haughey responded with a £30 contribution. On another occasion while canvassing, he noticed that the fireplace in the home of an old woman living alone was damaged, so he paid to have it repaired. On learning that a family in Donneycarney had lost their carpets and furniture due to a fire, Haughey instructed that the carpets and furniture were replaced, and he again paid the bill.

Of course, the cynics might say that it was not really his money, that other people had given it to him. It was a case of 'easy come, easy go'. No doubt, the recipients of those gestures welcomed the kindness. Charlie was prepared to help people and be generous, even where there was no political advantage to be gained.

'Come off it,' Conor Cruise O'Brien wrote in the *Sunday Independent*, 'it surely ought to be obvious that the "enormous popularity, especially in his own constituency" was precisely "the political advantage to be gained", and that Charlie Haughey duly gained it.'

'I had the rather unpleasant but instructive experience of sharing a constituency (Dublin North East) with C. J. Haughey and I saw his machine at work, at close quarters,' Cruise O'Brien continued. 'He had lots of money to throw around and he duly threw it in copious free drink at election times and multiple small handouts between elections ... Haughey was the legendary Robin Hood, taking from the rich, in order to give to the poor. Of course Haughey got a lot more from the rich than he ever gave to the poor. But the poor readily forgave that, and admired him for what he could get away with.'

In November 1940 a Luftwaffe seaplane with five German airmen made a forced landing off Innisvicillaun, the island that Charlie later bought. They waited on the island hoping for help. While there they killed a sheep for food and lit a fire, but after five days nobody had yet noticed them, so they made their way in a couple of rubber dinghies to the Great Blasket. Having bought the island, Haughey heard the story and traced the five men. He met them in Luxembourg and invited them to spend a holiday on the island together. There were no votes in that for him, and he never sought any publicity for the gesture.

'Every aspect of his character attracts curiosity,' Bruce Arnold declared. 'No man so dominated his period, in and out of power.'

In time, it would become apparent that much of his money was borrowed or bummed. For those who saw his wealth as the proof of his success, that success would prove ethereal and they would come to see him as a great failure. He was roundly condemned for his performance before the McCracken tribunal when he exposed himself to the charge of consistently lying. But, ironically, the findings in relation to receiving money from Ben Dunne should not have hurt his place in history.

Daniel O'Connell – arguably the most famous and influential Irishman of all time – lived beyond his means for much of his life. He lived extravagantly in the confident expectation that he would inherit an uncle's fortune, but the uncle lived to the ripe old age of ninety-seven. Having entered politics in the 1820s, Daniel gave up his practice at the bar and financed his lifestyle out of public subscriptions. He managed to support his extravagance with the help of national subscriptions from ordinary people amounting to about £13,000 a year, but on one occasion shortly before the outbreak of the Great Famine, it amounted to around £50,000. Charles Stuart Parnell also lived beyond his means and was the beneficiary of a public subscription of some £20,000 in 1882.

Unlike those who accepted money from people living in a state of virtual subsistence, Haughey got much of his money from a fabulously wealthy person in Ben Dunne. Nobody has shown that Dunne received any kind of favouritism, other than being invited to family occasions. Other famous men also built up great debts. Thomas Jefferson, the author of the Declaration of Independence and arguably the father of modern democracy, was in so much debt when he died that his heirs had to sell off his property to pay those debts, and Winston Churchill was so profligate that he was heavily dependent on the support of some wealthy admirers.

Ever since 1967 when George Colley complained about 'low standards in high places', Fianna Fáil bumbled from one scandal to another, and never cleaned up any of them. The arms crisis was essentially covered up, only to be raised again ten years later when Vincent Browne published the Berry Papers in *Magill*, showing that serious issues had been glossed over in Jack Lynch's handling of the whole affair.

Likewise with the telephone-tapping, there was no real inquiry and it was resurrected almost ten years later to force Haughey to resign as Taoiseach. The most serious aspect of the arms crisis was the conspiracy subverting the constitution in which Jack Lynch was involved, either wittingly or unwittingly, because he turned a blind eye and thereby ignored his sworn obligation to uphold the constitution. If he did not know what was going on, it was because he chose to ignore what was happening. Haughey stated that he did not know himself but even his sworn testimony on the matter was unbelievable.

If he had only said, 'I did it, so what?' He would still have been acquitted at the arms trial, and the telephone-tapping could not have been resurrected to haunt him in 1992, because the opposition had also tapped journalists. If he had admitted that he had received money from Ben Dunne, the real issue would have been whether Dunne had received any undue favours. It would seem that he did not, and it was noteworthy that he continued to give money to Haughey after he was out of office and out of politics. Had Charlie come clean about the Dunne money, he might have avoided the most damaging revelations at the Moriarty tribunal, such as the misappropriation of the money intended for Fianna Fáil and for Brian Lenihan's operation. His behaviour in accepting money from people with whom the government was doing business was at best irresponsibly reckless because it left him wide open to the suspicion of corruption by betraying the public trust for his own selfish gain. As an accountant Haughey had to have known that he should have kept the Lenihan money separate from the leader's fund, but this would have created difficulties when he helped himself to what was left over, and even got some more by pretending that more was needed.

Charisma, in its proper sense, is often confused with charm or popularity. A politician with real charisma possesses a kind of superhuman quality in the estimation of his admirers. Thus, it is not a quality that someone necessarily possesses but rather a perception in the minds of others. Haughey's charisma was based on his ability to survive a whole series of political scandals and escape from tight, seemingly inescapable, political corners. The perception of his personal invincibility was tarnished, perhaps irrevocably, by the disclosures that he had misappropriated money intended for Fianna Fáil and for Brian Lenihan's operation

He was facing charges of obstructing the McCracken tribunal, and he was exposed as having evaded a considerable amount of tax at a time when his government was extracting exorbitant taxes from the Irish people. Moreover, his financial adviser, Des Traynor was not only facilitating Charlie to evade tax, he organised a massive tax evasion scheme to facilitate a kind of golden circle that included many of Haughey's associates and financial supporters..

Throughout his career, Charlie confounded his critics and bucked the system. He may well be remembered as the greatest bucker of all time, but he was well and truly exposed in retirement. His enemies seemed to gloat with a sense of vindication, but they were part of the problem. Instead of seeking the truth, they were more intent on destroying Haughey politically. He survived because they were just playing politics.

John Healy really captured the essence behind Charlie's survival when he noted that Haughey was as 'blessed with his enemies as he is cursed with his friends.'

In the end, Haughey probably destroyed his political legacy. It was a great pity, because he was unquestionably a very talented politician.

BIBLIOGRAPHY

Arnold, Bruce, *What Kind of Country*, London, 1984.

_____ *Haughey: His Life and Unlucky Deeds*, London, 1993.

Boland, Kevin, *The Rise and Decline of Fianna Fail*, Cork, 1982.

_____ *Up Dev!* Dublin, 1977.

_____ *'We Won't Stand (Idly) By'*, Dublin, 1974.

Brady, Conor, *Guardians of the Peace*, Dublin, 1974.

Brady, Séamus, *Arms and the Men*, Dublin, 1971.

Browne, Noel, *Against the Tide*, Dublin, 1986.

Bugliosi, Vincent, with Gentry Curt, *Helter Skelter*, New York, 1974.

Collins, Stephen, *The Haughey File*, Dublin, 1992.

_____ *Spring and the Labour Party*, Dublin, 1993.

_____ *The Power Game*, Dublin, 2000.

Coogan, Tim Pat, *Ireland Since the Rising*, London, 1966.

Cruise O'Brien, Conor, *States of Ireland*, London, 1972.

Dáil Éireann, *Dáil Debates*, Volumes 192–370.

Downey, James, *Them and Us*, Dublin, 1989.

_____ *All Things New*, Dublin, 1989.

_____ *Lenihan*. Dublin, 1998.

Duignan, Seán, *One Spin on the Merry-go-round*, Dublin, 1995.

Dunlop, Frank, *Yes, Taoiseach*, Dublin, 2004.

Dwyer, T. Ryle, *Charlie: The Political Biography of Charles J. Haughey*, Dublin, 1987.

_____ *De Valera – The Man and the Myths*, Dublin, 1991.

_____ *Nice Fellow: A biography of Jack Lynch*, Cork, 2001.

_____ *Short Fellow: A Biography of Charles J. Haughey*, Cork, 1999.

Edmonds, Seán, *The Gun, the Law and the Irish People*, Tralee, 1971.

Feehan, John M., *Operation Brogue*, Cork, 1985.

_____ *The Statesman*, Cork, 1985.

_____ *Apology to the Irish Nation*, Cork, 1988.

FitzGerald, Garret, *All in a Life*, Dublin, 1991.

Horgan, John, *Seán Lemass*, Dublin, 1997.

Joyce, Joe and Murtagh, Peter, *The Boss*, Dublin, 1983.

Keena, Colm, *Haughey's Millions*, Dublin, 2001.

_____ *The Ansbacher Conspiracy*, Dublin, 2003.

Kelly, James, *Orders for the Captain?*, Dublin, 1971.

_____ *The Thimble Riggers*, Dublin, 1999.

Kennedy, Tadhg, *Charles J. Haughey*, Dublin, 1986.

Kenny, Shane, *Go Dance on Somebody Else's Grave*, Dublin, 1990.

Lenihan, Brian, *For the Record*, Dublin, 1991.

Mac Intyre, Tom, *Through the Bridewell Gate*, London, 1971.

O'Brien, Justin, *The Arms Trial*, Dublin, 2000.

O'Byrne, Stephen, *Hiding Behind a Face*, Dublin, 1986.
Oireachtas Éireann, *Report from Committees*, Volume 19, Parts 1 and 2.
O'Mahony, T. P., *Jack Lynch*, Dublin, 1991.
O'Malley, Pádraig, *Uncivil Wars*, Belfast, 1983.
O'Reilly, Emily, *Candidate*, Dublin, 1991.
O'Sullivan, Michael, *Seán Lemass*, A Biography, Dublin, 1994.
O'Toole, Fintan, *Meanwhile Back at the Ranch: The Politics of Irish Beef*, 1995.
Ryan, Tim, *Albert Reynolds, The Longford Leader*, Dublin 1994.
_____ *Mara, P. J.*, Dublin, 1992.
Smith, Raymond, *The Survivor*, Dublin, 1983.
_____ *Garret*, Dublin, 1985.
_____ *Haughey and O'Malley*, Dublin, 1986.
Smyth, Sam, *Thanks a Million Big Fella*, Dublin, 1997.
Tobin, Fergal, *The Best of Decades*, Dublin, 1984.
Walsh, Dick, *The Party*, Dublin, 1986.
_____ *Des O'Malley*, Dingle, 1986.
Young, John N., *Erskine Childers*, Gerrards Cross, 1985.

NEWSPAPERS AND PERIODICALS:

Cork Examiner, The
Crane Bag, The
Economist, The
Evening Herald
Evening Mail
Evening Press
Guardian, The
Hibernia
Hot Press
In Dublin
Irish Independent
Irish Press
Irish Times, The
Magill
Phoenix
Sunday Independent
Sunday Press
Sunday Review
Sunday Tribune
This Week

INDEX